JUDGE DINGAKE

SELECTED SPEECHES AND WRITINGS

KGOPOLO NTSEANE

notionpress.com

INDIA · SINGAPORE · MALAYSIA

Contents

Part II

Published Articles

Foreword

By Thomas Sibusiso Masuku, Justice of the High Court of Namibia, and former Judge of the High Courts of Botswana and Swaziland.

This book: *Judge Dingake – Selected Speeches and Writings* by Kgopolo Ntseane, a Senior Magistrate in Botswana, captures the cream of Judge Dingake's speeches and writings.

It is a rare feat for one person to offer permanent residence to both judicial acumen and sagacity, on the one hand and academic excellence on the other - and simultaneously master both and in equal measure. If truth be told, the one feeds off the other as the occasion demands. These rare species come once in a long season and are to be recognised, eulogized and emulated. A fitting candidate in this category that readily comes to mind, is Madame Justice Kate O'Regan. She is not, however, subject of this foreword.

I write about my friend and 'judicial sweetheart', Mr Justice and Professor OBK Dingake, that judicial and academic luminary born on the dusty streets of Bobonong, in the Republic of Botswana. I say judicial sweetheart for the reason that our outlook on the law, its significance and application coincide, even on those issues that are topical, divisive and controversial.

He has traversed various legal systems and traditions across the globe. In this connection, he has had the honour and privilege to serve as a Judge of the High Court and Industrial Court in Botswana, the Court of Appeal of the Seychelles and the Residual Special Court for Sierra Leone. Presently, he is plying his trade as Judge of the National and Supreme Courts of Papua New Guinea.

I commented during the celebration of his 50th birthday and conferment of Professorship by the University of Cape Town that it seems that whereas we, the lesser mortals have been allotted 24 hours in a day to make a difference in this the world of the living, he seems to be afforded some largesse of extra hours, like 30 in a day.

I said this because of his dexterous ability to mix judicial work in its multifarious facets - an extremely demanding and at times exhausting task and the capability and insatiable drive of writing books, articles and other legal publications. This is not to mention his added responsibility and passion of teaching law as a visiting professor in some renowned law schools around the globe. This includes lecturing to and shaping up judicial minds in this ever changing world, where the constant and the evolving need to be identified and developed with conscious and deliberate finesse.

'*Judge Dingake - Selected Speeches and Writings*' is a pleasure to read. From reading the pages of the works, his judicial mind and soul are laid bare and painted on the canvass.

He comes across as a man of the law through and through. He is judicious in his disposition and has a passion for constitutional law and the pervasive influence and impact it has on human and people's rights. This is so for the reason that human beings, regardless of their beliefs, practices, persuasions and inclinations, are and must be regarded as human even where they appear to be an island surrounded by a massive ocean.

His view of the law is not merely superficial - aimed at a good, short and acceptable outcome. It is microscopic as well - attending to the minute details that hold judicial philosophies in place. These are scrutinised sinew by sinew.

From reading the pages of the various articles in this publication, one can attest to a good human being - one with great passion for the law - one who makes the law work for the ordinary woman and man. One who, when the judicial mantle and the occasion demand, holds those who wield power to account, as envisaged by the Supreme Law.

No one, in his judicial world, is above or beyond the reach of the law, whatever his or her station in life, their acquirements or the massive health of their balance sheets.

A reading of the articles in this publication, depicts a stalwart and defender of the rule of law, judicial independence, coupled with accountability of judges.

In his unique and poignant manner, laced at times with humour, he traverses the lives of some stalwarts of the law - some of whom are at irreconcilable ends of the legal and judicial divide. In this regard, departed luminaries like Nganunu CJ, Marumo J, Legwaila J, are appropriately eulogized for their unique impact and contribution to the development of the law in Botswana.

He also traverses other legal fields, including judicial interpretation of the Constitution, the African Charter on Democracy, Elections and Governance, the protection of minority rights in Botswana, Sexual Diversity and Gender Identity, case law of judicial case management, to mention but a few.

This offering is a one stop shop necessary in everyone's legal and judicial bookshelf. This is because it traverses many seminal topics which are treated with forthrightness passion and deep analysis.

I am certainly waiting for my copy once it is publicly available and will be referring to it time and again as the occasion demands.

Part 1
Speeches

Chapter 1

Reflections of My Life Journey and African Leadership Challenges

A speech delivered to the 2023 cohort of Future elect Southern Africa Public Leadership Fellows – September 2023

Director of Proceedings, thank you for your kind invitation to address future leaders of our continent. I bring you greetings from Alotau in Milne Bay, where I am currently on circuit, in this earthly paradise called Papua New Guinea – the land of the unexpected. It is truly a humbling opportunity to share some thoughts with you in accordance with your invitation letter.

I must congratulate all the participants gathered here today for undergoing an intensive 9-month interdisciplinary public leadership program that prepares them for leadership in government or elected political leadership careers. Organizers of this event have informed me that the participants come from such countries as Botswana, Madagascar, Malawi, Zambia, South Africa, and Tanzania.

Your invitation requires me to do three things: to traverse my life story, give insights into the Constitutional review process in Botswana, and give some advice to participants on leadership. I propose to do so now following the order I just stated.

My life journey from a village peasant boy in Bobonong to Port Moresby, in the Pacific, serving as a judge of the Supreme and National Courts of Papua New Guinea, was totally unplanned, but it happened because education, other than being the greatest equalizer, is also the greatest enabler.

My life journey is long. By way of introduction and for present purposes, it is sufficient to say I am a native of Bobonong village in Botswana. I was born to peasant parents. Life appeared blissful then: we were free to roam the forests to catch birds and other animals for sustenance; splash in the streams and rivers, breathe clean air, and spend peaceful nights counting the stars on the Milky Way. Wild fruits were also in abundance. We were a close-knit family and shared everything that came our way. Being the last born in a family of 13, I was spoiled to the core.

I know the pain of going to bed hungry and going to school barefoot, traversing very long distances. We were not rich, but we were happy. I owe my broad world outlook to the background I sketched above. I am a product of the circumstances of my upbringing. Perhaps it is because of these circumstances that I yearned for a just world in which everyone's needs were catered for. At the University, I immersed myself in theories that gave impetus to the just world I dreamed of for every person. I was a member of the Botswana Student Council that required us to attend study groups every weekend at which we would study various economic and philosophical theories, including theories on why Africa is underdeveloped.

I will not go into the details of that background, but I will cut to the chase. Did I set out to be a judge? The answer is yes! In one of my books, I tell a story of how, when I was hardly 12 years old, I wrote my brother, then serving 15 years in Robben Island, for furthering the aims of a banned organization, the ANC, asking him to advise me on what qualifications I needed to obtain to be either a judge or president. I also asked him to advise on the applicable pay package.

In my naivety, I thought that to be President, one must be the most educated person in the country, and I was readying myself to scale the heights of the education ladder! I later learned that the Constitution only required me to be a Motswana, aged above 30 years, able to speak English, and read and write to run for the Presidency!

The pay package my brother mentioned for both roles was attractive, and at that point, it became clear that I had reached a point of no return as far as my career choice was concerned. By the time I was in high school, my resolve to be a judge was firm. I studied hard and ended up acquiring an LLB degree from the University of Botswana and an LLM from the University of London. My thirst for knowledge was not quenched by obtaining my LLB and LLM degrees, so I continued studying until I acquired my PhD in Law from the University of Cape Town, which in 2013 honoured me with an Honorary Professorship.

At the University of Botswana, I was a student leader – Vice President of the Student Representative Council (SRC). As a student leader, I led student protests and demonstrations on a variety of issues, but mostly, on our demands that students' allowances should be increased. I also led demonstrations denouncing American aggression in Libya. I was also active in the international student movement, which activism occasionally took me to such places as Finland, Norway, Denmark, Russia, Bulgaria, Czechoslovakia, Hungary, the United Kingdom, and the USA. In one of my visits to the USA, then, I was awarded honorary citizenship in the city of Harrisburg.

My role as the SRC Vice President was a leadership position that required planning, resource mobilization, and taking responsibility for decisions made. Looking back, I am proud of the role I played as a student leader, organizing protests, demonstrations, and other tasks. As we all know, the right to peaceful assembly is very important for several reasons. Peaceful demonstrations have played a significant role in shaping the world in which we live today.

We merely need to watch the news to see that people across the globe continue to engage in demonstrations to press their demands. During the last few decades, demonstrations have played a major role in bringing about positive social changes, such as the end of colonialism, the fight against racial discrimination in the USA, the fall of the Berlin Wall, the battle against apartheid, the Arab Spring revolt, and the demonstrations to demand the rollout of Nevirapine in South Africa to halt mother-to-child transmission of HIV, to mention just a few examples. The right of peaceful assembly and demonstrations gives participants an opportunity to connect with each other and to collectively assert themselves. It is also a major vehicle through which other rights in the human rights discourse have gained meaning and power. It is hard to imagine any fundamental human right that has not, in one way or another, been given life by demonstrations, marches, and other forms of protest actions. The right to vote, which was denied to women in some parts of the world until recently, came about because of collective action that included marches and demonstrations.

After my post-graduate studies, I was fortunate to return to the University as a Law lecturer, mainly focusing on Constitutional law and human rights. Still driven by the idea of a better world, I had to take calculated risks to advance that world outlook. For example, one career-limiting decision I made was to represent the SRC (following a class boycott and closure of the University) at court when I was employed by the University as a lecturer. I refused to withdraw from the case when the Dean of the Faculty of Sciences, under which the Law Department fell advised us (three law lecturers who had decided to represent the students) that "we cannot bite the hand that feeds us."

After my stint at the University and as a private law practitioner, most of my clientele were students, workers, and other marginalized groups. It was a human rights law practice. In many respects, my journey as an attorney and my overall law practice were not commercially driven; they were cause-driven!

My battle to secure a better deal for the vulnerable brought great satisfaction. It occurred to me then that it is the poor who need justice more than the rich because the poor have no money to hire good lawyers. In some jurisdictions, we often hear that the justice system treats you much better if you are rich and guilty than if you are poor and innocent.

Disrupting the oppressive status quo to minimize adverse consequences for my clients was a calling for me. I somehow believed that the seeds of the destruction of all oppressive regimes lay in the belly of their stomachs.

As a practicing lawyer, I learned a few things that law school didn't teach me. I learned that to be successful in the courtroom, it's not enough to know the law; you must also know your judge. Judges come in many shapes and forms. No one comes to the bench as an ideological virgin. So, whenever I rose to address a judge to champion my client's cause, I would tailor my arguments to meet the profile or taste of my judge. To dry-letter law judges, I gave them the dry law. To philosopher judges, I gave them philosophy. One example will drive the point home. Some years back, while in practice, my client was convicted of causing grievous bodily harm to another person and sentenced to an effective prison term of seven years, which I thought was harsh. In my assessment, the conviction was well-founded, so I filed an appeal with the High Court against the sentence only. However, when I rose to address the court, the judge, notwithstanding that I had not appealed against conviction, kept discussing the conviction, suggesting that the case against my client was not proven. When it became clear to me that the judge was bent on acquitting my client, at all costs, even though I had not appealed against conviction, I turned around to suggest that I understood the judge's concern and conceded he may be right. With that concession, my client was acquitted!

My practice at the bar revolved around challenging conventional wisdom that paid lip service to human rights and often used the law as a tool of oppression rather than as a tool that can promote the welfare of society. My law practice and academic pursuits were a blissful forerunner of my later life on the bench, to which I now turn.

Being a judge is not a job; it is a calling. Being appointed a judge is akin to priesthood. Today, the idea that judgeship is akin to priesthood subsists because of the belief that judges epitomize righteousness, fairness, and justice. Acceptance of the calling is like entering a monastery, a place of worship occupied by monks living under religious vows.

Judges are usually appointed by the President of the country or the Head of State on the recommendations of the Judicial Services Commission (JSC), the body specially set up to appoint judges. I was first appointed to the Botswana bench by former President Festus Mogae, in PNG by the Governor General, in Seychelles by the President of Seychelles, and for the RSCSL by the Secretary-General of the United Nations.

For all the above appointments, I took an oath, not worded exactly the same way, but each obliged me to be faithful to the Constitution and to administer justice to all persons alike without fear, favour, or prejudice.

The method of appointing judges is important. The practice in which the bodies appointing judges are dominated by the Executive is not ideal for the rule of law. It does not inspire confidence in the Judiciary as a non-partisan, independent body that is committed only to administering justice to all without fear or favour. A transparent, merit-based selection system inspires more confidence than an opaque one.

Speaking of merit, you may well ask, what then are the qualities of a good judge? Many decades ago, a British Lord Chancellor is alleged to have said, speaking about his power to appoint judges:

"I like my judges to be gentlemen. If they know a little law so much the better."

I am certain that today, many may have objections to the above remarks, insisting, correctly, that the qualities required of a judge should include independence, impartiality, knowledge of the law, experience, industry, excellent communication skills, and clarity of thought, among other qualities.

A famous story is told that a former US President was asked by a journalist whether he ever made a mistake. The President answered: "Yes, I made two mistakes, and both of them are sitting in the Supreme Court."

The President was reported to have been referring to Chief Justice Earl Warren and Justice William Brennan, who turned out to be more liberal than the conservative appointing authority had thought. As many of us may be aware, once appointed, judges are no respecters of any person, but the law; they choose their path. It is often said that: "You shoot an arrow into a far distant future when you appoint a justice."

Closer to home, in South Africa, one of the most significant cases of a post-independent South Africa, the Nkandala case, in which the Constitutional Court, led by Chief Justice Mogoeng Mogoeng, held that President Zuma breached the Constitution over the home upgrades in Nkandla, and ordered him to repay the government money he spent on the house upgrades, may be seen by some as a confirmation that appointing a judge does not mean that he or she will always be beholden to your interests.

The judgment was unequivocal, saying that: "The President has failed to uphold, defend, and respect the Constitution as the supreme law of the land." These words fell from the lips of none other than Chief Justice Mogoeng. Prior to his appointment as Chief Justice by President Zuma, Chief Justice Mogoeng was vilified as Zuma's lackey.

In the above case, Chief Justice Mogoeng led from the front, intellectually, and by exhibiting courage and fearlessness. Being a judge casts one in a leadership role that is different from that of a politician. It obliges one to be a servant and ethical leader. Judicial services are government services, and judicial time is a national resource. As it is often said, the ultimate role of a judge is to promote the welfare of the people. Experience has taught that only judges that are independent and impartial are the best guarantors of justice – not politicians. There is a point, however, where the appointed national leadership and elected leadership meet. With respect to these two types of leaders, it is true to say that an intellectual, educated, and informed mind makes good leadership. Leaders are required to be visionary and exhibit a high level of industry and deep thought.

Leaders are expected to hold a vision of a better tomorrow. They are supposed to be progress- driven. They should initiate, drive, and manage change to achieve progress that suits their vision. Leaders take educated and calculated risks without which no progress can take place.

And as for judges, they should also understand and appreciate that the good of the people is the chief law and as intellectual leaders of their nations and communities, they must understand that the law's sustainability depends on its ability to meet the needs of the people.

The law is not written in stone; it is dynamic and seeks to satisfactorily answer recurring questions concerning human life. Judges make life and death decisions concerning their fellow human beings. I have done many cases in which those who were unfairly dismissed from work were reinstated and those who were unfairly disinherited because they are women, given back their inheritance.

Some aspects of a judge's work can be depressing. For instance, divorce cases. In my court, women sought divorce more than men. The evidence seemed to cast men in a bad light. To get a divorce, the pleadings of the complainant, called the plaintiff, were chillingly familiar:

"I was married to the defendant. He was a good man when I married him. He has changed.

He is not the man I married many years ago; all love is now lost; my husband now stays with another woman as a man and wife. I want out. Marriage has broken down irretrievably." In most cases, the evidence would be compelling in favour of a divorce, and I would invariably mutter: a decree nisi for divorce is granted. Thereafter, one is often left in deep thought; thinking: the line between love and hate is indeed very faint!

In the judicial system, we place a high premium on arriving at correct decisions even as we know that no human being is infallible. This explains why the legal system provides for appeals often to a court with as many as 3 – 9 justices sitting. The rationale, of course, is to stop or reduce the likelihood of a wrong judicial outcome. No appeal can guarantee fault-free outcomes, but all must be done to avoid a wrong judicial outcome.

Socrates, a Greek philosopher, writing in the Fourth Century BC, said that there are four qualities of a judge: to hear courteously, to answer wisely, to consider soberly, and to decide impartially.

It is important that at the end of the day, it must be said of the judge by the community that the judge served that he acquitted himself with dignity and honour. Let it also be said that the judge was a good listener. Let it also be said that the judge was always impartial. On impartiality, Patrick Devlin (1905 – 1992) says: "I put impartiality before independence, simply because without the reality, the appearance would not endure." In truth, however, the appearance of impartiality is equally important, if not more so because, as it is often said, "the judge who gives the right judgment, whilst appearing not to do so, may be thrice blessed in heaven; but on earth, he is of no use at all".

The wretched of the earth: the homeless, the landless, those unjustifiably discriminated against, the hungry, and those without immediate name recognition or status in society, once they enter our courts, litigating against whosoever, the rich and powerful, expect the same treatment. Even an all-powerful State, once it is sued, becomes just another litigant and is not entitled to any special treatment.

Judges should not consider themselves sacred cows. We are not. We are as fallible as any other human being. We are not entitled to do what we please or to be the overlords of the Constitution, but its true servants.

Before I conclude this segment of my address, I must say something about judicial accountability. Judges are accountable to the people by the judgments they give, which can be read by anyone. They also sit in open courts. They are accountable to the people who delegated judicial power to them. The open court system increases transparency in the whole adjudicative process. In some jurisdictions, the Judiciary publishes annual reports, which are important information tools that promote public debate concerning the Judiciary's activities.

A story is told of a conversation between Mr. Justice Learned Hand and his Clerk, which went thus:

"Sonny… to whom am I responsible? No one can fire me. No one can dock my pay. Even those nine bozos in Washington, who sometimes reverse me, can't make me decide as they wish. Everyone should be responsible to someone. To whom I am responsible?"

The judge then turned and pointed to the shelves of his library and said: "To those books about us. That's to whom I am responsible." It is also said that Lord Donaldson, the former English Master of Rolls, once said: "Judges are without constituency and answerable to no one except their consciences and the law."

It seems to me that any society would be better if all leaders, not just those in the Judiciary, aspired to the same attributes as those of judges, which I discussed briefly earlier.

I turn now to the second part of my talk: insights into the Constitutional review process in Botswana. I want to precede those discussions by briefly discussing the value of Constitutions:

Why Constitutions?

Firstly, Constitutions provide the foundation for almost every nation's legal system. A Constitution is a statement of values and embodies a contract between the government and the people of any nation.

Secondly, in many legal systems, Constitutions are superior to all other laws, making them critical tools for overturning discriminatory legislation. For instance, in India, in 2017, the Supreme Court ruled that the traditional practice of "instant divorce" in Islamic marriages, which allowed men to legally divorce their wives by saying the Arabic word for divorce three times, violated the Constitution's protection for gender equality.

Thirdly, modern Constitutions refer to or acknowledge the binding nature of certain international human rights instruments. This enhances the protection the Constitution offers to people.

Fourthly, Constitutions can protect people from policies that undermine equal rights.

Fifthly, Constitutions are important in shaping public policy and programs.

Finally, Constitutions are an important tool for civil engagement, education, and activism. In India, activists undertook a 115-day march to establish a Constitutional right to education. In Kenya, civil society groups published copies of Constitutions in Braille. In Germany, newly arriving refugees receive copies of a Bill of Rights in Arabic.

With all the above in mind, it is important to say, as I always do, that a Constitution is not a panacea for all societal ills. It is a promissory note. It requires judges who can transform these promises into tangible deliverables when called upon to do so.

A Constitution must guarantee human rights to all, good governance, and accountability. It must make it possible for ordinary people to enjoy the fruits of their labour; to enable them to access opportunities in a fair manner and encourage them to generate wealth for their families and the nation; it should guarantee security for everyone and oblige the government to meet the basic needs of life: food, health, water, shelter, and clothing. It needs to ensure a caring and transparent government that translates into opportunities for all by ensuring that the laws are just and observed by all, including the rulers.

With the above in mind, a constitutional review is a rare opportunity offered to a nation to ensure that everyone contributes to the establishment of ground rules that will ensure that each one of us and future generations have a fair and equal chance in life to succeed and be happy people.

Every constitution review process might be approached from the history and circumstances of a given country. There is no one-size-fits-all model of constitutional review. Most of the post- independent African countries entrenched human rights in a half-hearted manner, introduced low-key accountability mechanisms, and concentrated power in the hands of the presidency or central government. The independence of many institutions meant to support democracy, such as human rights commissions, the office of the public protector, anti-corruption bodies, and judiciaries, was suspect.

An Overview of the Botswana Constitutional Review Process

The 1966 Botswana Constitution is a colonial relic. It has served us well generally, but it is no longer fit for purpose. It is overdue for far-reaching renewal. It has many weaknesses that can be instantly fixed, such as requiring it to expressly state that it is the supreme law of the land and to expressly recognize separation of powers, key components that, in my mind, constitute the unalterable basic structure of the Constitution.

The Constitution is not gender- sensitive, and the electoral system mandated by the Constitution tends to exclude women from national political decision-making. As it is often said, no country can claim to be democratic if half or more of its population is excluded.

The Constitution lacks independent institutions that support democracy, a bill of rights that recognizes all human rights, and concentrates too much power in the Presidency. The Constitutional architecture is such that Parliament ends up being a rubber stamp of Executive decisions. The Constitutional review process raises opportunities for devolving power to local government units, strengthening equality and non-discrimination clauses in the Constitution, and outright outlawing many other discriminatory legal provisions and practices.

A review of the Constitution would also provide opportunities for the Botswana Government to domesticate all international, regional, and sub-regional treaties or protocols it has signed, such as the Maputo Protocol.

Review of the Constitution of Botswana

A committee that was established to consult Batswana on the review of the Constitution is called The Presidential Commission of Inquiry into the review of the Constitution of Botswana. The above name, in many respects, tells a substantial part of the story about the nature and character of the Commission. The review process that started in December 2021 was one of the quickest in history. It was carried out over a period of about 9 months and was not preceded by any stakeholder engagement or civic education. The absence of civic education was apparent from most of the commentary that was offered in many public platforms that the commission addressed. Based on the commentaries that were made, one wished that civic education preceded the process. Having taught Constitutional law at law school, I know for certain that if I were to walk into a law class and without offering the lecture, asked the students to evaluate the strengths and weaknesses of the Botswana

Constitution, many may find the question difficult, but the appreciation of the subject matter may improve substantially after the lecture. The same is true with the Constitution review process, in which we want people to assess the strengths and weaknesses of the Constitution.

In December 2021, President Masisi appointed a Constitutional Review Commission headed by former Chief Justice Dibotelo. The Commission was established under the Commission of Inquiries Act, which required the Commission to report directly to the President. This approach, quite self-evidently, gave the impression of a partisan approach. The process could not be said by any standard to have been 'people-driven'.

The terms of reference of the Commission included the following:

- ascertain from the people of Botswana their views on the operation of the Constitution and in particular, the strengths and weaknesses of the Constitution;

- assess the adequacy of the Constitution, in particular by asserting Botswana's identity, principles, aspirations, and values;

- articulate the concerns of the people of Botswana as regards the amendments that may be required for a review of the Constitution;

- conduct inquiries and obtain information from sources that the Commission considers relevant in the exercise of its mandate; and

- make any recommendations on the review or amendment of the Constitution.

It is difficult to assess the extent to which civil society engaged with the process. What seems clear is that a significant section of civil society and political opposition considered that the process was not inclusive and transparent. The political opposition rejected the process as illegitimate. It is unclear to many people what exactly remains to be done and when exactly should Batswana expect a revised Constitution. The Botswana Constitutional Review process is, in my respectful view, "a dream deferred".

There are two important features of Constitution making or review: process and content. The two features are equally important. I will discuss them briefly.

Inclusivity

The Constitution-making process must be inclusive. All key stakeholders must be involved in the key elements of that process. There is, of course, no single approach to a constitutional review exercise. But best practice suggests that calling a stakeholders' conference in which key stakeholders like political parties and civil society can participate is a good idea. At this initial stage, where such a conference is called, stakeholders would deliberate about the Constitution as it is, and the need to review, debate and agree on the best way of going about the exercise, including who the commissioners would be, their terms of reference, criteria for selection, the need for the commission to represent the demographics of the nation, the scope, civic education, how it will be carried out, the need for a referendum, and timeliness for each activity.

It is common and acceptable that these processes are often led and facilitated by the government, which is also expected to set aside adequate resources for the exercise. But facilitation does not mean the imposition of anything.

In South Africa, the process was understandably drawn out. The consultation was thorough. The parties developed 34 Constitutional principles that would guide the process. The Constitutional Court had jurisdiction to determine any complaint relating to non-compliance with the agreed principles, and about 2 million submissions were collated from the people.

Legitimacy and educating the people about the Constitution are some of the key advantages of a people-centred Constitutional renew process.

Costs

The costs of an inclusive process are that it is expensive and highly time-consuming, and the temptation to take shortcuts is always very high. The other disadvantages are that power brokers can always hijack the process. Popular participation can also add legitimacy to populist pressures that infringe or violate minority rights.

Process Gaps

One of the outstanding and glaring gaps is manifested by the name of the Commission. This was a Presidential Commission established in terms of the Commission of Inquiries Act. As the name suggests, it is accountable to the President. It was not people-driven. And the fact that it was accountable to the President means it cannot be said to have been non-partisan or independent. The first term of reference requires Batswana to be consulted about the strengths and weaknesses of the Constitution. This term presupposes some functional knowledge of the Constitution. This term may have served its purpose if the process was preceded by civic education.

A Cloud of Illegitimacy

The fact that civil society and political opposition played no meaningful part in the conceptualization of the process and its operationalization suggests that the process may lack public ownership and raise questions of illegitimacy.

Reflections on Substantive Receptions

Under this section, I propose to deal with only four or so possible areas of reforms that civil society may focus on, for purposes of advocacy and lobbying. These areas are a transformative bill of rights (equality and anti-discrimination clauses), reform of the electoral system, and strengthening the independence of the institutions that support democracy.

Inclusion of Socio-economic Rights

Botswana's Bill of Rights was fashioned along the European Convention of Human Rights of 1952. It does not recognize socio-economic rights. It is hoped that the new constitution will recognize socio-economic rights.

Equality and Non-Discrimination

The discussion under this head focuses mainly on women and persons with disabilities.

Equality and non-discrimination are core international human rights. It is not enough to entrench formal equality provisions in the Constitution that do not consider the historic discrimination and inequality that women have and continue to experience.

An effective approach to covering all sorts of discrimination in a Constitution is to offer a broad definition of discrimination that includes (i) both direct and indirect discrimination; (ii) recognition of multiple forms of discrimination; (iii) application of prohibitions to both private and public persons/institutions; and (iv) a clear complaints process with remedies.

Article 14 of the Botswana Constitution embodies the general principles of equality before the law and equal protection of the law. Article 15(1) and (2) prohibit the state from discriminating against any citizen on any of the listed grounds, which include the following: race, tribe, place of origin, political opinions, colour, creed, or sex. The ground of sex was initially not there. It was added after 1992 following the locus classicus case of Dow v. the Attorney General. Since then, the courts in some cases have ruled that the list is not closed and that any ground that is irrational is not permissible. As a result, the courts have ruled that it is not permissible to discriminate based on health and marital status.

The definition in the Constitution of 'discriminatory' is narrow, thereby narrowing the scope of the protection. Equality is formal but not substantive. The protection is limited to discriminatory laws and does not equate to a prohibition on discriminatory behaviour or practices in society more broadly.

The Constitution contains several exceptions to the prohibition of discriminatory laws. These exceptions include laws making provisions for adoption, marriage, divorce, burial, and devolution of property on death or other matters of personal law; These exceptions authorize discriminatory laws in these areas of law and contribute significantly to the inequality between men and women in Botswana.

The Constitution review process is an opportunity to expand the scope of Section 15 of the Constitution to include a definition of discrimination against women, covering all prohibited grounds of discrimination and encompassing both direct and indirect discrimination, in line with Article 1 of the Convention on the Elimination of All Forms of Discrimination against Women (CEDAW).

The list of grounds upon which it is not permissible to discriminate leaves out other grounds such as membership of a national minority, property, birth, age, or other personal or social circumstance, gender, pregnancy, marital status, and sexual orientation.

It may be good for civil society to prepare papers around the following themes that include the actual wording of the Constitutional provisions:

- Review the definition of discriminatory; in Section 15(3) of the Constitution to include direct and indirect discrimination.

- Expand the list of protected attributes in Section 15(3) of the Constitution to include gender identity, sexual orientation, age, marital status, disability, pregnancy, and parental status.

- Expand Section 15 prohibition on discriminatory laws to also apply to policies; eliminate the exceptions in Sections 15(4), (5), and (7).

Stand-Alone Provisions on Women's Rights

It may also be a good idea to have stand-alone provisions on women's rights like the provisions in Malawi and Zimbabwe:

The Constitution of Malawi states: Any law that discriminates against women on the basis of gender or marital status shall be invalid, and legislation shall be passed to eliminate customs and practices that discriminate against women;

The Zimbabwe Constitution provides that: [T]he State must take all measures, including legislative measures, needed to ensure that (i) both genders are equally represented in all institutions and agencies of government at every level; and (ii) women constitute at least half the membership of all Commissions and other elective and appointed governmental bodies established by or under this Constitution or any Act of Parliament;

Discrimination Based on Disability

Research has established that persons with disabilities are among the most discriminated. In most countries, as indeed is the case in our country, adults and children with disabilities have the lowest access to education and work opportunities. In some countries, children with disabilities are excluded from schools or put in separate schools. Similar patterns play out in the workplace.

Research has also established that both children with and without disabilities learn well in inclusive classrooms. It has been proven repeatedly that inclusive classrooms enable interaction between students with and without disabilities and reduce bias. It is true that equality cannot be proved through segregation.

Our Constitution would be enriched if it domesticates certain core features of the UN Convention on the Rights of People with Disabilities (CRPD), which was adopted in 2006.

The CRPD made history as the treaty with the largest number of signatories (82) on its opening day and thereafter became one of the most quickly ratified treaties ever adopted.

Botswana is among the countries that have ratified the Convention. The CRPD acknowledges that how societies are constructed shapes whether a given situation is disabling. It says that disability results from the interaction between persons with impairments and attitudinal and environmental barriers that hinder their full and effective participation in society on an equal basis with others;

Reforming The Electoral System

Botswana operates the first-past-the-post system, in which the winner takes all. Although the system has been said to be good on accountability, it allows a government elected by the minority of the population to govern, to the exclusion of other power blocks with a significant following.

Reforming the Botswana electoral system can improve our democracy. Although our electoral system has many strengths such as stability and accountability, it tends to exclude many disadvantaged groups, such as women, youth, and persons with disabilities.

It may be a good idea to debate whether we need the Constitution to prescribe quotas for women and other disadvantaged groups. The first-past-the-post electoral system is against women and other marginalized groups based on resources and historical reasons.

If quotas are considered necessary, say to improve women's representation, they can be applied in any one of the three most common electoral systems: first-past-the-post (FPTP), proportional representation (PR), or mixed-member proportional representation (MMPR).

The most effective combination is candidate quotas in a PR or list system, especially when this is based on a style list of one woman and one man. In this case, regardless of what proportion of seats a party wins, women will constitute half of those who win. In several Southern African countries with a PR system, such as South Africa, Namibia, and Mozambique, ruling parties have adopted voluntary quotas that have led to a substantial increase in women's representation.

Strengthening the independence of the institutions that support democracy.

Comparative Constitutional law suggests that there are many institutions that may be established to support or enhance democratic order. These institutions include the anti- corruption body, the Office of the Public Protector, Media Commission, Gender Commission, police complaints commission, and the Judiciary.

In Botswana, the independence of the anti-corruption body has been questioned. It has been suggested that it should be removed from the office of the president. The independence of the Independent Electoral Commission (IEC) has similarly been questioned. For instance, its inability to determine election dates has been a concern in some circles. The Judiciary is generally considered independent, especially when compared to all other institutions set up to support democracy, but of recent voices have been heard questioning the transparency of the process of appointing judges. As for the office of the public protector, both academic and public commentary suggests that it will best serve its functions if it is constitutionalized, and its powers expanded.

Botswana may also consider establishing in its revised Constitution, the Media Commission, the Human Rights Commission, and the Independent Police Complaints Commission, which it currently doesnt have. This may help enhance democracy and protect the nation better.

African Political Leadership – Reflections

Politics matter to everybody, even those who think it is a dirty game and would rather have nothing to do with it. If you try to disengage from politics, politics will never leave you alone.

It is because of this all-pervasive phenomenon called politics that it would be dangerous to leave politics to politicians alone. Politics is too important to be left to politicians alone. This is because politicians exercise public power, for better or for worse. They are the primary holders, controllers, and distributors of power and resources in any given country. They can make or break any country. Africa is a living example of endless wars, conflicts, poverty, bad governance, an epidemic of bad laws, exclusion arising in part because of poor leadership.

For decades, our resources have been plundered by foreigners and our own political leadership. Corruption and greed have drained the continent of any growth potential. If truth be told, there is enough beneath the African soil to ensure that the needs of all our people are met. However, to the contrary, we see famine, disease, and want.

Post-colonial leadership is characteristically neo-patrimonial, afflicted by greed and an over- concentration of power in central government, leaving out local government structures that are closer to the people.

We have witnessed unconstitutional takeovers of governments, election rigging, and the general subversion of democracy without consequences on a disturbing scale. We seem paralyzed to act against the unconstitutional takeover of power, and this paralysis is fuelling coups in our continent. Our continent is experiencing a democratic recession of a fundamental kind. Democratic recession, absence of the rule of law, poor governance, weak and fragmented opposition, constrained civil society and media, and politicized armies remain issues of concern. The new crop of African leaders must be personally committed to the values of democracy, the rule of law, and governance in both words and deeds and must be rooted among the people they lead. They must regard politics as a relay and run their part and give others the opportunity to do the same. We must break down the debilitating cycle where every outgoing president weaponizes the criminal justice system to hound the incoming president and learn to respect the voice of the people. Corruption and subverting the will of the people in any way and form must be treated as treasonable offenses.

The African transformative governance architecture, which includes the African Union (AU), the New Partnership for Africa's Development (NEPAD), and the African Peer Review Mechanism (APRM), although timely and important, continues to be government and elite- driven. Important legal frameworks such as the African Charter on Human and Peoples Rights, the African Charter on Democracy, Elections, and Governance (ACEDG), the Southern African Development Community (SADC) Treaty (and other regional instruments) that commit the continent to democracy, the rule of law, and good governance are honoured more in breach than in compliance. Sovereignty has become the ready-made antidote to democracy, the rule of law, and good governance.

As a new crop of African political leaders, it is your duty to reverse the current democratic backsliding that we see on the continent; find ways to end conflict, violations of human rights, and hunger, and create independent institutions that can support democracy and effectively address the underlying causes of Africa's underdevelopment. I support the call that has been made by many before me that the continent must invest in an effective, well- resourced Leadership Academy under the auspices of the AU and continental civil society to ensure that the continent produces leaders fit for the purpose.

Finally, I hope that as our future leaders, you can embrace a new mindset that enables you to appreciate that true leadership is not about control but service, and that any exercise of public power must be justifiable and primarily geared towards empowering people. Your duty as future leaders is to inspire your followers to be better than yourselves in rendering service to the people. As it is often said, inspiration is what makes people submit to the leader's vision.

It has been a pleasure and a true honour to share my thoughts with you on varied matters that are important for our continent to reawaken and realize its true potential. The future of our continent is in your hands. All the best. I thank you for your kind attention.

Chapter 2

Judicial Accountability

A Paper delivered at a Conference of the Commonwealth Magistrates and Judges Association (CMJA), 9th – 12th of September, 2019, Port Moresby, Papua New Guinea.

My Lords and Ladies,

I am very pleased and honored to stand before you to share my thoughts on the topic of judicial accountability. I express my sincere gratitude to the Secretariat of the Commonwealth Magistrates and Judges' Association for their kind invitation.

Before, I delve into the topic of today, I beg your indulgence to digress for a minute or so. In January, 2018, I set out to travel to Papua New Guinea to take up an appointment as a judge of the Supreme and National Courts of Papua New Guinea. It was in many ways a leap of faith. I had just known, a few months before my departure, that there is a country called Papua New Guinea. That illustrates how bad my geography was! Some of my colleagues and friends thought that I was out of my mind. They could only say to me "make sure you come back alive". Another friend actually suggested I should not end up in the pot. My kids, ever forward looking, would say in a chorus: "Go dad, go"!

Nothing I read online prepared me for the outpouring of love and affection I received from my colleagues on the bench and the ordinary people in the street. In the public spaces I visited, I was welcome like a long lost kin. I was called wantok. (A person with whom one has a strong social bond). Every time I travelled out of Papua New Guinea, airport officials would say to me: "we are the same". Once at Cuppa Café at Vision City one elderly man came to greet me and said: "welcome to Papua New Guinea. This is your home. When you go back to your country, tell them you saw family in PNG". I have not read archaeological evidence on the connection between the people of PNG and Africa but the similarities are striking!

It is a pity that many of you may not find time to experience the pure beauty of this country. Papua New Guinea is a stunning collection of beautiful islands, river systems, swamplands, jungles, mountain ranges and extremely warm people. I am proud to add my voice to the chorus of welcome messages you have already received – welcome to PNG the land of the unexpected.

I return to the topic of the day.

I propose to discuss the topic in broad terms and deal with issues of personal and institutional accountability, without in anyway being prescriptive, because, in my mind, "one size fits all" model to hold judicial officers accountable does not

exist, and it would not be prudent to attempt to develop same. The topic: Judicial accountability is very broad and has many elements. It includes: the process of selecting judges, disciplinary proceedings against judges, criticism of judges, recusal and declaration of assets and liabilities, and many more.

I have been privileged to serve as a judge in several jurisdictions, at the national and international level, including in this beautiful country, PNG, the land of the unexpected, and I am able to say, without fear of contradiction, that in all of them the issues surrounding independence and accountability are essentially the same.

Across the globe, judicial accountability has received increasing attention in recent years. It is generally accepted that judges must be held accountable for their involvement in human rights violations, breaches of ethical obligations and corruption. Yet in many developing countries judicial accountability remains a sensitive topic. Some take the view that judicial accountability is incompatible with judicial independence.

A prevailing theme in contemporary discourse on the rule of law is whether judicial independence and accountability are compatible, or whether accountability should be viewed as a correlative obligation of independence?

The extent to which the judiciary as an institution is accountable depends, to a large extent on the attitudes, mindset, orientation and behaviour of individual judges. It is my considered and respectful opinion that we must have a mindset that says we are the servants of the people.

Legal systems across the world have been grappling with balancing the independence of the judiciary and judicial accountability. While respecting the independence of the judiciary, a right balance must be struck between judicial independence and accountability. In my mind Judicial Independence and accountability complement each other. Whilst there is no specific formula to balance these two ideals, any mechanism meant to foster judicial accountability must nevertheless not endanger judicial independence.

My basic premise of departure is that in any democratic state all exercise of public power, necessarily demands some form of accountability and that the judiciary is no exception.

In this paper, I suggest that accountability is not only complimentary to independence but is essential in terms of ensuring public confidence. In addition to enhancing public confidence, judicial accountability also reinforces the legitimacy of the judiciary as a third co-equal arm of the state. It is important that judges should not consider judicial independence to be a shield against being accountable.

The judiciary in any democratic state exercises delegated power by the people and it is entrusted with providing a very important service to the people – the dispensation of justice. It may be true that many amongst us never think of the judiciary as a service provider. The truth is that it is. The people have genuine and legitimate expectations of how the judiciary should exercise its mandate.

The judiciary provides justice to the litigants and the public according to law. In order to earn the confidence and trust of the people the judiciary must be efficient. We need, at all times, to be conscious of our duty to deliver expeditious, affordable and quality justice to the people. The public expects their judiciary to deliver justice in a transparent manner. As is often said publicity and openness is the very soul of justice. The public expects their judicial officers to be independent, impartial, fair and competent.

The wretched of the earth: the homeless, the landless, those unjustifiably discriminated against, the hungry and those with no immediate name recognition or status in society, once they enter our courts, litigating against whosoever, the rich and the powerful, expect same treatment. Even the all – powerful state once it is sued, in the eyes of the law becomes just a litigant, and is not entitled to special treatment, unless as may be prescribed by law.

The public desire a justice system that is fair, predictable and accessible, one that produces reasonably predictable outcomes and in the event of a departure from what precedent has laid, a compelling or reasonable explanation for it.

Whilst we should not be unduly enslaved by precedent we should not lightly and without justifiable cause cast it aside. We must account why we depart from precedent if we decide that a particular precedent that has governed the lives of people must be cast aside as untenable. We must, as may be necessary, develop the law to keep pace with societal development.

Judges should not consider themselves sacred cows. We are not. We are not free to do what we please in accordance with our whimsical preferences, neither should we be a law unto ourselves or in any way be the overlords of the constitution that created us. Being accountable is essentially about being answerable to the people, through the constitution, the wielders of sovereign power. In suggesting that we are accountable to the people, through the constitution, I am not suggesting that public opinion directs us. Public opinion cannot and should not override the constitution.

Judicial accountability, of necessity differs in character, extent and approach from the accountability expected of the executive and the legislature. Judicial accountability must be balanced by a sufficient degree of protection for judicial independence. The executive and the legislature are directly accountable to the electorates. We are accountable to the people through the constitution.

As I indicated earlier, judicial accountability is necessary to secure the legitimacy

of the courts and to enable them to withstand possible incursions on their authority from other branches of the state and be able to deal with concerns that are often expressed, directed often at common law countries, where judges are not elected, that by virtue of not being elected, they are "anti – democratic" or "counter- majoritarian". As is often said, the legitimacy of the administration of justice, is a function of the extent to which the courts enjoy the broad confidence of the public.

I have often heard members of the public, including some lawyers, suggest that we are not accountable. However, many of us here would take the view that we are more accountable than the other branches of the state. Our long training, ethics, traditions and conventions make it obligatory to account. We account for our decisions by sitting in public, giving reasons for our decisions and delivering judgements openly, in public, and permitting those who may not be happy with our decisions to appeal.

One cannot over emphasize the importance of giving reasons for a decision. This is a primary means of judicial accountability. On occasions the urgency of the matter may necessitate an immediate order granting or refusing the relief sought. Such a decision is often followed by reasons for the decision.

Closely connected to the duty to give a well-reasoned judgment is the fact that the decisions of the lower courts are subject to review or appeal within the legal system. This is one of the tried and tested means by which judicial accountability is pursued in a number of jurisdictions across the world.

Another important aspect of external accountability relates to regular publication of judgements and reviews by scholars. This tends to promote sound court decisions as the judges will be conscious of the fact that the decisions that they render will be scrutinized.

A further aspect of judicial accountability is the need to deliver judgements expeditiously. Long delays in resolving disputes and in delivery of judgements in particular, is function of many reasons, including availability of resources and conditions of service. Whilst any undue delay is regrettable, delays in matters concerning the liberty of the subject are to be avoided at all costs.

The question that often arises is to whom are judges accountable? Most judicial officers would say to the constitution and our conscience.

A story is told of a conversation between Mr. Justice Learned Hand, of the United States and his clerk, which went thus:

"Sonny…to whom am I responsible? No one can fire me. No one can dock my pay. Even those nine bozos (justices) in Washington, who sometimes reverse me, can't make me decide as they wish. Everyone should be responsible to someone. To whom am I responsible"?

The judge then turned and pointed to the shelves of his library and said: "To those books about us. That's to whom I am responsible."

It is also said that Lord Donaldson, the former English Master of the Rolls once said: "Judges are without constituency and answerable to no one except their consciences and the law".

A friend of mine, Justice Moroka of the Botswana High Court, our literary giant, finds being accountable to the conscience problematic become some consciences are not compatible with the constitution.

The powers of the courts to strike down legislation as being ultra vires the constitution has led to renewed calls for greater judicial accountability. Judicial corruption has also dominated judicial accountability debates especially in Africa and many other developing countries. There is a general perception that high rates of judicial corruption are prevalent in developing countries, and this makes judicial accountability an important tool in promoting the judiciary's responsibility to society.

A distinction is sometimes made between the individual accountability of judges and the institutional accountability of the judiciary as a whole. A survey of the literature on judicial accountability identifies four basic elements of it, which are transparency, political accountability, personal accountability and public accountability. These elements of judicial accountability hinge on identifying to whom judges are accountable to and the mechanism to ensure that accountability.

Transparency is an essential and critical prerequisite to judicial accountability. It necessarily follows that, transparency is the key to both judicial independence and accountability. Transparency entails several factors. First, judicial accountability is strengthened when judges are appointed on merit using a transparent judicial appointment criteria.

It seems incontrovertible that an open and participatory judicial selection system has better prospects of selecting more competent judges. Invariably, judges appointed in such a manner are better placed to administer their judicial functions in a fair and impartial manner. They are more likely to be sensitive to their obligation to account. What then are the qualities a candidate of judgeship must possess? Many decades ago, a British Lord Chancellor is alleged to have said, in speaking of his power to appoint judges:

"I like my judges to be gentlemen. If they know a little law so much the better".

I know that by today's standards the above statement may be objectionable on many grounds, including that it appears sexist. I am certain that today, many amongst us would prefer a much more elaborate and rigorous criteria that

includes the following: experience in the practice of the law, demonstrated superior knowledge of the law, superior analytical skills, clarity of thought as demonstrated through written expression, ability to work under pressure requiring ability to go through voluminous documents in any area of the law, integrity, courage, discretion and open –mindedness.

A famous but probably untrue story is told that a former US President was asked by a journalist whether he ever made a mistake. The President said: "Yes, I made two mistakes and both of them are sitting in the Supreme Court".

The President is reported to have been referring to the appointment of Chief Justice Earl Warren and Justice William Brennan, who turned out to be more liberal than the conservative appointing authority had thought. As many of us here may well know, once appointed judges choose their own path. In the US they say: "You shoot an arrow into a far distant future, when you appoint a justice."

The process of appointing judges is as important as the process of their removal. Both processes must be done in a transparent manner. The removal of judges must be fair and should never be politically motivated. A transparent mechanism of registering complaints against judicial impropriety is an important aspect of judicial accountability. It leads to greater public confidence in the judiciary. Disciplinary proceedings against judges should not be held in a secretive manner as that tends to undermine public confidence and trust in the judiciary. To this extent, an open disciplinary system coupled with public access to court records increases transparency in the whole adjudicative process.

In some jurisdictions, the judiciary publishes annual reports which are an important information tool which promotes public debate concerning the judiciary's activities.

It is also important as a form of accountability for Chief Justices to regularly report to the public about their performance and challenges. Many countries are increasingly fostering judicial accountability through judicial codes of conduct which go a long way in promoting internal accountability.

Judicial codes of conduct are primarily meant to ensure that the judiciary behaves in a manner that is consistent with their constitutional mandate and the expectations of the people.

In some jurisdictions such as South Africa, the Judicial Services Act establishes some structures to deal with judges' discipline: Judicial Conduct Committee (JCC) and Judicial Conduct Tribunal (JCT). The JCC which meets from time to time to consider complaints against judges is chaired by the Chief Justice. In PNG, judges have since independence been accountable under the Leadership Code which recognizes the special roles judges play as leaders in society and the corresponding responsibility that it entails.

Disclosure of assets and liabilities is an important form of accountability. In some jurisdictions judges are required to disclose their registrable interests which

include: immovable property, shares, directorships and judges are prohibited from holding any office of profit, or receiving payment for any service, other than that rendered by virtue of being a judge.

Other mechanisms of enhancing judicial accountability have been formulated such as performance evaluations and judicial training for judges. Performance evaluations for judges are now a common feature in many jurisdictions. In other jurisdictions judges are required to report to the Chief Justice about their load, disposal rate and the extent and age of reserved judgements. If properly done performance evaluations can encourage high standards of professionalism on the part of judges. However, care must be taken that such evaluations must not be a mechanism for witch-hunting especially if judges render politically unpopular decisions. A performance evaluation of judges is a sensitive area and must be done with extreme care.

The other way of accounting to the public is to accept that the judiciary is not above genuine and informed criticism. Any criticism against the judiciary must be sincere and well informed and not malicious and simply intended to bring the judiciary into disrepute. Judicial officers should not take the title "My Lords/Ladies and "Your worships" literally and as suggesting that they cannot make mistakes. Judges are human. They make mistakes. Even the apex courts make mistakes.

As former justice of the US Supreme Court, Robert H Jackson, once said of the apex courts: "We are not final because we are infallible, but we are infallible only because we are final".

In regard to criticism of the Judiciary, Sir Anthony Mason in an article, entitled: "The Judiciary, The Community and the Media (1998) ALJ 33 at 40, stated that: Like other public institutions, the judiciary must be subject to fair criticism and, if the occasion demands it, trenchant criticism. What I am concerned with is response to criticism, particularly criticism that is illegitimate and irresponsible."

In India, Mr. Justice Bhagwati, the former Chief Justice of India, in an article entitled: "Independence of the Judiciary In a Democracy, Human Rights Solidarity – AHRC Newsletter – Vol.7 (April-July 1997) at p.34 stated that:

"There is a pernicious tendency on the part of some to attack judges if the decision does not go the way they want or if it is not in accordance with their views. Of course, there is nothing wrong in critically evaluating the judgment given by a judge because, as observed by Lord Atkin, justice is not a cloistered virtue and she must be allowed to suffer criticism and or respectful, though outspoken, comments of ordinary men and women. But improper or intemperate criticism of judges stemming from dissatisfaction with their decisions constitutes a serious inroad into the independence of the judiciary and, whatever may be the form or shape which such criticism takes, it has the inevitable effect of eroding the independence of the judiciary..."

As many of us here would agree a malicious and ill-informed attack on decisions of judges represents an attempt on the part of those who indulge in such criticism to coerce judicial conformity with their own notions of justice and preconceptions.

It is often an attempt to influence the decision-making process. The best protection against such ill-informed attacks is to deliver well- reasoned judgements based purely on facts and law.

It is of critical importance, in a democratic country governed by the rule of law that every decision be made independently and impartially by judges having regard to the evidence and the law and not under the pressure of one group or a litigant who is simply unhappy with the decision of the court.

No judge should feel pressured by any one, whether a pressure group or the media as that would certainly undermine the independence of the judiciary. And if malicious and ill-informed criticism is permitted, as we see happening in many countries, the standing of the judiciary is often damaged.

Recusal is another form of accountability. It is common for judges to be asked to recuse themselves. Usually these applications are made in open court and the reasons for such applications are made known. The judges are required to dispassionately consider such applications and either grant or refuse same.

However, it must be stated that judges should not too readily and without justifiable cause accede to applications for disqualification, whereby parties may effectively influence the choice of a Judge in their case. A Judge may disqualify himself in circumstances where a fair minded and well informed observer, with knowledge of the material facts, might entertain a reasonable apprehension that the Judge might not decide the matter in an impartial manner.

A Judge should disqualify himself for reasons of apprehension of bias, where it is proven, by cogent and credible evidence that, he has an interest in the case before him, which interest may be direct, indirect, pecuniary or otherwise. Judges should not recuse themselves to avoid complex and involving matters. The onus rests with the applicant. In considering recusal it must be borne in mind that sometime absolute neutrality is impossible – and may even be undesirable.

In conclusion, it is worth reminding ourselves that to do justice according to law is what we are about. That is our core mandate. We come from different jurisdictions; at different stages of development and with unique challenges. Our approaches to the rule of law – particularly the approach of the executive to decisions of the courts often differ. Two examples illustrate this point.

It is recorded that in 1832 the Cherokee Indians won a landmark case upholding their land rights against the invasion of white colonial settlers. The then President sent troops to ensure that the decision was not enforced. In 1955, in Brown v Board of Education, the US Supreme Court ordered an end to segregated education, under the infamous "separate but equal doctrine". Contrary to the position indicated above, in India, the then President of the US, notwithstanding his personal misgivings and considerable public opposition to the Supreme Court decision, sent federal troops to ensure that the ruling was enforced.

Judicial accountability is linked to judicial independence. The former must not suffocate the latter. The Rule of law, which includes the independence of judges has to be continuously fought for and improved. Judicial independence earns judicial officers respect. Such respect must be earned and not demanded – and we can only earn it if we are accountable.

It is suggested that Chief Justices must make judicial accountability a priority for judicial reform if they want to have maximum impact towards the fair and efficient administration of justice and respect of human rights and the law.

It is also suggested that judiciaries must develop (those that have not) judicial codes that contain precise and detailed definitions of prohibited conduct, constituting grounds for disciplinary proceedings. In countries with professional associations of judges, it is important that they be involved in the drafting of such codes. It is a good idea for judicial officers to have professional associations that can represent their interests and defend judicial independence and the rule of Law.

It has been a pleasure and a rare honour to share my thoughts with colleagues on a subject that is critically important to our core mandate: dispensation of justice. I thank you for your attention and the pleasure of your company.

Chapter 3

Judicial Independence and The Right To Equality

A paper presented at a Seminar on the Courts' Role in Protecting the Right to Equality of Vulnerable groups – July 2014 - Gaborone

'The Independence of the judiciary is crucial. It constitutes the ultimate shield against that incremental and invisible corrosion of our moral universe, which is so much more menacing than direct confrontation with visible waves of barbarism...Subvert that independence and you subvert the very foundations of constitutional democracy. Attack the independence of judges and you attack the very foundations of freedoms articulated by the Constitution to protect humankind from injustice, tyranny and brutality. (Chief Justice Mohamed, in an address to the International Commission of Jurists, Cape Town, 21 July 1998).'

Introduction

In this paper, I propose to interrogate the issue of the Independence of the Judiciary and link it with the concept of equality and perhaps indicate how only an Independent Judiciary can demonstrate an unequivocal fidelity to the Constitution and effect the promise of the Constitution in so far as issues of human rights are concerned.

The concept of Independence of the Judiciary has been interrogated ad infinitum, in countless legal forums of this nature. It is now widely accepted that the Independence of the Judiciary is indispensable in any democratic order. As it is often said, there can be no Government of law without a fearless and Independent Judiciary. A Judge must be free from all external influence and subservient only to his own conscience.

Both the Universal Declaration of Human Rights of 1948, of which my sister Monageng J, of the ICC fame, spoke eloquently about earlier, and the International Convention on Civil and Political Rights of 1966, indicate in very clear terms that an Independent Judiciary is one of the essential elements of safeguarding human rights.

An Independent Judiciary is the one that harbours no fear of any adverse consequence that may result from any unfavourable ruling against a litigant, whether a litigant is an ordinary person or a government.

The role of an Independent Judiciary hinges on its ability to deal with cases impartially and in accordance with the law, especially those concerning grave and sensitive constitutional issues. A Judge must not fear to take the path least travelled because there is a chorus moving in the opposite direction, as long as his/her conscience and understanding of the law allows that cause of action- for at the heart of the discipline of law is not only institutional independence but the independence of the individual judge.

In my experience, an independent Judge must not be a slave of precedent if the said precedent will yield injustice. He must possess a mind-set that ruthlessly scrutinizes all ideas old and new. This, in my experience, is how the law is developed to keep pace with a fast changing society.

Law, it must always be remembered, exist for the purposes of establishing justice and when they fail in this purpose, they demean and debase the title that precedes every Judge's name. In the contemporary society we live in, the concept of justice is represented by the Roman goddess Justitia, or Lady Justice. Lady Justice, as can be seen atop the High Court Building, in the CBD, is usually portrayed as a blind folded woman with a sword in one hand scales in the other. The symbolism is profound: Justice should be blind; it must pay no regard to class no colour. Before the courts of law, all are equal. The scale communicates the idea that the evidence must be weighed and the issues viewed in a balanced manner.

Only an Independent Judiciary can do so.

It has often been said that the dispensation of justice is an attribute of God. Indeed, blessed are those on whom that Godly assignment has befallen. Even more blessed are those who are fearlessly independent and decide cases independently, impartially, and with integrity, even if in doing so, they risk the heavens falling on them. This may appear polemical, falling from the lips of a Judge, but every Judge, is oath bound to 'walk the talk' if I were to borrow the contemporary lingo of the current generation.

It makes sense therefore that ordinary mortals holding so much power must be truly independent. A Judge has the power to grant the freedom of living or the sentence of death. He has the power to keep historically marginalized groups - many on account of prejudice and stereotyping, in bondage or to free them. A Judge's mind and how it translates into a judgment can turn riches into rags and a pauper into a millionaire. The mere power Judges have, the more humility, rationality, and balance must be, among their possession.

An assessment of the performance of African Judiciaries in the post-colonial period - specifically with regard to sensitive and grave constitutional issues has revealed that a combination of timidity and undue deference to the executive has arrested the development of the law and its capacity to come to the rescue of the marginalized people especially in areas of discrimination based on gender or sexual orientation.

It must also be said that Judicial Independence includes the right of the Court to get its decision wrong as well as right.

According to Fombad, the actual role that Judicial Independence plays has been underscored in some empirical studies that have demonstrated that the extent of Judicial Independence does have an actual impact on the state of human rights behaviour in any country.

Judges must at all times exemplify the virtues of independence and impartiality by refraining especially in Court from making ill considered remarks that reveal them as prejudicial and incapable of bringing to bear on a dispute an open and logical mind. To this extent, I am tempted to share with you an instructive remark by an eminent jurist of the High Court of Australia, Hon Justice Michael Kirby, who in commenting on ill-considered prejudicial commentary by a Judge said:

'One of my judicial colleagues was given to making inappropriate jests at the expense of women and minorities (in court). When next he attempted such a remark, I observed that he neither spoke for me nor the Court. Soon his jests were a thing of the past.'

Emerging Jurisprudence on the Right to Equality

Recent comparative studies have commended the Botswana Judiciary for being independent and for their enthusiasm to protect the right to equality. The recent decision of the High Court and Court of Appeal in Mmusi v Ramantele, has been praised, on the main, for making it clear that any discriminatory practise based on gender would not pass constitutional muster. This decision by both the High Court of Botswana and Court of Appeal has received widespread commentary. Some commentary is quite critical.

The High Court has been criticized for being too quick to suppress customary law by inappropriately referring to comparative case law and international legal instruments to validate its decision. The Court of Appeal has been admonished for glossing over the High Court extensive use of comparative case law and international legal instruments.

It is clear when reading the case of Mmusi/Ramantele that the decision has been inspired by the high water mark case of Dow v Attorney General, which until recently, in my knowledge at least, has been treated as the sacred cow!.

However, in a recent article by Lekgowe both the Dow and Mmusi decisions have been slammed as incorrectly decided.

According to Lekgowe, Mmusi did not implicate Section 3 because the complainant was complaining about her right to inherit which is not a fundamental right. He also argues that both Dow and Mmusi should have been determined on the basis of Section 15, which in essence is the equality provision. Mmusi located the principle of equality in Section 3 of the Constitution of Botswana in so far as reference is made in that section to 'equal protection of the law' and did not resolve the issue in terms of Section 15 because the applicant had abandoned the challenge based on Section 15.

It has been suggested, in some literature that the Court should have resolved the matter in terms of both Section 3 and 15 - the latter being the main section on equality.

The principle of equality is generally considered by some authorities as being intertwined with the principle of discrimination. Benson has pointed out that:

'Generally speaking, equality and non-discrimination are positive and negative statements of the same principle. One is treated equally when one is not discriminated and one is discriminated against when one is not treated equally.'

It would seem that both the Botswana High Court and Court of Appeal hold the view that the 'protection of the law' in Sec 3(a) of the Constitution also means that laws must treat all people equally.

In the Dow Case, the Court of Appeal stated that Section 3(a) conferred the right of equal protection of the law on individuals, likening it with the language of the 14th amendment of the United States constitution which forbids the State to 'deny any person within its jurisdiction the equal protection of the laws'.

In the Kamanakao case, the High Court held that the 'protection of the law' in Section 3(a) of the Constitution was more than protection by law enforcements but mandated that laws must treat all people equally.

In Mmusi, the High Court held that the principle of equality seeks to ensure that:

'No member of society should be made to feel that they are not deserving of equal concern, respect and consideration and that law is likely to be used against them more harshly than others who belong to other groups.'

Sexual Orientation and Discrimination

The sad reality of our contemporary world is that human rights are still contested. Many, even within the ranks of the Judges still pay lip service to the truism that human rights are universal, interdependent and indivisible. There is still resistance and even opposition from conservative elements in society, and in the judiciary in particular, to accommodate sexual minorities in the human rights discourse. Yet it must be said, unequivocally, that discrimination based on irrational grounds is totally unacceptable. For no one can deny that sexual minorities are human beings.

In the South African Constitutional Court, Ackarmen J in the National Coalition for Gay and Lesbian Equality v Minister of Justice and Others, stated the following on the topic of criminal prohibition on sodomy:

'It punishes a form of sexual conduct which is identified by our broader society with homosexual. Its symbolic effect is to state that in the eyes of our legal system all gay men are criminals. The stigma thus attached to a significant proportion of our population is manifest. But the harm imposed by the criminal law is far more than symbolic. As a result of the criminal offence, gay men are at risk of arrest, prosecution and conviction of the offence of sodomy simply because they seek to engage in sexual conduct which is part of their experience of being human. Just as apartheid legislation rendered the lives of couples of different racial groups perpetually at risk, the sodomy offence builds insecurity and vulnerability into the lives of gay men. There can be no doubt that the existence of a law which punishes a form of sexual expression for gay men degrades and devalues gay men in the broader society. As such it is a palpable invasion of their dignity and a breach of section 10 of the Constitution.'

The court thus unanimously concluded that the common law crime of sodomy was inconsistent with the Constitution, and accordingly, invalid.

The Botswana Court of Appeal in Kanane v The State, seemed to take a different view to the South African case cited above. Their decision has been criticized as retrogressive in a piece crafted by Chilisa, in one of the journals published by the Botswana Network on Ethics Law and HIV/AIDS (BONELA) a few years ago. What is clear from reading Kanane is that the Court did not interrogate the relevance of the right to dignity, which is a fundamental right or value to any bill of rights. It may well be that this was so because the right to dignity was not argued, perhaps because it is not expressly provided in the Constitution. Yet no one can credibly contest the view that the concept of human dignity is what informs the entire bill of rights.

As anyone familiar with the discourse on human rights would easily testify, majoritarian preference can often be harsh and oppressive to minorities who exist outside the mainstream. It is the function of those charged with dispensing justice, consistent with the test and logic of the Constitution, to come to the rescue of the minorities and to validate their humanity - as long as, in doing so, no prejudice is done to the fundamental right of any person or group. Equality does not mean uniformity. It also recognizes divergence, even if such divergence may be uncomfortable to some.

International human rights treaty bodies and Courts have increasingly recognized that sexual orientation falls within the prohibited grounds of discrimination - either as falling within the grounds of 'sex' or other 'status' or as an aspect of diversity, akin to the listed grounds, and therefore an analogous ground.

In Tooney v Austria the HRC held that 'sex' includes 'sexual orientation.' The HRC made a similar finding in the case of Young v Australia and X v Colombia which both related to different treatment of pension benefits for same sex partners, and held that it violated the right to be free from discrimination on the grounds of sex or sexual orientation.

In Suratt and Others v Attorney General of Trinidad and Tobago, the Court of Appeal, per Archie JA, held that irrespective of whether same-sex sexual activity is a crime, sexual orientation is not a reasonable basis for distinction:

"The effect of specifically excluding a particular category of persons, on the ground of sexual orientation, from the protection afforded by the Equal Opportunity Act to others, is to deny them a fundamental right on a basis analogous to one of the grounds enumerated under section 4 of the Constitution (i.e. sex). It is a denial of the protection of the law and of equality of treatment under the law."

Conclusion

In my experience, grave and sensitive constitutional cases such as the ones concerning discrimination on the basis of the grounds not listed in Section 15 require more than a positivist outlook. According to Austin, the classical role of a Judge is that of a mechanical interpretation of the law as enacted by parliament. Such an approach gives extreme deference to the value judgements of parliament or the executive.

With respect to cases involving equality and non-discrimination, especially concerning the grounds analogous to the ones stated in Section 15 of our Constitution, upon which is not competent to discriminate, no Judge can afford under the Austinian approach. They must, instead, engage in transformative jurisprudence to the extent permitted by the Constitution. In the world we live in, characterized by the ever changing nature of human rights issues, the Courts in some countries, such as The United States, India, and South Africa, to mention but a few, have devised a number of strategies to expand the scope and quality of human rights protection.

Chapter 4

Financial Independence and Autonomy of The Judiciary

A Paper presented at the Judicial Conference held on the 25 -26 July 2023 at Palapye.

"At the moment that a court accepts jurisdiction over a controversy between government and an individual", government is demoted – it loses its claim to be the exclusive representative of the state. At the same time, the individual is promoted to a public role, to one with an equal claim to represent the state. The court, then, in deciding between these claims, articulate a vision of what the state is and publicly draws the line between law and politics… In order to articulate this vision, the court needs to be independent…" (David Dyzenhaus: 1998)

Introduction

An independent judiciary lies at the heart of democracy. Various international treaties including the Universal Declaration of Human Rights (1948) (UDHR), the International Covenant on Civil and Political Rights (1976) (ICCPR) and the African Charter on Human & Peoples rights (1981) contain provisions affirming the importance of an independent judiciary in a democratic society.

The principle of judicial independence has two components: individual independence and institutional independence. Institutional independence refers to the existence of "structures and guarantees to protect courts and judicial officers from interference by other branches of government", while individual independence refers to judicial officers' acting independently and impartially.

One of the accepted facets of 'institutional independence' is the one concerning the financial resources and financial freedom or autonomy that is to be given to the judiciary. Today, this concept has been developed and accepted in most of the democracies governed by the rule of law. The doctrine of separation of powers has been suitably modified and adjusted to achieve the above goal of financial freedom of the judiciary. The principle of judicial independence is almost universally accepted.

This paper focuses on how to strengthen the institutional independence of the judiciary, so that the judiciary does not become the weakest link in the tripartite arrangement of our constitutional order.

In the scheme of power, and of the efficacy of institutions, the Judiciary is not able to compete with an Executive which has its roots in the Legislature. Alexander Hamilton, in relation to early constitution-making in the Unites States of America, observed that.

"Whoever considers the different departments of power must perceive that…the judiciary, from the nature of its functions, will always be the least dangerous to the political rights of the constitution…the executive not only dispenses the honours but holds the sword of the community. The legislature not only commands the purse but prescribes the rules by which the duties and rights of every citizen are to be regulated. The judiciary, on the contrary, has no influence over the sword or the purse; no direction either of the strength or the wealth of the society and can take no active resolution whatever. It may truly be said to have neither Force nor Will but mere judgment…" –

Financial Independence and Autonomy of The Judiciary

While Judicial Independence may be guaranteed under most constitutions, the financial and administrative aspects of the judiciary in some jurisdictions in reality continue to be controlled by the Executive. As Chief Justice Gicheru of Kenya put it:

"The institutions that control the purse and the administrative support of the judiciary can also directly control the extent and efficiency in the execution of the role. It is simply a case of he who pays the piper calling the tune. The necessary judicial independence of the judiciary cannot be achieved if the court finances are determined and dictated by the political organs of the Executive and the Legislatures over whom the court should exercise judicial control"

According to Justice Browne – Wilkinson, lack of "financial support" by a Government is a clear "threat to the independence of the legal system". He says:

"Control of the finance and administration of the legal system is capable of preventing the performance of those very functions which the independence of the Judiciary is intended to preserve, that is to say, the right of the individual to a speedy and fair trial of his claim by an independent Judge.....the enforcement of the rule of law by the Judges could be wholly frustrated by the refusal to appoint Judges, to provide court rooms for them to sit in or staff to service those courts....there is a failure of the provision of adequate courts and court staff to meet society's current demands for Justice....It is that aspect of the independence of the Judiciary which I wish to consider...."

In many jurisdictions, judiciaries complain of insufficient funds; that the funds availed to them by the executives are grossly inadequate to meet the requirements of the judiciary. It is all too common for the judiciaries to beg for resources to enable them to build courts, to hire adequate staff, to avail funds to afford judicial officers to attend conferences in furtherance of their professional development; to provide accommodation, vehicles, security and all other matters that are incidental to secure the proper independence of the judiciary.

Institutional independence requires that the judiciary must have its own budget sourced from the consolidated fund; and that it must have a separate accounting system. The judiciary should be able to have a budget that enables it to procure all that it needs to function efficiently and independently in that going down on its knees to beg the executive which is a regular litigant before the courts.

A Synopsis of Funding The Judiciary on Botswana

Budgeting in Government is done in terms of Chapter two of the Financial Instructions and Procedures (from Financial Instructions 201-207) and the Finance and Audit Act.

The budget of the judiciary is not paid directly from the consolidated fund but comes from a warrant voted to the Minister of Finance for the entire Government. The Accounting Officer of the Judiciary follows the same procedure prescribed for all other Ministries and Departments for getting the budget approved for the Judiciary. There is therefore no special procedure prescribed for voting the budget of the Judiciary.

The budgeting process starts with the Permanent Secretary in the Ministry of Finance issuing a circular concerning the preparation of Recurrent Estimates for the next financial year. This is done six months before submission of the Estimates to the National Assembly. The Accounting Officer then prepares the estimates of his organization in accordance with the format and submits them to the Ministry within the prescribed timetable. The draft estimates must reflect the needs of the Judiciary and must be consistent with the National Development Plan. The National Development Plan is an agreed six-year plan mapping out the plans for Government during that plan period. For instance, NDP 10 which started in 2010 to 2016.

The submissions for the estimates are then examined by a committee normally chaired by the Permanent Secretary in the Ministry of Finance. Accounting Officers are questioned by this committee on their submissions. The Committee has extensive powers of reducing or increasing the budget estimates of an Organisation within the Cabinet set ceilings and also guided by the economic outlook. The committee then reports to the Minister who in turns makes recommendations on the budget to Cabinet.

Parallel to the preparation of the budget, the Budget speech is also prepared. Cabinet considers the estimates and once it is satisfied with them, the Budget Speech is finalized and estimates will now be ready to be submitted to the National Assembly for approval together with the necessary appropriation Bill required to authorize the expenditure contained in the estimates. When the Bill has gone through all the stages of Appropriate Bill is promulgated.

The Minister of Finance then makes a warrant for expenditure to the Permanent Secretary of Finance.

Ministries and Independent Departments through the Minister responsible submit their budget to the Committee of Supply for approval. The Budget of the Judiciary is submitted by the Minister of Defence Justice and Security who must also debate it in Parliament.

Once the Committee of Supply has approved the budget of the Judiciary, the Permanent Secretary responsible for finance, make a warrant to the Accounting Officer of the Judiciary to start spending within the limits of his warrant.

Accounting for Resources of The Judiciary

The Registrar is by virtue of that position an accounting officer for the Judiciary. In that position he is responsible for administering the functions prescribed in the Finance and Audit Act and Regulations made there under and the Supplies Regulations & Procedure. He/she therefore account for all the resources that have been approved for the judiciary. For instance, financial allocation, human resources, development of infrastructure, procurement, transport etc. He/she must manage all the resources allocated to Administration of Justice efficiently for the maximum productivity of the Judiciary. Accounting Officer is defined in the Financial Instructions and Procedures as;

"…….. the public officer designated by the Minister responsible for Finance in accordance with the provisions of the Finance and Audit Act (Cap 54:01). Such officer will normally be the Permanent Secretary of the Ministry or Head of an Extra Ministerial Department and on appointment to his office he will be issued by the Permanent Secretary of the Ministry responsible for Finance with a letter setting out in general terms his responsibilities and duties in connection with financial administration and control and his relationship with the Ministry responsible for Finance, the Public Accounts Committee, the Auditor General, and the Minister."

As accounting officer, the Registrar is responsible for:

a. the control of expenditure

b. the collection of revenue and the payment thereof into the consolidated fund, the Development Fund or a Special Fund, as the case may be:

c. the control, custody, issue and use of all public stores

d. the custody of public monies for the Head in respect of which he is designated: and

e. the control and reconciliation of all other public funds for which he is responsible.

Funding for the Judiciary in Botswana continues to be a challenge. Every year the Judiciary runs out of funding towards the end of the financial year resulting in cases being halted due to the courts inability to pay witnesses allowances, pro deo fees, travelling and subsistence allowances for judicial officers and support staff. In turn this impacts on the constitutional rights of accused persons in particular those held in custody as they cannot be heard. Hearing of cases within a reasonable time (Sec 10 of the Constitution) is seriously compromised resulting in applications for dismissals of cases for delays in prosecutions.

In summary

a. The budgeting process of the Judiciary takes the same form and follows the same procedure as the budget of any Ministry of Independent Department of Government.

b. The budget is determined by the viability of the economy

c. Reviews between the budget processes (Mid-term reviews) may depending on the performance of the economy result in reduction of the allocated budget or suspension of some of the projects/programmes approved for the Judiciary in the financial year.

d. The budget of the Judiciary does not enjoy any protection as it is not paid directly from the Consolidated Fund.

It is absolutely important that the judiciaries be entrusted with sufficient financial and administration autonomy to support its day-to-day operations and activities. Control of funds by the executive obviously breeds bureaucratic delays and redtape and negatively affects the efficiency of the judiciary.

The performance of the judiciary in its constitutional mandate depends directly upon financial autonomy of the court because efficiency and efficient administration requires resources to support the remuneration of necessary staff and acquisition of equipment and facilities. In the interest of the independence of the judiciary, it is important that the administration of the judiciary be carried out by the judiciary itself or/by a professional agency under the superintendence of the judiciary."

Comparative Review of the Position

USA

In the USA, the Judicial Conference of the US is a statutory body for the Federal Courts created in 1922 and it is the policy making body and it acts through its various Committees including committees for long-range Planning, Budgeting, space or Accommodation and Technology. It has its own bureaucracy – under its control – the Administrative office of the Courts in the USA. Statute vested the entire judicial administration in 1939 in this Administrative Office under the control of the Judicial Conference after shifting it from the office of the Attorney General. The staff and officers of the Courts are under the control of Courts. Budget for the Federal Courts is prepared on the basis of the policies of the Conference, the data prepared by the Administrative Office, in consultation with the Courts. It normally takes 18 months to prepare a budget. The Conference has to meet twice in one year. The Administrative Office gives it two reports in advance before each meeting. The budget proposals do not go to the Executive but are submitted direct to the Congress.

England

In England, Judges are not involved in any policies or planning. The court officers are integrated into the civil service. The officers in the Lord-Chancellor's office are also part of the Executive. Judges are not consulted in the budget formulations. The matter is under the exclusive control of the Lord Chancellor's office. The Lord Chancellor's office prepares the budget. The budget is not directly submitted to Parliament but is submitted through the Executive. There is no place for the Judges in any of these matters. The Vice Chancellor has grave doubts whether such a system is conducive to judicial independence… Thus in the area of Court finances the Judges have no say in UK. But in the matter of salaries, UK is far ahead of all countries. With the setting up of the 'Top Salaries Review Board' for Judges, Permanent Secretaries and others. The Advisory Group for Judiciary in that Board has thought it fit to consider that Judges' salaries must bear a reasonable proportion to the salaries received in Industry and to the net income of leaders of the Bar. Because of this approach, Judicial salaries which at one time were below (and later equal to) those of the Permanent Secretaries have now gone ahead of the salaries of Permanent Secretaries and also gone ahead of inflation.

Australia

In Australia, at least in the High Court, the Federal Courts and Family Courts – the control over the staff and financial budget is within the Judiciary. But the budgets are presented to the legislature by a Minister. The Legislature makes a 'single line' appropriation and there is flexibility in shifting the budget grants from one head to another. In all other courts, the staff and budgets are under executive control. There the budget is an identifiable part of the budget of the Ministry of Justice. Policies are not made in consultation with the Judiciary. However, salaries are increased according to inflation and the matters can go before Tribunal manned by a former judge and his decision is placed before the legislature for approval or deemed approval.

India

In India, there is an advantage of the Court officers and staff being under the complete control of the Judiciary from the highest court to the lowest courts. That way, the system is better than that of UK and France. But the main problems are in regard to policy-making and finances.

The Judges are not involved directly in any policy making. All the judges are not involved in the preparation of the budget. The Chief Justice of India and the Chief Justices of the Courts no doubt prepare a budget with the help of their Registrars but these are routine budgets based upon a notional increase of the figures of previous years. They are not based on any long range or short range plans for the Judiciary. The budgets are sent to the Executive and suffer serious cuts. The budget is so even at the State level.

There is neither an independent judicial council or conference with statutory status, nor an independent bureaucracy of court administration who can prepare the budgets and who can independently spend the lump sum allocation under various heads, subject to supervision by the Judges' Council. The judiciary's budget is part of the executive budget.

Lesotho

The Lesotho Constitution casts an obligation upon "the Government to accord such assistance as the courts may require enabling them to protect their independence, dignity and effectiveness" and to discharge their functions under the Constitution to the law.

In practice the judiciary lacks financial autonomy and its finances and administration have been directly controlled by the Ministry of Justice.

The Judiciary should not be treated as if it is another administrative department and the Ministry of Justice for it is not. It is an institution under the Constitution which qualifies as an independent institution; whose accountability and responsibility should go hand in hand. Judicial independence without administrative and financial autonomy may turn out to be meaningless. Autonomy implies control of resources both human and material and without this autonomy there can be no accountability to speak about. The needs of the judiciary and its corners can only be addressed if and only if the judiciary can itself assess and determine these needs and concerns.

Conclusion

It is our considered view that sufficient and sustainable funding should be provided to enable the judiciary to perform its functions to the highest standards. Such funds, once voted for the judiciary by the legislature, should be protected from alienation or misuse. The executive should not be allowed to use funding as a means of exercising improper control over the judiciary.

Appropriate salaries and benefits, supporting staff, resources and equipment are essential to the proper functioning of the judiciary.

As a matter of principle, judicial salaries and benefits should be set by an independent body and their value should be maintained."

As part guaranteeing the institutional and personal independence of the judiciaries, judicial salaries and benefits should be set by an independent body and their value should be maintained.

It is our respectful view that the manner in which the judiciary is funded in Botswana needs to be improved. It may be helpful to source the funding of the judiciary from the consolidated fund and for the judiciary to have control over its budget

Chapter 5

A Synopsis of Justice Delivery Constraints and Challenges In The Administration of Justice In Botswana

A Paper delivered at the Annual Judicial Conference held at Mahalapye on the 30 -31ˢᵗ July 2015.

"At a conceptual level, one cannot talk about the judiciary as a genuinely independent and autonomous branch of government if it is substantially dependent upon the executive branch not only for its funding but also for many features of its day-to-day functions and operations. The practical dimension flows directly from this. While the judicial officers may be free to operate independently and to hand down fair and impartial decisions according to law, their ability to do this may be constrained in various ways, notably by the financial, human and physical resources available to perform their tasks. A key element of this is the extent to which the judiciary has control over its own resources and thus is liable to determine its policy and strategic priorities and how funds are to be allocated to pursue those priorities"

Source: Justice Ngcobo "Delivery of Justice: Agenda for Change" (2003) 120 SALJ 688.

1. Introduction

In this brief paper, I locate and discuss the constraints and challenges of service delivery within the theme of the independence of the judiciary – which is the golden thread that informs the paper.

It is incontestable that for the entire post-colonial period, the judiciary in Botswana has been treated as a unit within the Ministry of Defence, Justice and Security or whatever the name of the line Ministry. It has no control over the budget, yet it is a third arm of the State.

2. Problematizing The Concept of The Independence of The Judiciary

In the broader constitutional discourse the means for securing judicial independence has, traditionally, been through the security of tenure and a prohibition on the reduction of the salary of judges. The above was considered sufficient to secure the independence of the judiciary. The underlying assumption was that if the executive or parliament was permitted to reduce benefits for the judicial officers, this would promote dependence that would be inimical to public interest. This assumption was not extended to include the administration of courts and such other relevant items such as the provision of accommodation to hold court, the furniture and other resources necessary for the courts to function.

Modern constitutional lawyers now accept that it is undesirable for the executive to have control over the basic resources that the courts require to function properly. It is now generally agreed that the executive may manipulate the control it has over some of the resources mentioned above to entrench dependency and undermine independence. In the olden days the latter point was not appreciated, partly because the courts' power had not grown as phenomenally as today, where the power of judicial review, has heralded serious power struggle and tension between the judiciary and other arms of government – with the courts having the last say on what is the position of the law.

The power that the courts wield has not only brought tension, it is also a source of envy of the other branches, who repeatedly ask: what is so special about the judiciary that entitles it to special treatment? It follows therefore that the control of the administration of courts poses the potential that such control may be manipulated either deliberately or otherwise to undermine the independence of the judiciary and interfere with the functioning of the courts.

Under our constitutional dispensation, the judiciary enjoys independence at two levels, firstly, at an adjudicatory level, (personal independence) and secondly, at an institutional level. The personal independence of the judicial officer must also be considered in light of a judicial officer's physical security.

The question that some of us often ask, is whether, having regard to the nature of our mandate, our security can best be provided by security guards? Many within our ranks would easily testify that the security around judicial officers is limited and ineffectual and needs to be tightened. Judicial officers create all sorts of enemies every day. The state is obliged to provide for their security. The sooner this is appreciated the better. More significantly, it is flawed logic to think that judges only need security during normal working hours - and that there is no risk to their lives thereafter.

An example from Uganda will illustrate the point better. His Worship Araali Kagoro Muhiirwa of Uganda highlighted an often-overlooked aspect of judicial services – the need to ensure the security of judicial officers. In his presentation, at a conference, he noted that in Uganda there have been incidents where Magistrates have been violently attacked. The incidents in point are; a serial killer who was appearing before a lady magistrate attempted to attack and strangle the Magistrate in the open court, a group of criminals abducted a lady magistrate and psychologically tortured her and a male magistrate who had gone to visit locus in a land dispute was attacked and injured using a machete.

I am certain that, in this jurisdiction, we are not immune to such incidents.

It is also important, as part of the personal independence of a judicial officer, that not only must a judicial officer's tenure and remuneration be constitutionally protected (to the extent that, in the case of the latter, it may not be reduced during his or her tenure), the quantum of the remuneration received must be adequate to allow for a standard of living commensurate with his or her standing in the community as a judicial officer. Adequate pay for judicial officers fulfills a number of societal functions that will bolster their confidence in maintaining their independence in decision-making and their commitment to justice.

For the judiciary to be efficient, competent and impartial two non-negotiable imperatives must be in place. These are financial security and organizational professionalism of the judiciary as an institution.

Generally, it may be said with some credibility that much of the inefficiency we experience in our court system is on account of the pervasive power of the Ministry of Defence, Justice and Security in the affairs of the Administration of Justice which is regarded as a department of the Ministry. The Ministry and other government entities often demonstrate a lack of appreciation of the real financial and true administrative needs of the judiciary.

It cannot be credibly contested that justice suffers when judicial officers are working under unfavourable conditions; it suffers when some courts have to contend with poor and inadequate support services; it suffers when those who are charged with budgeting for the judiciary are frustrated to fashion and defend an appropriate budget because of a number of barriers such as arbitrary ceilings and negative attitudes of those with the power to accept or reject budgetary proposals.

3. A Synopsis of The Problems Affecting The Administration of Justice

Below, I summarize some of the constraints and challenges in the Administration of Justice. The list is by no means exhaustive.

- The tools of our trade such as computers are often insufficient and not fit for purpose. This has adverse effect on the functioning of CRMS and typing of court orders and judgments.

- Essential personnel is often inadequate. For instance, inadequate number of drivers has adverse effect on many things – including service of court process, executing other court related duties, such as service of cars. Inadequate court reporters, as is the case in some courts, may lead to cases being postponed, in the event a court reporter, for instance, is not able, for whatever reason, to report to work. And as we often say justice delayed is justice denied.

- Inadequate and inappropriate office space or offices.

- Accommodation challenges for judicial officers.

- Insufficiently trained staff who may struggle to produce proper records or orders.

- Unnecessary transfers that affect staff performance and negatively affect team building. For instance, sudden transfer of reporters, at the magistracy delays preparation of records, because new reporters may find it difficult to read the other's shorthand. Delays in processing court records may be prejudicial to litigants.

- Poor and out-dated Court infrastructure [e.g. no air-conditioning in Judges and Magistrates' Chambers and Courts and some other court offices, making it difficult and unbearable for court staff to undertake their duties to the best of their ability.

- Transport constraints which affect the adequate running of Courts – this extends to Judges when their vehicles have gone for service or are afflicted with frequent breakdowns leading to such vehicles being at the garages for long period of times. At times Judges end up using administration vehicles as they will be no other vehicle to use and this stalls the day to day running of courts without vehicles.

- Real time recording – Courts need this in order to alleviate the current appeal backlog. This is a serious issue as it affects the basic rights of convicts; puts presiding officers in a quandary as at times they end up having to determine issues of bail without records in order to safeguard the right of an accused or convicted appellant; it defeats the core of case management as it takes the control away from presiding officers who are at the mercy of the system that is clearly not working.

- Lack of qualified research assistants for Judges, making their work too cumbersome and leading to long delays in judgment delivery.

- Lack of continuous training for presiding officers and staff.

- Lack of career path - even for judges.

- Lack of incentives for administration staff.

The above constraints and challenges are in large measure on account of insufficient funding. In one way or the other they impact upon access to justice. When cases are postponed because a court reporter could not avail herself or himself, for whatever reason, or there was no vehicle to transport a magistrate to hear some part-heard matters in some locality, access to justice is denied.

Quite often when we talk about access to justice we assume that this is confined to the High Court or Court of Appeal only. However, the engine of our justice system lies with the lower courts.

It is at the lower courts that a majority of our people experience justice or lack thereof. It is at the lower courts that our faith in justice is reaffirmed. If people do not have access to the lower courts then we are missing voices, problems, and perspectives that enrich the ideals of the law enunciated at the top or at any other level of the judiciary.

Access to justice means that everybody —regardless of race, ethnicity or orientation, irrespective of wealth or poverty, whether we are mighty or weak —each and every one of us gets his or her day in court. Equal justice, that defining principle of our country, requires that every human being has access to the courts of the republic.

4. Budgeting

Our budgeting system needs to change if we are to meet the imperatives of access to justice. Below I outline, briefly, the challenges of our budgeting system.

The judiciary does not have control over the allocation of funds to run the courts. All they do is to prepare budget estimates; it ends there. As to how much is eventually allocated to them may be a product of the whims and caprices of top bureaucrats in various layers of government. Funds usually allocated are insufficient. The court system often run out of funds, very early in the financial year, leaving the courts with no funds to pay witnesses, special interpreters and travelling allowances – and in some cases even stationery. This also means that when funds run out, some courts, such as Stock Theft Courts, Traffic Courts may be forced to postpone cases whilst awaiting further allocation of funds. I mention these courts because these are the courts close to the people, whose confidence is critical for our legitimacy.

It seems clear from what I have stated above that institutional independence of the judiciary can only be realized if it is allocated with sufficient operating funds.

There is an ongoing debate on the extent to which the branches of the Executive and the Legislature should have an input in the budgetary allocation to the judiciary.

One school of thought says that the judiciary should be budgeted by an independent body and that the Executive should not arbitrarily reduce the budget allocation. Another school of thought is that the judiciary's budget should be provided for in the Constitution (eg. Singapore). In the same vein, there is an ongoing debate as to how the judicial organ can be held accountable in the way it is run.

In our case, the court budget is a line item in the overall budget of the Ministry of Justice; and although the budget is prepared by officials of the judiciary who make their own assessment as to the needs of the court, this process counts for less because their budget compete with many other 'units' or 'departments' in the big ministry and the result is that the budget is invariably cut, more often it would seem arbitrarily, without regard to the needs and priorities of the judiciary.

In addition, the budgetary process takes place in the context of a pre-determined ceiling which makes budgeting a nightmare experience for Administration of Justice staff. The budgetary process is littered with far too many bureaucratic layers presided over by people with insufficient knowledge of how the judiciary functions. The result is that the judiciary hardly obtains the funds it needs to carry out its mandate.

5. Training and skills building

If the machinery of justice is to run smoothly, every part must function in harmony. The court employees are a key component of the machinery – issues such as career development opportunities, adequate and fair payment structure, further training and a motivating work environment are important.

An example of one component of the machinery will drive the point home. Interpreters are central to the administration of justice. They should interpret accurately. Failure to interpret accurately may occasion injustice. Interpreters need to be trained on a sustainable basis. They must have clear job descriptions and guidelines. Their career path must be clear.

Speaking on the matter of training and skills building, former Justice Mokgoro, of the Constitutional Court of South Africa, pointed out that continuous education and training for judicial officers is essential so as to sharpen the competence and efficiency of the Bench.

The need for sensitivity training, judicial accountability, how to manage judicial power and the judicial function, including the efficient and expeditious delivery of judgments, how to manage the nuanced aspects of the judicial function, including the judicial temperament, are critical as part of our society's reality.

Importantly, the inculcation of fierce individual independence and the importance of legal competence, proper judicial insights and effective delivery of access to justice cannot be overemphasized.

6. Judicial Governance/Leadership

There is also an urgent need to look into the judicial governance structure of the judiciary as one way of enhancing efficiency of service delivery. It is perhaps time that the three high court divisions have statutory designated Judge Presidents, whose functions, inter alia, shall include, supervising the magistracy in their respective jurisdictions. In other words, Judge Presidents would have over sight roles in their respective areas, which bodes well for more efficiency and effectiveness in the entire court system.

7. Modernization

About 10 years ago the judiciary in Botswana introduced CRMS which has facilitated efficient management of cases, and reduced the phenomenon of disappearance of documents which used to plague the pre-CRMS period. We now need to introduce further reforms such as (a) electronic filing; (b) imaging, to put documents brought to court by litigants without equipment for electronic filing; (c) video conferencing facilities; and (d) Automatic payment by debit or credit card.

8. Conclusion

In conclusion, permit me to return to the theme of this paper, which is the constraints and challenges in the delivery of justice and pose polemical and yet potent question: what is to be done?

Our duty is to administer justice to all without fear, favour or prejudice. We have a duty to make our system of justice work better. We have a duty to establish a world class judiciary with depth of talent and whose independence is beyond reproach.

We should aim for a system of justice that dispenses justice speedily and is not plagued by unnecessary postponements on account of resource constraints.

To this extent, it is imperative that we must review our system of justice and all its components on a continuous basis. Our justice system suffers from certain weaknesses that threaten the delivery of justice. Our challenge is to fix it. We must begin by examining our administrative machinery and the management of our courts. We must find ways of doing our best even in the midst of financial challenges.

Our courts have discharged their constitutional obligations admirably over the years notwithstanding operating consistently on a shoestring budget. Resource constraints have the potential to cripple our work. Adequate stuffing, transportation and infrastructure is indispensable to our work. For instance, magistrates can hardly afford inadequate transport facilities because they have to travel to hear part heard cases, court processes has to be served and many other work related imperatives. Decent accommodation for all judicial officers is an imperative to an efficient justice system.

We must not tire to point out that we are not a department of government. We are an organ of the State. The lack of institutional independence is perceived by many, to be in conflict with the Constitution. We need a radical paradigm shift, from the current executive court administration system to one that is led and controlled by the judiciary. Yes, it is critical that we be permitted to dream of utopias; to ask not just what is, what seems possible, but what could be. Justice is central to the welfare of our people. For this reason, it is critical that the judiciary must lead in shaping the judiciary that is fit to serve the demands of our courts in the 21st century.

Lastly, but not least, we need to build on the success of judicial case management and implement court annexed mediation urgently, before we are overtaken by others who started much later than us.

Chapter 6

Judicial Interpretation of The Constitution

A Jurist's reflections at a Roundtable of African Judges – Stellenbosch October 2016

1. In a constitutional democracy, the power to say what the law is resides in the judiciary and no other organ. The judiciary is best suited to do this because of its learning and integrity. An independent and impartial judiciary, insulated from the passions of the moment and the pressures occasioned by the ebb and flow of politics is best placed to render decisions without fear or favour.

2. Alexander Hamilton said, independent courts serve as an "excellent barrier to the encroachments and oppressions of the representative body," and they play a "peculiarly essential" role in safeguarding individual rights and liberties. On the other hand, "the judiciary "has no influence over either the sword or the purse"; it has "neither FORCE NOR WILL, but merely judgment.

3. The voice of the judiciary on constitutional questions must ultimately draw its authority from the public's acceptance of its institutional role, even when its specific decisions are controversial. The Court's judgment must reflect the nation's best understanding of its fundamental values, "[f]or the power of the great constitutional decision's rests upon the accuracy of the Court's perception of this kind of common will and upon

the Court's ability, by expressing its perception, ultimately to command a consensus.

4. In interpreting and applying the Constitution, the judiciary independence from politics and reflect the common will in order to secure the democratic legitimacy of its decisions. These institutional features frame the challenge that the judiciary uniquely faces in interpreting the Constitution.

5. In interpreting the Constitution, a judge must pay heed not only to the text, but to the values of the Constitution. He or she must also be consistent and not render an interpretation that renders the Constitution unpredictable. Inconsistency is a form of infidelity.

6. A Constitution is not a museum piece. It must be interpreted generously in order to meet both the aspirations of the current and generations yet unborn. This means that a constitutional meaning must be able to evolve over time. The idea that constitutional meaning is capable of evolving over time is not license to disregard text or precedent or to undermine the rule of law. As we explain below, these criticisms are more often based on caricatures of judicial decision-making than on a careful examination of the methodology that judges actually use.

7. That constitutional meaning must evolve over time suggest that a Constitution is a living organism capable of growth. A meaning attached to a particular provision may have a changed meaning in the course of time. It is the judges, who as society evolves, must be able to breathe life into the Constitution. The assertion that a Constitution is a living organism has been vulnerable to the criticism that our Constitution is a written document and, as such, does not grow or evolve except by formal amendment. The metaphor of a "living Constitution" misleadingly suggests that the Constitution itself is the primary site of legal evolution

in response to societal change and that the Constitution can come to mean whatever a sufficient number of people think it ought to mean.

8. It must be made clear though that to say a Constitution is a living organism does not in any way suggest that a Constitution has no enduring character. It does. The meanings, interpretation assigned to particular provisions of the Constitution may change, but the Constitution itself does not change until properly amended.

9. There has never been and they can never be one and only one legitimate, mechanical, and time-less way to derive constitutional meaning, and notably the Constitution itself does not prescribe a specific method of interpretation. Interpreting the constitutional text and principles in light of changing norms and societal consequences is not radical. What is radical is an insistence that the Constitution's meaning is static and divorced from contemporary context.

10. Some jurists of conservative persuasion do not approve of the view that although the constitutional text may not change, but that its meaning changes as back door judicial legislation. They consider the view that the Constitution is a living organism as somewhat radical.

11. As a matter of general rule in giving appropriate meaning to the Constitution, the courts usually adopt a multi-pronged approach that considers such diverse considerations as the Constitutions, history, text, values, purpose and structure. To this extent, at least two approaches are discernible from the case law and constitutional literature. There are authorities of respectable lineage that suggest that Constitutional meaning is a function of both text and context. In many instances, a court cannot be faithful to the principle embodied in the text unless it takes into account the social context in which the text is interpreted.

12. Most judges in constitutional democracies take oath to be loyal to the Constitution. Constitutional fidelity serves not only to preserve the Constitution's meaning over time, but also to maintain its authority and legitimacy. The words and principles of the Constitution endure as our fundamental law because they have been made relevant to the conditions and challenges of each generation through an ongoing process of interpretation.

Originalism

13. Originalism is the approach to constitutional interpretation that gives weight to the intentions of the original authors of the Constitution. Originalism requires a judge confronted with a constitutional dispute to ask how informed individuals living at the time the Constitution was ratified would have applied it to a similar dispute.

14. Originalism as a constitutional interpretation approach ignores the evolving nature of society and the significance of the dynamic of time to constitutional interpretation. As society evolves society's understanding and application of constitutional principles deepens and the notion of expansive interpretation of rights gains traction.

15. Originalism by invoking the Framers' understanding of how the Constitution should apply to specific situations – actually diminishes their accomplishment. In writing the Constitution, the Framers sought to vest a set of fundamental principles with authority and permanence. At the same time, they understood that the Constitution could not spell out answers to every important controversy.

Judicial Restraint

16. Judicial restraint is constitutional. Interpretation approaches that urges judges to be restrained in interpreting the Constitution. It

is the opposite of judicial activism – that is considered to be an unacceptable way of using judicial power to achieve, personal and even partisan objectives.

17.   Proponents of strict construction hardly provide a clear definition of the term. It is often said that judges should not "legislate from the bench" and should not "make law" but apply it. Beyond these agreeable platitudes, strict constructions seems to suggest a method of interpretation that takes the words of the Constitution literally. Proponents of strict construction argue that judges must read the Constitution to mean simply what it says, nothing more and nothing less. In this way, its proponents say, strict construction limits judicial discretion.

18.   Strict constructionism is unattractive to the extent that it suggests that judges should be enslaved by the text and not pay heed to other considerations such as purpose or values of the Constitution. A text should not be construed strictly but reasonably for purposes of realizing the core values and vision of the Constitution.

19.   At the end of the day what accounts for our enduring faith in the Constitution is not that we have rigidly adhered to original understandings frozen in amber or to so-called strict construction of the text. It is that we have continually interpreted the Constitution's language and applied its principles in ways that dynamic and advance a society based on human dignity and equal worth of every person.

Chapter 7

The African Charter on Democracy, Elections and Governance

1. Director of Proceedings, permit me to express my sincere gratitude to the organizers of this event for their kind invitation to deliver a keynote speech at today's gathering. It is not quite often that a member of the judiciary finds time to interact with members of civil society on issues as important as democracy, elections, and good governance.

2. I understand that the Democracy Works Foundation (DWF) together with its partners seek, through the Charter Project Africa, to promote the African Charter on Democracy and Elections and Governance (ACDEG). They aim to use digital democracy technologies to strengthen participatory democracy. It would also appear that civic education lies at the heart of their work.

3. The ACDEG is inspired by the objectives and principles enshrined in the Constitutive Act of the African Union, particularly Articles 3 and 4, which emphasize the significance of good governance, popular participation, the rule of law and human rights. It seeks among other things to entrench a political culture of constitutional change of government based on the hholding of periodic free and fair elections.

4. Article 3 of the Charter requires State Parties to implement the Charter in accordance with the following principles: (a) respect for human rights and democratic principles, (b) access to and exercise

of state power in accordance with the constitution of the State Party and the principle of the rule of law; (c) promotion of a system government that is representative; holding of regular, transparent, free and fair elections; (d) separation of powers; (e) promotion of gender equality in public and private institutions; (f) effective participation of citizens in democratic and development process and in governance of public affairs; (g) transparency and fairness in the management of public affairs, (h) rejection of corruption, (j) strengthening political pluralism, recognizing the role, rights, responsibilities of legally constituted political parties.

5. It is plain from the above that The African Charter on Democracy, Elections and Governance is an important blueprint intended to put constitutional democracy at the centre of the African governance system. It is a norm setting document which all African states must subscribe to through, not only ratification but execution. It is plain from reading the Charter that it was informed by many important regional, sub regional and international legal instruments including the Universal Declaration of Human Rights- which asserts among other things, that the authority of any government shall be derived from the will of the people.

6. The Charter (ACDEG) recognises the above principles and the nexus between democracy, elections and good governance. Elections are fundamental to the legitimacy of any government. Such elections must truly reflect the will of the people, they must be free and fair. In a constitutional democracy envisaged by the Charter, the judiciary has a special role to adjudicate over electoral disputes. It is therefore important that the independence of the judiciary should not be open to credible doubt.

7. As we consider how we can use ACDEG to advance democracy we must spare a thought on the state of democracy in Africa. I will give a very brief synopsis to provide the context. The state of democracy in Africa is far from satisfying – there is a protracted

democratic recession marked by erosion of civil liberties, shrinkage of civic space, the undermining of the will of the people through electoral manipulation, the uneven playing ground as illustrated by the lack of funding of political parties in some countries, unequal access to public media during elections and the death of independent institutions.

8. The above instances of democratic recession have been accompanied by a concentration of power in the executive and the corresponding emasculation of parliament. The reality in many African states is that parliaments', as the repository of the will of the people are often weak compared to the executive, their independence is doubtful, and they are often under resourced to be an effective watchdog of the executive and can hardly pass effective laws for the "good order and peace of the country". As a result of this power imbalance, parliament is often dominated by the executive and cannot hold the executive accountable – mainly on account of the dominant party system. In some cases, the last line of defence in a democracy being the judiciary has not been spared interference in one form or the other.

9. In the African region a view is increasingly gaining traction that while Parliaments are central to ensuring separation of powers and checks and balances, they do not always fulfil this role effectively due to various reasons, that include the dominance of the party system and a lack of resources.

10. In many countries in Africa, separation of powers is loose, as members of the executive tend to be drawn from members of Parliament. This has the potential to compromise the necessary separation of powers and the checks and balances that can hold other organs of the state accountable. The dual membership of ministers to the executive and legislative branches of government as well as their proportionately large number, have in some cases resulted in decreased Parliamentary oversight capacity.

11. There are many recorded instances of harassment of the opposition, free media, disdain for civil society, state sponsored social media terrorism against political opponents. The latter has reached alarming proportions in many countries. Corruption is rampant and pervasive. Private money that sponsors political party campaigns has proven to be a danger to democracy as the monied are able to buy governments in waiting ahead of elections – a phenomenon that often results in state capture by private interests with the result that governments become accountable to those who sponsored them to win power than the people. Private funding of political parties needs to be regulated.

12. All the above instances have led to massive civil society disengagement from the electoral process and the death of participatory democracy. Democracy should never be understood as simply voting every election cycle. It must involve continuous participation of the people in the manner in which they are governed. International law guarantees the right of the people to, "take part in the conduct of the public affairs directly or through freely chosen representatives". International Law also requires countries to hold, "genuine" and periodic elections. How many amongst us can attest to the "genuineness" of the elections we hold?

13. A democratic recession in our continent has been evident for decades and there are no signs that the situation is improving.

14. Democratic recessions suggest a reversal of democratic gains that may have occurred in the past decades, it is characterised by weakening of democratic institutions, the emergence of a big man syndrome. It entails the erosion of political accountability, conducting elections fraught with fundamental irregularities, rampant corruption, violation of human rights. Research suggests that there has been a gradual decline of democracy in Africa with

more than 15 active violent conflicts across the continent in 2021. The continent has moved from 3 democracies and 42 authoritarian regimes in 1985 to only 18 democracies, 19 authoritarian regimes and 13 hybrid regimes in 2015. The occasional occurrence of unconstitutional changes of government and military aided transitions account for much of Africa's democratic recession.

15.   One of the tools that can be used to halt and even reverse the democratic recession is constitutional building or constitutional review.

16.   In the recent decades many countries have sought to review their constitutions, many of which were colonial inheritances. Countries such as South Africa, Namibia, Malawi, Kenya, Zimbabwe and Botswana- all with varying degrees of success. In other countries such as South Africa, Namibia and Kenya, people's participation was put at the centre of the process. In other countries the constitutional review processes was infected with illegitimacy as politicians imposed their wishes on the citizenry resulting in constitutions that can hardly be called people's constitutions. Best practice teaches that the best constitutional review process must genuinely be people driven and involve all key stakeholders. A constitution that the people cannot proudly call their own is not worth the paper it is written on.

17.   The above challenges, notwithstanding the picture is not entirely bleak. We, the people, can use tools at our disposal such as ACDEG, to demand that our government not only ratify, but execute the letter and spirit of the Act. Africa has an epidemic of bad laws that would fail a democratic index audit. Our governments record in ratifying regional, sub regional instruments is very good, but their record of domestication and implementation of that which they agreed is poor.

18.   I conclude by commending Democracy Works Foundation (DWF) and its partners to remain resolute in promoting the

values and dictates of ACDEG and urge them to be rooted among communities and roll out civic education programmes, using technologies and face to face community meetings.

19. The existence of the African Continent's regional instruments has provided an opportunity for supranational accountability- and although these instruments have been allowed to gather dust and have sometimes served as vehicles for norm diffusion, the historical, political and socio-economic context and peculiarities of countries have led to a mixed bag in terms of democratic consolidation results.

Chapter 8

Protecting The Rights of Minorities and Marginalized Populations In Botswana – A Judge's Perspective

ICJ Meeting on rising instances of persecution of human rights defenders in Africa: 16 -17 July 2015.

The purpose of this paper is to reflect on the role of the judiciary in protecting the rights of minorities and marginalised populations, more particularly sexual minorities in Botswana.

The basic premise of departure is as simple as it is problematic, being that human rights remain heavily contested.

This meeting takes place hardly a month after the US Supreme Court handed down a historic landmark case legalizing same sex marriage in the whole of the United States of America. I mention this, with the full knowledge that this particular matter in Africa is highly problematic and culturally sensitive, and in some respects a taboo subject.

In the context of Africa, it may be unwise – or as some scholars maintain, to advance LGBT rights in the region by placing undue emphasis on US jurisprudence, in view of the often-expressed standpoint that we must free our jurisprudence from the clutches of western influence. Whilst this line of reasoning is contested or even misguided, it is always good to rely on Indigenous African jurisprudence in order to avoid misplaced perceptions of western bias. Furthermore, in dealing with sensitive issues of sexual minorities, in particular, we, the current generation of jurists – who have the historical mission to dismantle the walls of prejudice and irrationality, must be ready to deal logically, with the argument often advanced that these are the issues that are best left to the popular will; and the courts have no business in making laws because there are not the legislature, they are not democratically elected, their duty, so the argument goes, is to say what the law is and not what it should be.

The above background provides a good context within which to interrogate the evolving jurisprudence in Botswana with respect to the rights of sexual minorities. During my over 12 years in the bench, I have noticed a shift, albeit minor, yet still significant, in the judicial perspective towards sexual minority rights. The ultra-conservativeness of the yesteryears seems to be giving way to an increasing recognition of what I call the morality of the Constitution – namely that all are equal in the eyes of the law. This notwithstanding, one can still say, it is not yet uhuru!

I turn now to the Botswana jurisprudence.

Kanane v The State

Kanane v The State Others 2003 (2) BLR 67 ("Kanane") was a case involving an application by Mr Kanane to declare Sections 164, 165 and 167 of the Penal Code unconstitutional. In essence, the question before the Court was whether homosexual acts between two consenting male individuals carried out in their private sphere should be decriminalized. Sections 164 and 167 of the Penal Code provide that "any person with carnal knowledge of any person against the order of nature, has carnal knowledge of an animal or permits carnal knowledge of him/her against the order of nature, is guilty of an offense and is liable for imprisonment' and 'any person... who commits any act of gross indecency with another person'.

In the High Court, Mr Kanane argued that the impugned provisions of the Penal Code (a) discriminates against male persons on the grounds of gender and offends their right to freedom of conscience, expression, and privacy, assembly and association as in entrenched in Section 3 of the Constitution; and (b) hinders male persons in their enjoyment of their right to assemble freely and associate with other persons as contained in Sections 13 and 15 of the Constitution by discriminating based on their gender. Mwaikasu J upheld the impugned provision of the Penal Code and found that homosexuality and venereal disease are among the benefits bestowed on Botswana by the West. Although I would not express any remarks on the unfortunate views made by the learned Judge, it is necessary to point out that the views are indicative of the fact that the impugned provisions are vague and open to arbitrary interpretation.

In light of the judgment handed down by the High Court, Mr Kanane was forced to approach the Court of Appeal. The same arguments were presented at the Court of Appeal. In particular, that unfair discrimination exists between heterosexual persons and homosexual persons in criminalizing same-sex sexual conduct. Citing international law authorities, he argued that modern society no longer stigmatized homosexual practices between consenting adult males and it has been decriminalized in several states. After considering all the evidence the Court, however, held that there was nothing to suggest a change in societal perception against homosexuality and in fact all indications show a hardening public attitude to the contrary. The Court considered the legislature and expansion of the law criminalizing sexual conduct by including women in passing the 1998 Amendment Act as reflective of society's disagreement with homosexuality and that the "court can take judicial notice of the incidence of AIDS both worldwide and in Botswana, and…the legislature in enacting the provision it did was reflecting public concern".

The implication of the Court of Appeal's reasoning is far-reaching and its failure to strike down the impugned provision under the Penal Code is highly problematic. First, the Court should have engaged with its role and mandate in terms of its constitutional obligations and in particular, it displayed a lack of judicial activism in applying international human rights values and standards. This was a clear case in which more than a mere routine application of the law was required. Second, and related to the latter point, the Court (with respect) placed undue reliance on the perceived morals of society and the relevance of public opinion, placing same at the core in the interpretation of the Constitution.

The Botswana Constitution provides for the protection of "every person" within Botswana and by placing public moral and majoritarian preferences at the heart of the inquiry of discrimination, the Court missed an opportunity to extend much needed protection to the most vulnerable in our society. Discrimination and stigma occur daily against sexual minorities and the Court missed an opportunity to ensure redress of the rights violated. Instead of redressing discrimination, the Court of Appeal's implied remarks on AIDS and homosexuality is also quite unfortunate, as this could potentially perpetuate and add to the stigma of homosexuality.

The Court's Role and Mandate-Failed?

Constitutional democracy requires the judiciary to interpret and develop common law, customary law and legislation in a manner that reflects the spirit, purport and object of the Bill of Rights. Indeed, the judiciary (along with the executive and the legislature) has a duty to develop and give content and effect to the Bill of Rights, including civil and political rights. Upholding these values and the ideals of the Constitution therefore requires more than the routine application of the law to the facts. Instead, constitutional adjudication requires a more ambitious judicial methodology, one that seeks to identify the underlying dispute between the parties and aims to forge new tools to bring about justice and equity and non-discrimination. Crucial to this project is the dismantling of existing power relations which contribute to or entrench civil and political disadvantage or marginalization of the most vulnerable in our society such as sexual minorities.

Although the judiciary should be mindful of separation of powers and the limits of their authority they are also mandated to bring about justice and equity as set out in the Constitution and the Bill of Rights. Simply put, where the legislature pass legislation (such as the Penal Code and 1998

Amendment Act) in which certain provisions fail to extend protection to "every person" in Botswana especially the most vulnerable such as sexual minorities, the courts should not be overly cautious and slow to intervene in a manner that would bring about equity and non-discrimination as mandated by the Constitution. The duty to bring about equality does not fall solely on the executive and the legislative branches of government. A constitutional democracy also commits the judiciary to the goal of achieving social justice and the improvement of the quality of life for all persons without discrimination. This will, however, require judges to be "informed and courageous" and to meaningfully engage with its mandate and "its duty to act as an independent arbiter of the Constitution" and not readily defer to the legislature. As part of this constitutional mandate and duty judicial officers are also required to consider foreign and international law as an important guide when interpreting and giving content to the constitution, legislation and other laws.

The Court of Appeal's decision in Kanane has been criticised as retrogressive and failing to build on from its own jurisprudence and international human rights standards. The criticism does not come without foundation though. By placing social norms and values as a core factor in considering the interpretation of the Constitution, the Court has in fact narrowed the space wherein the judiciary can contribute toward the meaningful advancement of justice and equity of all persons and particularly sexual minorities.

In fact the approach taken in Kanane is a far cry from the generous approach adopted by the Court in Attorney-General v Unity Dow ("Dow"). Here the Court held that the Constitution is supreme and where there is conflict with another law or culture the Constitution must trump them. Also, when interpreting the Constitution "a broad and generous approach should be adopted in the interpretation of its provision; that all relevant provisions bearing on the subject for the interpretation be considered together as a whole in order to effect the objective of the Constitution, and where such rights and freedoms were conferred on persons by the Constitution, derogation from such rights and freedoms should be narrowly or strictly construed". The Court therefore agreed that although sex or gender were not included in the definition of discrimination, the interpretation has to be broad allowing for a read in of the words rather than the exclusion of the right.

Based on the level of judicial activism displayed in Dow one would have therefore envisaged that the Court would have adopted a more generous approach than what it has taken in Kanane by including sexual orientation as a prohibited ground of discrimination. An approach in which the Court would have given full effect to the right of equality, by including sexual orientation in those forms of discrimination set out in Section 15(3) of the Constitution and thereby providing protection to a vulnerable sector of our society. In doing so, it would have not only strengthened the role of the judiciary in advancing equality to all persons but it would have also upheld international human rights principles. Instead of interpreting the impugned provision in line with Botswana's international obligations, the Court adopted an approach diminishing the realisation of the judiciary's constitutional mandate.

Limitations of Rights: The Role of Public Opinion in Constitutional Adjudication

The Court of Appeal in Kanane held that in interpreting the Constitution, social norms, values and public opinion are relevant in matters of sexual freedom. Indeed in Kanane, the determining factor in the inquiry into the lawfulness of the discrimination was whether "the time has arrived when society in Botswana" is ready to include sexual orientation as a prohibited ground for protection under Sections 3 and 15 of the Constitution. In reaching this decision, the Court with approval quoted the Zimbabwean decision of Banana v State where the Supreme Court held that it did not believe "that social norms and values of Zimbabwe are pushing us to decriminalise consensual sodomy. Zimbabwe is, broadly speaking, a conservative society in matters of sexual behaviour". Unfortunately, it was ultimately on this very basis upon which the Court quite remarkably found that gay men and women do not represent a group worthy of protection under the Constitution and that the impugned provision of the Penal Code therefore passes constitutional muster.

Interestingly, the Court adopted this approach without any evidence or research available as to whether public opinion and attitudes are indeed against homosexual acts but it never-the-less deemed the laws passed by the legislature as indicative of and "reflecting public concern". It is submitted that the Court's reliance on public opinion and social norms, and the fact that it viewed legislation enacted by Parliament as reflecting public concern is quite unfortunate and with respect totally misplaced and not line with its role as an independent arbiter.

Nevertheless, and notwithstanding the absence of evidence before the Court on societal attitudes towards same-sex sexual conduct, this should not play a core role in constitutional adjudication. In fact, even if one were to accept that the views of the majority was to criminalise same-sex sexual activity, this ultimately has no bearing on the interpretation of the Bill of Rights. In this vein, Justice Powell in his dissenting judgment Furman v Georgia made the following observation:

"...the weight of the evidence indicates that the public generally has not accepted either the morality or the social merit of the views so passionately advocated by the articulate spokesmen for abolition. But however, one may assess amorphous ebb and flow of public opinion generally on this volatile issue, this type of inquiry lies at the periphery - not the core - of the judicial process in constitutional cases. The assessment of popular opinion is essentially a legislative, and not a judicial, function"

By relying on public opinion and morals at the core of constitutional interpretation the judiciary in effect steps into the terrain of and blur the lines with the legislature and disregards and misconstrues its role under the Constitution. It is of course open to the legislature which is democratically elected to adopt laws which it deems to be favourable amongst the majority of its electorate. However even these laws do not fall short of constitutional scrutiny. Where laws such as the impugned provisions of the Penal Code and the 1998 Amendment Act fail to advance constitutional guarantees of human rights and freedoms, including equality, the Court has a duty to interpret the law generously and extend protection to all persons regardless whether this approach may be considered to be unfavourable amongst the majority.

In this light the High Court of Kenya in interpreting the right to freedom of association and non-discrimination held in Eric Gitari v Non-Governmental Organisation Co-ordination Board and 4 others that

"The Constitution is to protect those with unpopular views, minorities and rights that attach to human beings-regardless of a majority views. The work of a Court, especially a Court exercising constitutional jurisdiction with regard to the Bill of Rights, is to uphold the Constitution, not popular views or the views of the majority".

The High Court of Kenya went further and quoted with approval the observation in the case of John Harun Mwau & 3 Others v Attorney General & 2 Others

"….The public and politicians have their own perceptions of when the election date should be. We must, however, emphasis that public opinion is not the basis for making our decision. Article 159 of the Constitution is clear that the people of Kenya have vested judicial authority in the courts and tribunals to do justice according to the law. Our responsibility and the oath we have taken require that we interpret the Constitution and uphold its provisions without fear or favour and with regard to popular opinion… our undertaking is not to write or rewrite the Constitution to suit popular opinion…."

Similarly the South African Constitutional Court in S v Makwanyana also considered the role of public opinion when interpreting the Bill of Rights and the Court said the following:

"Public opinion may have some relevance to the enquiry, but in itself, it is no substitute for the duty vested in the Courts to interpret the Constitution and to uphold its provisions without fear or favour. If public opinion were to be decisive there would be no need for constitutional adjudication. The protection of rights could then be left to Parliament, which has a mandate from the public, and is answerable to the public for the way its mandate is exercised, but this would be a return to parliamentary sovereignty, and a retreat from the new legal order established by the 1993 Constitution....The very reason for establishing the new legal order, and for vesting the power of judicial review of all legislation in the courts, was to protect the rights of minorities and others who cannot protect their rights adequately through the democratic process. Those who are entitled to claim this protection include the social outcasts and marginalised people of our society. It is only if there is a willingness to protect the worst and the weakest amongst us, that all of us can be secure that our own rights will be protected."

Though mindful that the above statement was in the context of South Africa whose Constitution was adopted under much different historical circumstances than Botswana, the Constitution of Botswana (as with South Africa) contains a Bill of Rights and such rights are universal in applications to all person without discrimination. Therefore, public opinion and morality should not be a core factor in the inquiry whether discrimination is justifiable under the Constitution. In fact Professor Mutua quite correctly states that,

"Constitutions are not meant to protect only individuals that we like, and to leave unprotected those who are unpopular, or those the majority may find morally objectionable. A person's identity- especially if it exposes them to ridicule, attack, or discrimination- must be reason for constitutional protection. Constitutions protect individuals from tyranny of the state and oppression from their fellow human beings".

It is important to note that it does not suggest that the State is barred from upholding morality, in fact as the South African Constitutional Court has held in the National Coalition for Gay and Lesbian Equality v Minister of Justice 1999 (1) SA 6 that,

"A State that recognizes differences does not mean a State without morality or one without a point of view. It does not banish concepts of right and wrong, nor envisage a world without good and evil. It is impartial in its dealings with people and groups, but is not neutral in its value system. The Constitution certainly does not debar the State from enforcing morality. Indeed, the Bill of Rights is nothing if not a document founded on deep political morality. What is central to the character and functioning of the State, however, is that the dictates of morality which it enforces, and the limits to which it may go, are to be found in the text and spirit of the Constitution itself".

In the premises, morality should not be determined through the lenses of the majority and what it regards as morally acceptable. The people of Botswana chose to be morally bound by the text of the Constitution itself. By placing public opinion and morality at the core of its inquiry, the Court of Appeal failed in its duty to meaningfully engage with its role as independent arbiter of the Constitution of Botswana and as a result failed to extend much needed protection to a vulnerable group in our society.

Registration of Lgbti Organisations

Botswana: LEGABIBO Case

This case involves a local LGBT group (LEGABIBO) who was refused registration in terms of the Section 7(2) of Societies Act. In the High Court, LEGABIBO successfully argued that refusal to register the organization amounted to a violation of the rights to equal protection of the law, freedom of association and freedom of expression. This case specifically emphasises the importance of the rights to freedom of expression, association and assembly in a constitutional democracy.

On 16 February 2012, the Applicants applied for the registration of LEGABIBO in terms of the Societies Act. On 12 March 2012, the Director of the Department of Civil and National Registration rejected the Applicants' application for registration on the basis that the Botswana Constitution does not recognise homosexuals and that the objectives of the organisation are contrary to Section 7(2) of the Societies Act.

The Applicants' appealed against this decision to the Minister of Labour and Home Affairs. The appeal was rejected on 12 November 2012. On 12 March 2013, the Applicants filed a case before the High Court of Botswana, asking the court to review the decision to refuse to register LEGABIBO.

The State, inter alia, argued that the Applicants' application was procedurally flawed, in that the Applicants failed to specify whether their application was a review application or a Constitutional violation application. The Court however held that, notwithstanding the procedural shortcoming, it will nevertheless hold that the application was properly brought under Section 18 of the Constitution of Botswana.

The right to freedom of expression and assembly and association is an important and powerful right critical to the engagement of other rights. It is a right which has, amongst others, been use to fight persecution of people on the basis of political opinions and convictions. The Court, by selecting substance over procedure and technicality, provided LEGABIBO and other organizations that might potentially be in a similar position with the enjoyment and full protection of the fundamental rights contained in the Constitution of Botswana. In doing so, the Court on the one hand meaningfully engaged with its constitutional mandate as independent arbiter and on the other also mindful of the importance of the right to freedom of association and that "the litigants before the Court should not be singled out for the grant of relief, but relief should be afforded to all people who are in the same situation as the litigants". Indeed, in a constitutional democracy it requires more than just a mere routine application of the law instead it requires the Court to "scratch the surface to get to the real substance below".

Similarly, the High Court of Kenya in Nation Media Group v Attorney General also found that substantive justice should trump procedural technicalities so as to avoid hindering the cause of justice. According to the High Court of Kenya,

"A Constitutional Court should be liberal in the manner it goes around dispensing justice. It should look at the substance rather than technicality.

It should not be seen to slavishly follow technicalities as to impede the cause of justice".

The Attorney General of Botswana has subsequently filed a notice appealing the High Court's decision. In its appeal, the State inter alia argue, based on Kanane that homosexuals are not a class of persons entitled to protection under Section 3 and 16 of the Constitution of Botswana – i.e. Because LEGABIBO is an organization that seeks to lobby for homosexual rights, it should also not enjoy the same constitutionally protected rights as other classes of person in Botswana. The State's basis for its argument is that the criminalisation of same-sex sexual acts, implies a criminalization of advocacy aimed at law reform. Though without going into the merits of the State's argument, it is important to note that the Court of Appeal in Kanane in declaring same-sex acts as unlawful nevertheless expressly made the observation that there is nothing in its decision to prevent LGBT groups from forming an association. Importantly, recently the High Court of Kenya came to a substantially similar decision to that of the Botswana High Court in LEGABIBO, where it was also required to determine the right to freedom of association of LGBT individuals in terms of the Constitution of Kenya.

Kenya: Eric Gitari Case

The High Court of Kenya was called upon to determine substantially similar legal issues to that in the LEGABIBO case. In granting the relief sought by the Applicant, the Court recognized the importance of the right to freedom of association in a constitutional democracy. The mere criminalization of same-sex acts does not criminalise the right of association of people based on their sexual orientation. In contrast to the Botswana Court of Appeal's decision in Kanane, the Kenya High Court held that public opinion and morality is not a core factor in constitutional adjudication.

In April 2013 Mr. Eric Gitari sought to register a non-governmental organisation (NGO) with the first respondent, the Non-Governmental Organisations Coordination Board (NGO Board). The purpose of the

NGO was to address the violence and human rights abuses suffered by LGBTIQ people. In accordance with the requirements for the registration of a NGO, the Mr Gitari sought to reserve with the NGO Board the names Gay and Lesbian Human Rights Council; Gay and Lesbian Human Rights Observancy and Gay and Lesbian Human Rights Organization.

Mr Gitari was advised by the Board that all the proposed names were unacceptable and should be reviewed. He then lodged the names Gay and Lesbian Human Rights Commission; Gay and Lesbian Human Rights Council and Gay and Lesbian Human Rights Collective 2 for reservation. He also sent a letter to the NGO Board asking why his application had been rejected.

The NGO Board advised that under Sections 162, 163 and 165 of the Penal Code same-sex sexual conduct is criminalised, and that this was the basis for rejection of the proposed names. The NGO Board relied on Regulation 8(3)(b) of the NGO Regulations of 1992, which provides that an application may be rejected if "such name is in the opinion of the director repugnant to or inconsistent with any law or is otherwise undesirable".

After three attempts to register the proposed NGO the claimant scheduled a meeting with Mr. Mugo, a member of the Legal Department of the Board. According to the claimant, Mr. Mugo advised him that any association bearing the names gay and lesbian could not be registered by the NGO Board because the association furthered criminality and immoral affairs. He subsequently commenced litigation proceedings on the grounds that his constitutional rights to freedom of association (Article 36) and freedom from discrimination (Article 27) had been violated. The respondents contended that the Mr Gitari's right to freedom of association had not been infringed and if it has been limited, such limitation can be justified on the basis of the criminalisation of same-sex conduct in the Penal Code. They further argued that 'sexual orientation' is not a prohibited ground of discrimination under the Constitution.

The right to freedom of association is guaranteed in Article 36 of the Constitution of Kenya which provides;

1. Every person has the right to freedom of association, which includes the right to form, join or participate in activities of and association of any kind.

2. A person shall not be compelled to join an association of any kind.

3. Any legislation that requires registration of an association of any kind shall provide that

(a) registration may not be withheld or withdrawn unreasonably....

The issue before High Court was twofold. Firstly, whether LGBTIQ people have a right to form associations in accordance with the law. If the answer is in the affirmative, secondly whether the decision of the NGO Board not to allow the registration of the proposed NGO because of the choice of name is a violation of the rights of the claimant under Articles 36 and 27 of the Constitution of Kenya, taking into account that these rights can be limited only in terms of law and only to the extent that the limitation is reasonable and justifiable in an open society based on human dignity, equality and freedom.

In dealing with the substance of the right to freedom of association, the Court held that an individual is a "person" for the purposes of the Constitution regardless of their gender or sexual orientation. That the Court is enjoined to apply the Constitution without prejudice, and must be able to distinguish between the right to assemble of those of a sexual orientation that is not socially accepted, and the homosexual acts that the respondents and the 3rd interested party argue are criminal acts prohibited by law. In particular the Penal Code does not criminalise homosexuality but rather certain sexual acts "against the order of nature" which is not defined. Moreover, the Penal Code does not contain any provision that limits the freedom of association of individuals on the basis of their sexual orientation.

Importantly, in determining whether Mr Gitari's right to freedom of association has been infringed, the Court had regard to various international and regional law and principles and particularly the importance of the right to freedom of association and expression in a constitutional democracy. In contrast to the Botswana Court of Appeal's decision in Kanane, the Kenya High Court quite correctly held that public opinion and morality is not a core factor in constitutional adjudication and particularly the right to association. In this regard the Court held that the Constitution and the right to freedom of association applies regardless of the popularity of the objects of the association.

Conclusion

In conclusion, it is apt to observe that the field of human rights is still heavily contested. There is still a yawning gap between theory and practice. Much of the reluctance or hostility to honour human rights of all is fuelled by an attempt to impose our perceptions of morality on everyone, yet in a constitutional democracy the perception of morality that must be imposed is that one of the Constitution. Prejudice, misinformation, stereotyping, ignorance remains major barriers to realising a vision of equality for all.

An independent judiciary is institutionally suited to safeguarding the rights of 'every person' - to employ the wording of the Botswana Constitution. Judges are not answerable to any constituency and are thus insulated from most political pressures. They are therefore in a better position than legislators or executive officials to protect the constitutional rights of individuals, even when that requires a politically unpopular decision. More significantly, the absence of direct political responsibility on judges and the "deliberative, contemplative" nature of the judicial process, results in more thoughtful decisions.

In jurisdictions where the legal and constitutional framework is not developed enough to protect human rights of minorities and marginalised groups international human rights law offers an opportunity to fashion appropriate remedies within the limits of the legal system that may be operative. Both monist and dual legal systems offer opportunities to use international law within the framework of the Bangalore Principles.

Courts, in our region are prepared, incrementally, to enforce rights of LGTB communities. The recent case law from Botswana and Kenya makes this clear. However, this has not been smooth sailing. In countries where the law is unclear, non-existent or vague, judges who have resorted to international law to reinforce the inadequacy of domestic law have been accused of legislating or being activist judges.

It is my considered opinion that judicial activism which has generated criticism in some circles is often fully justified. By judicial activism, I simply mean the ability to develop the law in accordance with the changing times and as may be permissible in law. Courts do not relish making hard and politically charged decisions. But the courts have a sacred duty to uphold the Constitution and its values. When a case or "controversy" is properly presented, the court may not shirk its own responsibility to uphold the Constitution.

I would like to conclude by saying that the responsibility for trends in the development of the law, whether in the retrogressive or progressive direction, do not belong solely to the judiciary. Lawyers play a vital role in shaping this development. The questions presented to judges are framed by lawyers within the context of actual controversies. They are obliged to bring before the courts cutting edge jurisprudence that can advance the vision of a better society for all – ensuring, at all times, that no one is left behind.

Anyone familiar with the workings of the law would readily testify that decisions of the courts are influenced by the advocacy of the lawyer; the depth of his/her research, his creativity and persuasiveness. In a nutshell, lawyers often determine whether the law stands still or moves forward. But as for whether justice is finally seen to be done that is the primary responsibility of the Judge.

Chapter 9

Sexual Reproductive and Health Rights (Srhr)

A Keynote speech at a Workshop on Advocating for SRHR rights through the Media.

Introduction

I wish to express my profound gratitude to the SADC PF Secretary General, Dr Chiviya, and the SADC PF Secretariat, for inviting me to share with this distinguished gathering of regional editors and journalists my thoughts on advocating for Sexual Reproductive Health Rights through the media.

My multiple roles as a parent, citizen of the region, Judge and interim Co-chair of the newly established Regional Think Tank on HIV, Health and Social Justice in Southern and Eastern Africa makes this intervention a matter of duty and a rare honour indeed.

It is not quite often that a member of the judicial arm of the State has an intellectual moment with members of the 4th Estate - the shapers of public opinion.

Most Judges pride themselves on their clarity of thought, the powers of persuasion which they bring to their judgments - and not necessarily their ability to make public speeches. So, if I fumble, stammer, and exhibit some incoherence, please bear with me! Judgments are generally not addressed to non-lawyers; and are rarely addressed to members of the public. It follows therefore that this is not a familiar territory for me. I am used to writing judgments, in which the manner of communication is somewhat rigid, couched in misleadingly neutral terms, dry and devoid of emotion. In the result, no one could credibly argue that Judges have any appreciable competence at public speaking. This constitutes my disclaimer. I can only hope it is effective.

In the tapestry of constitutional literature, the media like the other three arms of the State is considered an indispensable component of any democratic society. It has a duty to entertain, inform, and educate. A free and critical media is indispensable in engendering an educated and enlightened citizenry.

One of the foremost American statesmen, Thomas Jefferson, expressed his belief in the value of the media/press in the following golden words:

"The basis of our governments being the opinion of the people, the very first object should be to keep that right; and where it left to me to decide whether we should have a government without newspapers or newspapers without government, I should not hesitate a moment to prefer the Latter"

The media has a huge and untapped potential to inform and educate the general populace about SRHR and HIV and governance issues – such as the imperative for the three arms of the State to be interested and indeed obligated to honor God given rights in executing their diverse mandates. In other words, the need to respect human rights should never be seen as the monopoly of the judiciary and the three arms of the State need to cooperate at all times to honour fundamental rights of all people.

Defining the Universe of Discourse

Reproductive health is not just a health issue - it is also a human right issue. Reproductive health is a state of complete physical, mental and social wellbeing, and not merely the absence of disease in all matters relating to the reproductive system, its functions and processes. Sexual and

Reproductive Health encompasses health and wellbeing in matters related to sexual relations, pregnancy, and birth.

It follows from the above that reproductive health deals with the most intimate and private aspect of people's lives, which can be difficult to write about and discuss publicly. Furthermore, cultural sensitivities and taboos surrounding sexuality often prevent people from seeking Sexual and Reproductive Health information and care. Yet, Sexual and Reproductive Health affects social and economic development of any country. When women die during child birth or from AIDS, children are orphaned.

When girls must take care of their siblings, they drop out of school and become an economic burden to their country.

Without education, girls often marry and begin having children early, which can jeopardise their health and limit their opportunities to contribute to their own development, those of their families, communities, and countries.

The media plays an important role in bringing Sexual and Reproductive Health matters to the attention of the people who can influence public health policies.

Journalists who produce accurate reports about Sexual and Reproductive Health issues can:

a. Bring taboo subjects in the open so that they can be discussed.

b. Monitor their governments' progress towards achieved stated goals.

c. Hold government official accountable to the public.

Reproductive health of necessity implies that people are able to have a satisfying sex life and that they have the capability to reproduce and freedom to decide, if, when and how often to do so. Implicit in the latter point, are the rights of men and women to be informed and to have access to safe, effective, affordable and acceptable methods of family planning of their choice and the right to access appropriate health care services that would enable among other things, women to go safely through pregnancy and childbirth.

Speaking for myself, it is imperative that efforts within the field of Sexual Reproductive Health Rights, HIV and governance issues, should be approached from a human rights perspective, where participation, inclusion and accountability are the central principles. This approach views citizens not as passive receivers of services or beneficiaries of programmes, but as active rights holders, who should be empowered to claim their rights. The Media can play an important role in empowering the people to claim their rights.

States have obligations to respect and protect their citizens against violations of their rights. The courts have a duty to hold the legislature, the executive and other entities to honour human rights, effect the promise of most constitutions that eloquently speak of the right to dignity. The courts in the region have enforced Sexual and Reproductive Health Rights with admiration even in the face of hostile executive stand points or inadequate legal framework.

This has been particularly the case in the area of HIV, non-discrimination and equality, notwithstanding that in our region, in particular, there is an epidemic of bad laws in the broad area of Sexual and Reproductive Health Rights, mainly because in most of our societies, the ideology of patriarchy still holds sway and even threatens to suffocate progressive constitutions. This state of affairs is exacerbated by religious dogma and intolerance. It follows in my view that fulfilling the rights to Sexual and Reproductive Health requires that both the Media and the three arms of the State be absolutely committed to the human rights enterprise.

In the case of Diau v BBS and Mwale v the Attorney General the Botswana High Court remarked that even in an underdeveloped legal framework that is not fully protective of those infected and affected by HIV, it is the duty of the courts to determine the extent, content and context of human rights of individuals and that the courts must not treat constitutions as museum pieces but rather as living documents intended to cover the interests, not only the current generation, but generations yet unborn. In Mwale, the High Court went further, and suggested that the right to life encapsulated in the Botswana Constitution is expansive enough to include the right to health especially in the circumstances of the applicant where he was denied the right to be provided with life-saving drugs simply because he was a foreigner. However, it must be indicated that this expansive definition of the right to life was rejected by the apex court in the land.

It must also be noted that Sexual Reproductive Health Rights embrace certain rights that are often recognized by national laws and international law. These rights rest on the basic right of all couples and individuals to decide freely and responsibly, the number, spacing and timing of their children and to have the information and means to do so. To this extent, it is imperative that women should have access to safe and legal abortion care. I want to put it plainly, and boldly, that without access to safe and legal abortion, women are not fully able to decide freely, on matters related to their Sexual and Reproductive Health, and thus, not able to fully enjoy their human rights.

I do not wish to be understood to be saying that abortion should be promoted as a method of family planning. The position I hold is that the best way to avoid abortions is through improved access to reproductive health services (contraception), information and the empowerment of women - through education which can be done brilliantly by the media.

I submit further, with respect, that gender equality – in terms of equal rights, (as the High Court of Botswana recently enunciated in the case of Mmusi) including Sexual and Reproductive Rights, equal access to resources and equal opportunities, is central for women to become fully integrated and equal citizens in their countries and thus fulfil their enormous potential for contributing and benefiting from the development of their countries.

It is for this reason that the Botswana High Court, recently, in the case of Mmusi, polemically indicated that, on matters of gender equality especially in under-developed legal environments, the courts have a duty to act as judicial midwives for the birth of a society based on equality between men and women – that is still struggling to be born. In terms of my experience and conviction, quite often it even becomes necessary for the courts to aid the birth of a new society based on equality by resorting to caesarean birth.

This is so because promoting gender equality demands changes to existing power relations. It must of necessity be based on acknowledgements of cultural and religious differences within the framework of universal human rights. However, it is worth emphasizing that religious and cultural values and traditions must never be used to serve as an excuse of depriving any individual of his/her freedom or rights.

Concerns around Media Coverage of SRHR and HIV Issues

There is concern in our region that the Media often fail to prioritize Sexual and Reproductive Rights, HIV and governance issues, or report them in an accurate manner.

In the SADC region, it is generally agreed that the media coverage of reproductive health issues is not satisfactory on account of weak capacity and motivation for reporting these issues.

According to some authorities, the interest of the media in the area of SRHR is often dominated by announcements of new drugs or official health campaigns. This criticism notwithstanding, it must also be pointed out that, the Media's lack of capacity or motivation is not the only problem; researchers also often lack the capacity to simplify their research or to present it in a way that captures the Media's interest.

In this era, where the ideology of patriarchy is still dominant and religious intolerance is high, a capacitated media can assist in promoting Sexual Reproductive Health Rights and in bringing down the walls of prejudice, discrimination and stigma that still haunt the fight against HIV.

The media can also help shine the spotlight on poor legislative frameworks and implementation capacity by the executive and even shine the spotlight on the jurisprudence of deficiency and retrogression that still dominates our law reports, mainly from the jurists of the yesteryear who pay lipservice to human rights.

The SADC Capacitation Programme of the Media

It is in the context of the above that this particular initiative by SADC PF must be appreciated as it seeks to inspire and build capacity of journalists to undertake evidence based reporting of reproductive health issues. It is important that the SADC PF approach must emphasis the following:

a. Enhancing journalists interest in and motivation for reporting on reproductive health issues through training and competitive grants for meaningful and effective reporting on SRHR:

b. Building the capacity of journalists to report simply and clearly, on reproductive health research and the capacity of reproductive health researchers to communicate their research to the Media using plain language, devoid of jargon, where practicable.

c. Establish and maintain trust and mutual relationships between journalists and researchers.

It is indisputable that Sexual and Reproductive Health is a major problem in our region. According to some sources, illness and deaths from poor reproductive health accounts for more than one-fifth of the global burden of the disease.

In our region, the use of contraceptives by married couples is not satisfactory and as with HIV prevalence our region is the epicenter of deaths due to unsafe abortion. We still have serious problems of women who die from complications associated with childbirths and too many of our adolescents are hospitalized every year with abortion related complications

Other indications of poor reproductive health rights include adolescents' lack of access to reproductive health information and services.

SADC PF must remain committed to the agenda of seeking to cultivate the interest and capacity of the media to educate the populace about the need to honor in words and deed, the constitutional provisions of member States that seek to honor the all embracing right to life – the umbrella provision under which SRHR can find protection. Amongst the issues that SADC PF must seek to unearth and resolve, includes understanding the drivers and consequences of population change in our region.

Conclusion

I am conscious that I have kept you listening for a long time and that I must conclude my address. I conclude by inviting you in covering SRHR, HIV and governance issues to remain critical in an informed and respectful manner. Don't hesitate to criticize the Judges if they betray their constitutional oath of office. We are not infallible. Neither are we untouchable angels. A critical appraisal of our judgments is necessitated by the fact that law is fraught with illusion; the illusion that law and justice mean the same thing. What I can say and say unapologetically is that the ultimate objective of law must be justice. The law can be a force for good; but also for bad. This is an incontestable reality. You must also, in covering the issues I have highlighted above, demystify the notion that the law is accessible to all irrespective of wealth or privilege.

You, the members of the 4th Estate, need to keep watch over us - those engaged directly in the enterprise of law – that we keep our faith in honouring the morality of our constitutions – whose central theme is equality. I am certain that if you remain focused on quality and evidence-based reporting, and reduce undue sensationalisation and distortion, in the context of the theme of this conference, this world shall be a better place to live in.

I thank you for listening.

Chapter 10

Protection of The Rights of Domestic and Illegal Foreign Workers In Botswana

A Keynote speech delivered at ILERA Africa 7th Regional Congress held at GICC, Gaborone, 14 -16th of September 2014.

Introduction

"Labour law … is a fundamentally important as well as an extremely sensitive subject. It is based upon a political and economic compromise between organized labour – a very powerful socio-economic force - on the one hand, and the employers of labour – an equally powerful socio-economic force – on the other. The balance between the two forces is delicate …" (McIntyre, J., in Re Public Service Employee Relations Act (1987), 38 DLR (4th), p 232)

Distinguished guests, ladies and gentlemen, I feel highly honoured to have been asked by the organizers to address this distinguished gathering on: "Protection of the rights of domestic and illegal foreign workers in Botswana". The common denominator between the two categories of workers is that they are vulnerable groups who have not always been sufficiently protected in national legislation of many countries.

It is on account of the insufficiency of protective legislation that Judges presiding in cases involving the aforesaid category of workers have often been challenged to rise above a mechanical interpretation of the law that yields injustice in favour of an interpretational approach that ensures that justice ultimately prevails. The law, it has often been said has no finer hour than when it cuts through formal concepts and transitory emotions such as xenophobia to protect the rights of vulnerable groups. A creative way of conceptualizing the position of illegal workers to provide for redress is evident from the jurisprudence of the Industrial Court.

I imagine that your organisation primary mandate is to advance, among other, objectives, workplace peace. Such a collective approach, in this global village, is to be commended. Usually, globalization summons images of corporations than labour relations practitioners, lawyers, courts and their formations.

It seems to me that the compression of distance and the dissolution of borders that drives globalization has proved far more efficient at producing global markets than global justice.

Information technology may transcend culture and a new generation of lawyers may weave together a global society, but judge made law, still seems inherently national. A new generation of jurists need to emerge to weave together a human rights driven jurisprudence based on rendering justice – the end of product that qualifies every judge's name.

Protecting the rights of vulnerable workers

From a point of view of social justice, the needs and interests of domestic workers and illegal foreign workers demand protection. These categories of workers wield limited bargaining power and are least able to negotiate better terms and conditions of employment and are vulnerable to intense pressure to work with no or little rest.

Domestic workers are the weaker party in an employment relationship for several reasons. Firstly, the nature of their work places them in vulnerable situation vis-à-vis their employer. They are generally isolated from other workers and are in close physical and emotional proximity to their employers. Secondly, domestic work often has a low social status, given its historical link to slavery and servitude.

Over the years, Botswana has attracted an increasing number of foreigners. Most of these foreigners came from Zimbabwe. The exact number of foreigners, a significant proportion of whom may be in the country illegally is uncertain as no official figures are published by the Ministry of Labor and Home Affairs. Foreigners, especially those whose presence in the country is illegal or unauthorized are vulnerable to abuse and exploitation in the workplace.

The question whether and if so, to what extent, illegal immigrants working in the country are protected by legislation is an important one in the light of both the number of illegal foreign employees and their vulnerability.

Domestic Work

Domestic work, as one ILO Report notes, is rooted in global history of slavery, colonization and some other forms of servitude. It is generally undervalued and poorly regulated. Many domestic workers remain overworked, underpaid, and unprotected. Within the privacy of the home, it is extremely difficult for labour inspectors to detect any such abuse.

Another defining feature of domestic work is the fact that it is done overwhelmingly by women. For many women, it is practically the only port of entry to the world of paid employment. Domestic work exposes women to all forms of discrimination, including sexual harassment.

It is in consideration of the above factors that the International Labour Conference (ILC), in 2011, adopted a convention, supplemented by a recommendation, on decent work for domestic workers. The convention enjoins member states, to take measures to ensure that domestic workers, like other workers, enjoy fair terms of employment as well as decent working conditions. It further enjoins member states to ensure that domestic workers are informed of their terms and conditions of employment, where possible through written agreements that capture, among other terms, the normal hours of work and paid annual leave.

The Regulatory Framework of Domestic Work in Botswana

Domestic workers are employees in terms of Section 2 (1) of the Employment Act Cap 47:01. Domestic workers do not have the same entitlements as other employees under the Employment Act. Some provisions of the Employment Act apply equally; such as those with respect to leave with pay, severance benefit and termination on notice.

In terms of the Employment (Domestic Employees) Regulations, domestic employees are not entitled to overtime. However, the regulations provide that domestic employees shall not be required to work more than 240 hours in any period of four weeks. On average, this translates into more than 8 hour working week. Although the 8 hour working day is now an internationally accepted legal norm, domestic workers are often exempted from this standard.

In France, the law sets normal weekly hours for domestic work at 40 hours per week. Uruguay's weekly limit is 44 hours and South Africa 45 hours per week.

South Africa's basic Conditions of Employment Act provides basic protection for all employees, including domestic workers, in respect of conditions of work, such as working hours, leave and dismissal.

In Finland, the law permits departure from ordinary hours of work only in cases of emergency. However, it must be stated that long and unpredictable working hours impose a high cost on worker's health and well being and, in turn erode the efficiency and quality of service they provide to their employer's households.

The principal challenge to policy makers in our country, and indeed in other countries, is to formulate legislation on terms and conditions of service of domestic workers that protect domestic workers' interests while taking into account the needs of the households that employ them. It is true, as it is often said, that the measure of every country's progress is how it treats its most vulnerable and marginalized.

Paid Public Holidays

Ordinarily and in terms of the Employment Act, employees in general are entitled to 8 paid public holidays. An employee who works on a paid public holiday shall be paid double pay or be granted a day off in lieu of that day. However, in terms of the regulations mentioned earlier domestic employees are entitled to only four paid public holidays, namely, New Year's Day, Good Friday, Botswana day and Christmas day. In practice, they are hardly paid for working over these public holidays.

Rest Periods

In Botswana, domestic employees are entitled to one day a week off as a rest day. It is doubtful whether this is done in actual practice. It must be emphasized that adequate rest periods and sleep make a big difference to a worker's state of mental and physical health and work performance. Studies have actually shown that there is a link between long working hours without rest and other poor psychological outcomes including depression, anxiety, and confusion.

It is therefore very important to ensure that domestic workers are granted rest periods.

Illegal Foreign Workers

That illegal foreign workers are vulnerable is to state the obvious. They are often employed on farms and household for a pittance.

The employment of foreign employees is governed by Section 4 of the Employment of Non-Citizens Act (Cap 47:02)

Section 4 of the aforesaid Act provides that:

1. "No non-citizen shall engage in any occupation for reward or profit unless-

    a. He is the holder of a work permit issued under this Act permitting him to be employed or to engage in and he is employed or otherwise so engaged in accordance with the terms thereof …

    b. He is the holder of a certificate of exemption issued to him under this Act.

2. No person shall employ a non-citizen unless

    a. The non-citizens is the holder of a work permit issued to him under this Act permitting him to be employed and he is employed in accordance with the terms thereof …

    b. the non-citizen is the holder of an exemption issued to him under this Act."

Contravention of the Act is punishable by a fine of P1000 or 12 months imprisonment or both.

Section 4 (1) forbids non-citizens from engaging in any occupation for reward. Section 4 (2) forbids employers from employing non-citizens.

For a long time, the Industrial Court took the view that illegal contracts cannot be enforced. And the early decisions tended to throw away the baby with the bath water.

(See Edrogan Cahit v Masto Olmetz (Pty) Ltd IC 89/95 (unreported); Musenza v J and P Security Services (Botswana) (Pty) Ltd 1997 BLR 274; Hattas v Kim's Auto (Pty) Ltd 1998 BLR 338)

The inspiration for our courts refusing to enforce illegal contracts could be partly explained by the remarks of Innes CJ, in the case of Schierhout v Minister of Justice 1926 AD 99 at 109, when he said:

"It is a fundamental principle of our law that a thing done contrary to the direct prohibition of the law is void and of no effect. … So what is done contrary to the prohibition of the law is not only of no effect, but must be regarded as never having been done – and that whether the law giver has expressly so decreed or not, the mere prohibition operates to nullify the act."

Whilst a few jurists can find fault with the correctness of the view that anything done contrary to statutory provision is null and void, many would also concede that there is injustice in an employee walking empty handed after working for an employer because the contract that was entered into was illegal. It is this concern that troubled the court in the case of Olena Molefi and Blue Blends Investments (Pty) Ltd t/a Nescafe 2004 (1) BLR 259 (IC). As they say, every era have its mood and the justices for that mood. The seminal decision of Molefi constituted a decisive turning point that sought to render justice to the parties in the face of legislation that on the face of it made that task difficult.

In the aforesaid case, the court whilst accepting that the contract entered into was illegal, took the view that the employer had been unjustly enriched by not paying the employee and ordered that the employer must pay the employee for services actually rendered so that it may not be unjustly enriched at the expense of the employee.

It is my considered view that ordinary justice frowns upon a powerful offender deliberately taking advantage of the law to enrich himself/ herself at the expense of a weaker party, an employee, who simply wants to put bread on the table for himself and his family. Where an employer knowingly employs a foreigner with no work permit, the maxim, "no polluted hands shall touch the pure fountains of justice", should not be applied against the employee to reward an employer who has engaged in the most reprehensible from of trickery, as the court observed in the case of Molefi, referred to above.

It is possible that they may well be some jurists who credibly take the view that nothing can be salvaged from an illegal contract – in that the contract is null and void ab initio – but one may say in response, that faced with injustice judges cannot fold their arms, wring themselves of any responsibility, and say our hands are tied.

After all, it was that doyen of the British bench, Lord Denning MR, who once poignantly observed that:

"A judge must not alter the material of which it (the law) is woven, but he can and should iron out the creases" (See Discipline of Law (Butterworths, 1979), p 12)

Justice Benjamin Cardozo of the United States in his much quoted treatise – The nature of the Judicial Process (Yale University Press, 1967) at pp 66-7 stated that:

"The final cause of law is the welfare of society. The rule that misses its aim cannot permanently justify its existence. "Ethical considerations can no more be excluded from the administration of justice which is the end and purpose of all civil laws than one can exclude the vital air from his room and live." Logic and history and custom have their place. We will shape the law to conform to them when we may; but only within bounds. The end which the law serves will dominate them all. There is an old legend that on one occasion God prayed, and his prayer was "Be it my will that my justice be ruled by mercy". That is a prayer which we all need to utter at times when the demon of formalism tempts the intellect with the lure of scientific order. I do not mean, of course, that the judges are commissioned to set aside existing rules at pleasure in favour of any other set of rules which they may hold to be expedient or wise. I mean when they are called upon to say how far existing rules are to be extended or restricted, they must let the welfare of society fix the path, its direction and its distance."

It is the duty of the judiciary, to do all they can to ensure that justice reigns supreme at all times and to skilfully and innovatively negotiate tensions in the law in order to render justice to the parties without necessarily usurping the powers of Parliament.

Shaping the law, in the words of Benjamin Cardozo or ironing the creases in the words of Lord Denning does not necessarily amount to making law.

While it can be hardly contested that democratically elected legislatures are the primary law making bodies, it can hardly be denied that in a limited way Judges make law. For Judges, law making is a refined art, one that accounts for past legal precedent and is based on a clinical and informed analysis of what the law "is" rather than what it "should be".

In the process of making law, in the manner I have suggested above, Judges need to be informed and courageous. They should not be timorous souls, fearful or biased.

In one of his most celebrated dissents on the Court of Appeal of England, the legendary common law jurist Lord Denning suggested the following classification of Judges: "On the one side there were timorous souls who were fearful of allowing a new cause of action. On the other side, there were bold spirits who were ready to allow it if justice so required."

According to Lord Denning, the progressive development of the law, is to be credited to judicial creativity and courage of bold spirits. He disapproved of timorous souls who showed blind allegiance to existing rules and precedent – the 'dead hand of the past' – and, in so doing, served a mechanical, not a constructive, role in the law. The case of Molefi, cited above, is a classical example of progressive development of the law of which Lord Denning eloquently spoke about.

In conclusion, I would like to emphasize that there is a limit to what judges can do to protect the rights of vulnerable groups in society. Parliament needs to step in and legislate to protect vulnerable categories of employees in line with relevant ILO conventions. The issue of protection of the rights of domestic workers and illegal foreign workers is bound to be contentious, but guidance may be obtained from the ILO conventions and other international treaties.

Thank you.

Chapter 11

The Role of The Judiciary In Promoting Prisoner's Rights and How Civil Society Organizations (Cso) Can Use The Courts

A Paper delivered at a Regional Dialogue on HIV, TB and Human Rights in Johannesburg, South Africa on the 6th of February, 2015.

Introduction

The purpose of this paper is to reflect on the role of the judiciary in promoting prisoner's rights and how civil society organizations can utilize law and the court to advance a vision of a more humane society that respects human rights of all people especially of prisoners, in the context of HIV/ AIDS and tuberculosis.

For the purpose of this paper the term "prisoner" is used to refer to adult and juvenile males and females detained in the criminal justice and correctional facilities during the investigation of a crime; while awaiting trial, after conviction before and after sentencing.

The basic premise of the paper is simple and straightforward. It is that prisoners, especially those with HIV and other health conditions, such as tuberculosis, are vulnerable groups that require protection by respecting their human rights. Respecting their rights is a good public health policy and also a good human rights practice.

The legal position, generally speaking, is that prisoners retain all rights that are not taken away as a result of imprisonment. Loss of liberty alone is considered sufficient punishment. What this means is that prisoners retain all their fundamental human rights, save for liberty.

In terms of international law, States are prohibited from inflicting inhuman or degrading treatment on people in detention. This prohibition compels States not only to refrain from inflicting inhuman and degrading treatment on prisoners, but also to take practical measures necessary to protect the physical integrity and health of persons who have been deprived of their liberty.

Of all the rights that prisoners have, the right that is often undermined or compromised is the right to medical treatment.

Background on HIV/AIDS in Prisons

HIV/AIDS is acknowledged the world over to be a health threat for prison populations. It is generally accepted that prisons and prisoners remain part of the broader community. This means that the health threat of HIV/AIDS within prisons, and the health threat outside prisons are invariably linked and therefore demanded coordinated action.

Worldwide, the levels of HIV infection among prison populations tend to be much higher than in the population outside prisons. This situation is often accompanied and made worse by high rates of other health conditions such as tuberculosis, sexually transmitted infections (STD's) and mental health problems in prison populations.

In many parts of Africa, the spread of HIV within prisons is related to sexual contact (primarily men having sex with men), as well as unsafe medical practices or sharing of razors.

The best way to understand the human rights concerns of prison population is to appreciate prison conditions that exacerbate their vulnerability to HIV infection and other infectious diseases.

As a general rule, prisons tend to be over populated; characterized by poor personal hygiene, poor ventilation, inadequate nutrition, lack of access to drinking water and inadequate medical services.

International law places obligations on States to meet human rights of prisoners. States are particularly precluded from pleading lack of resources as an excuse of not meeting its international obligations.

International Legal Instruments and Guidelines governing prison management and HIV/AIDS

The human rights of prisoners are articulated in a number of international legal instruments, declarations and statements. These include the following:

- Universal Declaration of Human Rights [1948]

- United Nations Standard Minimum Rules for the Treatment of Prisoners [1955]

- International Covenant on Civil and Political Rights [1966]

- United Nations Principles of Medical Ethics relevant to the Role of Health Personnel, particularly Physicians, in the Protection of Prisoners and Detainees against Torture and Other Cruel, Inhuman or Degrading Treatment or Punishment [1982]

- United Nations Basic Principles for the Treatment of Prisoners [1990]

- Body of Principles for the Protection of All persons under Any Form of Detention or Imprisonment [1988]

- United Nations Standard Minimum Rules for Non-custodial Measures (The Tokyo Rules) [1990]

- World Health Organization's Guidelines on HIV Infection and AIDS in Prisons [1993]

- Joint United Nations Programme on HIV/AIDS (UNAIDS) Statement on HIV/AIDS in Prisons [April 1996]

- Recommendation No R (98)7 of the Committee of Ministers to Members States Concerning the Ethical and Organisational Aspects of Health Care in Prisons [council of Europe: April 1998]

- International Guidelines on HIV/AIDS and Human Rights [1998]

- World Medical Association Declaration of Edinburgh on Prison Conditions and the Spread of Tuberculosis and Other Communicable Diseases [October 2000]

- Declaration of Commitment on HIV/AIDS ("UNGASS Declaration") [United Nations General Assembly Special Session on HIV/AIDS: June 2001]

- Prison, Drugs and Society: A consensus Statement on Principles, Policies and Practices [WHO Europe/Pompidou Group of the Council of Europe: September 2001]

- United Nations Committee on Economic, Social, and Cultural Rights: Geneva Comment on the Right to the Highest Attainable Standard of Health. Twenty-second session, Geneva [2002]

- International Labour Office Code of Practice on HIV/AIDS and the World of Work [2002]

- Warsaw Declaration: A Framework for Effective Action on HIV/AIDS and Injecting Drug Use [November 2003]

- Moscow Declaration: Prison Health as part of Public Health [WHO Europe: October 2003]

- Dublin Declaration on HIV/AIDS in Prisons in Europe and Central Asia [February 2004]

- Policy Brief: Reduction of HIV Transmission in Prisons [WHO/UNAIDS: 2004]

- Policy Statement on HIV Testing [UNAIDS/WHO:2004]

- Substitution maintenance therapy in the management of opioid dependence and HIV/AIDS prevention [WHO/UNODC/UNAiDS:2004]

- Effectiveness of sterile needle and syringe programming in reducing HIV/AIDS among injecting drug users: Evidence for action technical paper [WHO: 2004]

- Recommendation Rec (2006) 2 of the Committee of Ministers to member States on the European Prison Rules [Council of Europe: January 2006]

A number of the legal instruments enumerated above are based on the Universal Declaration of Human rights of 1948, which has the status of Customary International Law and as such binding, as a general rule, on all States. What is plain is that countries that have ratified or acceded to any of the above listed covenants, declarations or charters have agreed that they are bound to respect, protect and fulfill human rights including the right to equality and non-discrimination; the right to life, the right to security of the person, the right not to be subjected to inhuman and degrading treatment and the right to health, to mention but a few, are some of the protected rights.

The Right to Medical Treatment

The right to medical treatment is often implicated when it comes to consideration of human rights of prison populations. Under international law prisoners are entitled, without discrimination, to a standard of health care equivalent to that available in the broader society, including preventative measures.

Vulnerability, Stigma and Discrimination in Prisons

It is a matter of record that prisoners are often the most vulnerable and stigmatized of the prison population. It is common knowledge that fear of

HIV/AIDS often places HIV positive prisoners at increased risk of social isolation; violence and human rights abuses from both prisoners and prison staff. This fear is often driven by misinformation about HIV transmission, and the false belief that HIV infection may be spread by casual contact.

Fear of discrimination discourages prisoners from accessing voluntary HIV testing and HIV/AIDS prevention and education measures.

Within the prison populations, they are minorities who are particularly vulnerable and require special attention. These include children, women, migrants, men who have sex with men, gay, lesbian, bisexual and transsexual and transgendered prisoners.

The Role of the Judiciary in Promoting Prisoner's Rights

The field of human rights in prisons, in so far as it implicates the right to health and other associated rights is seriously contested. Amongst the general populace and within the judiciary there is no agreement on such issues as distribution of condoms in prison. In some sections of the populace and the judiciary, there is even denial that sexual activity between men takes place in prisons. In some jurisdictions, immigrants are still fighting to be provided with ARVs just like locals. Much of the hostility to honour human rights is fuelled by misinformation, prejudice, stereotyping and ignorance.

During my over 12 years at the bench, I have witnessed some of the prejudice referred to above. In the early days of my career, at the bench, courts, in the region, appeared reluctant to review prisoners' complaints with respect to alleged violations of human rights in prisons. Courts were generally reluctant to intervene because the courts involvement would be prejudicial to the proper maintenance of prison discipline. The other reason that was often proffered was that the administration of prisons was entrusted to the discretion of the executive branch and therefore judicial intervention would violate the principle of separation of powers.

Of recent, courts in most of our jurisdictions have discarded the policy of judicial restraint and now take the view that when a prison regulation or practice offends fundamental constitutional rights, courts will discharge their duty to protect such rights.

An independent judiciary is institutionally suited to safeguarding constitutional principles. Judges are not answerable to any constituency and are thus insulated from most political pressures. They are therefore in a better position than legislators or executive officials to protect the constitutional rights of individuals, even when that requires a politically unpopular decision. More significantly, the absence of direct political responsibility on judges and the "deliberative, contemplative" nature of the judicial process, results in more thoughtful decisions.

In jurisdictions where the legal and constitutional framework is not developed enough to protect human rights of prisoners international human rights law offers an opportunity to fashion appropriate remedies within the limits of the legal system that may be operative. Both monist and dual legal systems offer opportunities to use international law within the framework of the Bangalore Principles.

Examples of Case Law on Prisoners' Rights

In South Africa, although the Constitution does not have explicit provisions regarding HIV and AIDS, it nevertheless guarantees prisoners the right "to conditions of detention that are consistent with human dignity", including adequate medical treatment. However, this right is limited in scope, as the State is required to take reasonable legislative and other measures, within its available resources, to achieve the progressive realization of this right. The following cases illustrate the important role the court may play to protect constitutional rights.

The Case of Van Biljon v Minister of Correctional Services

In Van Biljon v Minister of Correctional Services, four HIV positive prisoners, who had previously received ART outside of prison, challenged the State to provide them with medication at its own expense, as part of the State's obligation to fulfill the prisoners' right to adequate medical treatment. The court had to decide (i) whether the applicants' medical condition or the advanced nature of their disease entitled them to medical treatment and (ii) whether this treatment should be provided at the State's expense. In emphasizing the term 'adequate' in the Constitution, the court observed that medical treatment does not have to be the 'best available' or even 'optimal', but must be equivalent and comparable to the treatment afforded to those outside the prison setting. However, the court went further and found that there was a stronger obligation on the State to provide medical care for particularly vulnerable prisoners, such as those living with HIV and AIDS, than there was to provide healthcare for comparable patients outside of prisons.

The court considered resource limitations under the constitutional clause relating to prisoners. This gave rise to criticism because the section does not have a specific limitation clause. If the right to medical treatment was being limited due to financial constraints, then this could only be done under the general limitation clause of the Constitution.

N v Government of Republic of South Africa

N v Government of Republic of South Africa dealt with the challenges of access to, and provision of, ARVs for prisoners. In this case 15 applicants, incarcerated at Westville Correctional Centre (WCC), were all infected with HIV and Aids, needed ARVs and brought an urgent application to court. Prisoners had attempted to access ARVs via regular channels but this failed, forcing the prisoners to litigate as a last resort.

The court accepted that the applicants and respondents had divergent views on the facts of the case, but did not dispute the applicants' claims that their constitutional rights to medical treatment were being violated. The respondents did not recognize that the applicants' actions aimed to speed up the provisions of ARV treatment in accordance with South Africa's Operational Plan, and believed that they were seeking to override the NDP and expected the court to prescribe treatment for them. However, the court regarded the applicants' complaints in a very serious light, stating that the case involved questions of life and death. The court referred to numerous precedents dealing with the medical care of prisoners, dating back to the turn of the century, and held that the DCS was obligated to provide, within its resources, adequate healthcare. However, the WCC failed to implement the court's order issued, and two further applications to court had to be brought before it finally complied

The failure of both the Executive and Legislatures to take action to remedy shocking conditions that exist in prisons has caused the courts to abandon the 'hands off" doctrine. Courts do not sit to supervise prisons, but to enforce the constitutional rights of all persons, including prisoners. The courts are not unmindful that prison officials must be accorded some latitude in the administration of prison affairs, and that prisoners necessarily are subjected to appropriate rules and regulations. But persons in prison, like other individuals, have the right to approach the courts for the enforcement of their constitutional rights.

Tapela & Another v Attorney General & Others MAHGB-000057-14

The applicants in this case, were Zimbabwean prison inmates. They approached the court arguing that the policy of the Botswana Government of denying them ARVs while availing them to citizen inmates denied them the rights to life, freedom from inhuman and degrading treatment, discrimination and equality.

In upholding the contention of the applicants, the court ordered the Botswana Government to provide anti-retroviral treatment to HIV positive foreign prisoners at State expense.

In the course of its judgment, the court highlighted the importance of ensuring that all prisoners have access to ARV treatment, not only for their own health, but also to protect other prisoners from acquiring HIV and other opportunistic infections such as tuberculosis.

How Civil Society Organization (CSO's) Can Use Courts to advance a vision of Equality and Non-discrimination in Prisons

Civil Society Organizations, including political movements, have historically turned to litigation to advance the cause they believe in. The resulting litigation is best described as strategic. In this context, litigation is strategic in the sense that it attempts to persuade the courts to use their learning and integrity to expand the democratic space or to enforce the rights, especially of marginalized and vulnerable groups.

Strategic litigation, in my respectful view, casts civil society organizations as some kind of a radical social critic of the unsatisfactory status quo and they litigate in order to exhort the courts to replace the present unjust reality with a just and equal future. Strategic litigation emphasizes the vision of justice as a continual struggle – rather than as a set of legal norms or procedures – and does not necessarily mourn over lost cases; because its primary purpose is to advance a vision of a better society.

Civil Society Organizations that use the courts to advance a vision of an equal society must regard law as a process of struggle, where they would be defeats and victories along the way – even causalities. Litigation, in terms of this view, arises from a conflict between a status quo that is unjust and civil society's vision to create a better society in which rights of all persons are respected.

In my mind, for Civil Society Organizations engaged in the task of effecting a better society, the symbol of justice is not the traditional scales, connoting calm and detached balancing of the scales but an imagery of a turbulent cascading river.

Strategic litigation uses courts as a forum of rational engagement especially with respect to enforcement of certain rights that may be politically unpopular. In addition to winning legal battles that may have immediate and concrete benefits, it also serves very important educational purpose.

Civil Society Organizations must however understand the limitations of law. Law cannot be a panacea of all societal ills. And much as it can be a force for good it can be a force for bad. This notwithstanding, law and the courts can be engaged successfully to move the agenda of a better society forward.

I guess my underlying message is as simple as it is profound. It is that litigation, even losing litigation can be an important mechanism for a narrative that is central to the creation of a better society. Even judgments dismissing cases in which civil society sought to bring about a fairer and better society leaves behind a narrative of resistance. The lessons learned by future generations is not that the case was lost, but that a civil society grouping and their lawyers found courage, energy and creativity to resist injustice in the face of overwhelming odds.

Conclusion

Prison conditions in many countries do not meet the requirements set out in the UN Standard and Minimum Rules for the Treatment of Prisoners, as well as other international and regional standards and norms.

It is incontrovertible that prisoners are vulnerable to HIV and other opportunistic diseases such as tuberculosis (TB). The prevalence rate of tuberculosis tends to be higher in prisons compared to the general population.

Prisoners, like any individual have rights that must be protected. The only right they lose by virtue of incarceration is their liberty.

Courts have used their powers to enforce the rights of prisoners, specifically their right to medical treatment. However, this has not been smooth sailing. In countries where the law is unclear, non-existent or vague, judges who have resorted to international law to reinforce the inadequacy of domestic law have been accused of legislating or being activist judges.

It is my considered opinion that judicial activism which has generated criticism in some circles is often fully justified. Courts do not relish making hard and politically charged decisions. But the courts have a sacred duty to uphold the Constitution and it values. When a case or "controversy" is properly presented, the court may not shirk its own responsibility to uphold the Constitution.

I would like to conclude by saying that the responsibility for trends in the development of the law, whether in the retrogressive or progressive direction, do not belong solely to the judiciary. Lawyers play a vital role in shaping this development. The questions presented to judges are framed by lawyers within the context of actual controversies.

Anyone familiar with the workings of the law would readily testify that decisions of the courts are influenced by the advocacy of the lawyer; the depth of his/her research, his creativity and persuasiveness. In a nutshell, lawyers often determine whether the law stands still or moves forward.

Chapter 12

Case Law of Judicial Case Management

A Paper delivered at the 2012 Judicial Conference held in Palapye on the 24th of October, 2012.

Introduction

1. This paper discusses the jurisprudence of the High Court and that of the Court of Appeal on the new rules dealing with judicial case management. This jurisprudence is still evolving. From the onset, one observes that the jurisprudence of the two courts is not necessarily consistent, as illustrated by the High Court's enthusiasm to apply the rules somewhat strictly and the Court of Appeals cautious approach that seems to emphasise the need to do justice to the parties and to grant an adverse order after all the parties have been fully heard.

Background

2. The 19th of May 2008 was a watershed moment marked a sea-change in the conduct of litigation in Botswana. That is the day upon which new and updated Rules of court were published and came into force. These rules introduced the new system of judicial case management. The new rules transfered control over the conduct of cases from the lawyers to the judiciary. Before the advent of the new rules litigation was largely driven by attorneys

with judges playing a subservient role. Prior to the promulgation of the new rules it was the Registrar, who allocated trial dates and set court rolls without input from the Judges. The system was inefficient and some cases took years to be concluded, and the confidence of the public was warring.

3. In terms of the new rules each Judge litigation is now judge driven and cases are allocated randomly by the computer upon registration. The rules require early disclosure of causes of action, defences. The rules also require parties to meet in advance of conferences called by the judge to manage the case. Once a judge has issued a scheduling order setting out timelines for the various stages of the litigation, the parties are expected to comply failing which adverse orders may be issued against them. and evidence is required and case management conferences are to be called by the Judge, where timetables are set by scheduling orders and amicable settlement of disputes is explored. Generally, time consuming procedural jousting between lawyers is minimized, and resolution of the real issues between the parties is hastened by setting firm trial dates at an early stage. The Rules provide for a strong response, in the form of adverse orders, when lawyers or their clients fail to attend conferences, or to comply with scheduling orders.

4. Order 1 Rule 2 of the new rules expresses the rationale behind case management. It reads:

    "2. Application of these Rules shall be directed towards the achievement of a just, efficient and speedy dispensation of justice."

5. Order 42 is the mother board of JCM. Rules 1 to 10 set out the obligations of the parties to meet with each other first and then with the Judge at case management conferences so as to set and execute scheduling orders and to expedite the early setting of trial dates on defined issues. The rules require pre-disclosure of witness statements and documentary exhibits if an early settlement is not achieved.

The attitude of the High Court to Judicial Case Management Orders

6. In order to realize the objectives set out in Order 1 Rule 2 of the rules of the High Court the justices of this court have taken a dim view of parties who disregard court rules and orders. They have taken the view that scheduling orders must be obeyed so that litigation moves forward quickly. As a result of this strict approach attorneys know by now, that those who disregard rules and court orders do so at their peril.

7. The rationale of the above approach is that disregard of court rules especially if that is done wilfully, undermines the authority of the courts; it is prejudicial to other parties as quite often undue delay escalates litigation costs; it is disrespectful to other litigants and its disruptive to the orderly disposal of the business of the court. It is a view shared by many of the justices of the High court that if the court does not strictly enforce scheduling orders we risk sliding back to the olden days where justice was often held hostage by Attorneys who, having initiated litigation or defended it appeared to develop cold feet and instead of retreating or bringing the litigation to an end, would instead drag it on for no good reason.

8. My brother Newman J eloquently expressed the significance of Order 42 in the case of Gowenius Keanang Error Rantabe v Gabriel Kanjabanga, Tshwaragano Mmereki and Attorney General Case No. Civil Case No. 2914-02 in the following terms:

"Order 42 rule 9 is not part of the rules, which took effect on 19 May 2008, by accident. Nor is it of minor significance. Fundamental to the successful implementation and operation of the 'JCM' system is the appreciation that, once registered, every case properly 'belongs' to the Court, and not to the parties or their attorneys. From that point on, the Court bears responsibility of dealing with the matter expeditiously and fairly, inter alia, by setting out what the parties are required to do, and when they are to do it. That is not to say that, in controlling the pace of the litigation, the judge will operate in a vacuum, or according to his own whims or personal schedule. (My emphasis)

The Learned Judge Continued to State That

'JCM' pre-supposes the full participation of the parties, at all material stages of the process between registration and trial. That is why meetings are scheduled for the parties to prepare case management reports and proposed final pre-trial orders, and why their attendances are required at the Case Management and Final Pre-Trial Conferences. Accordingly, by the time the Final Pre-Trial Order is issued, all interlocutory motions will have been disposed of; all factual and legal issues to be determined will have been identified; all evidence proposed to be tendered, in the form of witness summaries and exhibits, will have been explored. The matter will then proceed purposively to trial, on a date, or dates agreed by all concerned parties."

9. In the case of Khono Boiki Motsamai v Mmamphula Boipelo Bodutu Matrimonial Case No. 274 of 2004, my brother Walia J expressed similar sentiments as those of Newman J, when he said:

   "The new rules have now been promulgated and this is perhaps a good time to remind attorneys that in furtherance of the objects of those Rules, the Courts will have zero tolerance for disregard of the Rules, orders of Court and slothful litigation."

10. The learned Judge continued:

   "New rules are now in place, Judicial Case Management is a reality, warnings have been sounded and orders unfavourable to the tardy and negligent, such as the one in this application, have been made. There can be no excuse for litigants before this Court not to conduct their cases with dispatch and if the laggards suffer adverse consequences, then they have only themselves to blame."

11. In the case of Regent Insurance v Sintala CVHLB-000946-10 my brother CJ stated that:

"Parties who recklessly disregard the Rules and have no respect for the court or its orders must realize that they do not have a place to abuse the judicial process and clog progress at the expense of more deserving cases."

12. It follows therefore that our courts frown upon unjustified disregard of court rules. The parties to litigation are expected, nay, required to always act with due diligence so as to meet the overriding objective of the new rules, namely: "the achievement of a just, efficient and speedy dispensation of justice." (Order 1 (2) of the High Court Rules).

13. In the case of African Directory Services (PTY) LIMITED v Botswana Telecommunications Corporation Case No. CVHLB – 002283-06, my brother Lesetedi J, at paragraph 9 of his judgment, when dealing with a non-diligent party stated as follows:

"Quite clearly, the plaintiff through its representative and/or has not shown due diligence to the court in its conduct of a litigation which it considered to have infringed rights. One would have expected especially with the new case regime that the plaintiff or at least its counsel would have diligently persuaded the claim and duly comply with the Orders of the Court which were made in their presence and with their concurrence. The Court takes dim of such conduct."

14. The High Court has not hesitated to impose any of the sanctions mentioned in Order 42 Rule 11 in an appropriate case. In a number of cases it has not hesitated to dismiss a case or enter final judgment for failure to participate in judicial case management. On a number of cases (if not the majority) the Court of Appeal has reversed the High Court.

15. It seems fairly settled that Order 42 Rule 11 must be applied judiciously and not arbitrarily. The rules were not designed, except

in the clearest of cases, to lock the door of the court to a litigant whose case has not been heard on the merits.

16. In Michael Jacobus Jordaan & another v Keetse Baitshupi CACLB-037-08 Foxcroft J.A. declared at paragraph 9 of the judgment that:

"9. The Court was required to exercise a proper discretion as to whether sufficient reason not to dismiss had been shown. Part of that consideration would have been an examination of the question whether Order 42 and not Order 23 should have been followed. After all, all that applicants awaited was a date of hearing of their application."

17. The Court of Appeal has also dealt with the question whether a 'final judgment' entered by a judge in terms of Order 42 Rule 11, may be rescinded or not. This was in the case of Tswedisang Gofhamodimo v Sam Koboyankwe & Others Civil Appeal No. CACLB-098-10.

18. The holding of the court was that a final judgment entered in default may be rescinded in terms of the common law.

19. At paragraph 46 Kirby JP articulated the position as follows:

"So, there is no reason why, in an appropriate case not covered by the Rules, an application for rescission under the common law cannot be made or granted. While it is desirable that, for the future, the Rules Committee should advise the Chief Justice to consider inserting a rule to fill the existing lacuna, rescission is the procedure which is presently appropriate when an aggrieved party who had notice of a pre-trial conference but was unable to attend due to acceptable unforeseen circumstances, has had a judgment or dismissal entered against him in absentia. It is also the appropriate procedure when the aggrieved party had no notice of the conference and thus failed to attend, and in such a case the onus of showing a lawful excuse will be more easily satisfied."

20. In the aforesaid case the court held that a judge, under Order 42 Rule 11 has a discretion to enter an order that is just, not necessarily limited to the ones appearing under the rule.

21. The Court of Appeal clarified that in exercising his/her discretion, the judge may adopt a three-stage approach as follows:

    a. First, he will consider, as a fact, whether there has been a default of one of the types listed, and if so, he will record that default;

    b. Second, he will consider whether the defaulting party has discharged his onus to show that he had a lawful excuse for such default (or, where failure to participate in good faith is alleged, whether the party alleging such failure has discharged his onus to prove that), and

    c. Third, where no lawful excuse has been shown, or a lack of good faith has been established, he must decide upon and enter an order which is just in all the circumstances, and record his reasons for doing so.

22. In a nutshell, the court held that a rescission of judgment entered in default ought to be allowed if there is a reasonable explanation for the default and a prima facie defence is raised.

23. The court went further to give some guidelines as to what order would be just. The test is an objective one. The order is just if it is fair and reasonable in all the circumstances of the case.

24. The court stated that relevant considerations will include the following:

    1. The need to enforce judicial case management in the interests of the just, efficient and speedy dispensation of justice, per Rule 21 Order 1.

2. The degree of non-compliance on either side, and whether there has been repeated non-compliance, thus significantly hampering the progress of the case.

3. Whether the conduct of the parties or either of them demonstrates a lack of seriousness in advancing their case or defence, as the case may be, or indicates a hope of delaying a likely adverse outcome.

4. The strength or weakness, prima facie, of the case or defence advanced, including the complexity of the issues to be determined.

5. The strength or weakness of any excuse put forward for the non-compliance.

6. The degree of fault attributable to the client, as opposed to that attributable to his attorney – and there will, in extreme cases, where the sins of the attorney may properly be visited on his client, of whom he is the agent.

25. The above approach is similar to the 5-stage test set out in the US case of (Romeo v Evans NO CV-02-2294 PHX-DGC (January 25, 2007)

26. The court emphasized that before granting judgment in default in the course of judicial case management the judge must be satisfied that on the evidence before him/her, such judgment is fully justified.

27. The Court of Appeal has also emphasized that it is desirable, where dismissal is a possible consequence of inaction; that the dismissal be effected at a hearing at which the defaulter has been given notice. (See paragraphs 65 of Tswedisang Gofhamodimo)

28. Generally, it is accepted that a dismissal must be a last resort.

29. In the case of Gast Botswana (Pty) Ltd v D&S Machinery & Plant Hire (Pty) Ltd t/a Excavator Hire Court of Appeal No. CACLB-054-10 Moore JA in discussing entering orders that are just stated that:

"By enjoining the Judge to enter such orders as are just, the rule mandates the Judge to do justice to both parties bearing the public interest in mind. For it is in the interest of the parties, as well as of the public that litigation be brought to an end expeditiously and justly after both, or in the case of multiple parties, all parties have been fully heard.

Accordingly, the framers of the rule have placed a range of options at the disposal of the Judge so that he or she may apply those alternatives which most appropriate to the circumstances of the case. These options all contain an element of sanction with varying levels of severity. It stands to reason therefore that the severest of the available sanctions, option (c), the so-called nuclear option- the option of making an order dismissing a claim or entering final judgment, and thus banishing a party from the judgment seat – must be made only in the most egregious of cases, and only if all the other options available, either individually or collectively, are found upon reasonable and justifiable grounds, to be completely inadequate to punish the errant litigant or his counsel for the mischief of which he or she stands condemned …"

"… Except in the rarest of cases, orders dismissing an action without the parties, and particularly the plaintiff, being heard on the merits can hardly be seen as just …"

"…Order 42 Rule 11 must be applied judiciously and judicially. It must not be applied wantonly like an implacable guillotine severing the heads of actions where the breach of the relevant rule does not warrant such draconian action. The new case management rules were designed to facilitate a more efficient, cost effective and timely dispensation of justice. They were not designed, except in the clearest of case, to lock the door of the court to a litigant whose case has not been heard on the merits." (my emphasis)

30. Commenting on possible dismissal Kirby JP in the Gofhamodimo case stated at paragraph 68 that:

"I also cannot agree that it is only in the rarest of cases that an order dismissing a case or granting final judgment without hearing both parties on the merits will be just. Each case is to be decided on its own facts and circumstances by the Judge, in the manner outlined above. If a party fails to attend a conference called by the Judge, and to convey an explanation for than non-attendance, then he fails to discharge the onus of showing that he had a lawful excuse for his default. His remedy, if in fact he alleges a lawful excuse, and an adverse order has been made in his absence, is to bring a common law application his explanation will be heard. There is no obligation upon the Judge to himself add a further layer to the procedure, or to delay the case, by scheduling another hearing so that the defaulting party can show cause why his claim or defence should not be dismissed."

31. A question has also arisen whether there is a duty on the plaintiff as the dominus litis to take steps to progress the matter, failing which, the matter may be dismissed. The question is not quite settled but there appears to be a view that such an order may be entered in an appropriate case.

Conclusion

32. On the whole, it still seems to be the view of the Court of Appeal that the justices of this court are more enthusiastic to enforce judicial case management at the expense of ensuring fairness to litigants.

33. The matter of enthusiasm of the justices of this court was referred to in the case of First National Bank of Botswana Ltd v Tau (2009) 1 BLR 112 CA at 116 where the court (per Tebbutt JP) stated that:

"While the amendment of Order 23 and the introduction of Order 42 are to be commended for seeking to clear the backlog of ancient cases and, by the case management system, those already registered and to be registered in the future, the enthusiasm for those procedures should not cloud the desirable requirements that courts should ensure fairness to litigants."

34.   The above sentiment uttered when judicial case management had been in operation for a year was recently endorsed by Kirby JP in the Gofhamodimo case.

35.   All what the above means is that the justices of this court must take heed and try as best they could to ensure compliance with the rules to be fair and to always exercise their discretion judicially.

Chapter 13

Continuing Judicial Education and Mentorship

A Paper delivered at the 10th Anniversary of Southern African Chapter on the International Association of Women Judges – (SAC – IAWJ) at the University of Pretoria on the 8 – 10th August 2014.

Introduction

Thank you very much for inviting me to share with you my thoughts, as an outsider and a neighbour, on continuing judicial education and mentorship. I also take this opportunity to salute you, the South African women judicial officers for celebrating the tenth anniversary of your existence as an organisation. This is a highly commendable achievement. Without an organized voice, you cannot achieve much to transform your judiciary into a representative, independent and impartial judicial arm. It is also befitting that you are also simultaneously celebrating 20 years of your democracy in which women, just like men, played a significant part to bring it into being.

Most countries recognize the value of continuing judicial education – and to a lesser extent, mentorship. By mentorship, I refer to a system where a junior or recently appointed judges/judicial officers could be linked to senior and experienced judges who can hold their hand, so to speak, and engage them whenever necessary.

A mentor shares what she/he knows and lives, shares personal experiences with the mentee. Mentoring is about having experienced it. You cannot mentor anyone beyond who or where you are. As a mentor, it is important that you know the aspiration of your mentee and direct them to excellence in the direction they have indicated. Mentorship is training by doing.

The manner in which continuous judicial education is carried out differs from one jurisdiction to another. In some countries, the approach is adhoc and or sporadic and the programme not scientifically organized or designed.

The objectives of judicial education may also differ from one jurisdiction to another. However, as a general rule, judicial education aims to reinforce impartiality, independence, efficiency and competency. Efficiency of judicial officers is important. It includes efficient judicial courtroom management. In my country Botswana, it places the judge, not the lawyer, in charge of case management. It encourages timely settlement of disputes. Competency relates to knowledge of substantive and procedural laws. Needless to say that it is not enough for a judge to be impartial, efficient, and competent. He or she should be effective in interpreting the law to achieve justice. This may be achieved among other things, by the use of judicially developed technique such as domestic application of international human rights norms.

The targets of judicial education vary from country to country. Generally, the following are often the targets of judicial education:

a. Aspirant judges

b. Newly appointed judges

c. Sitting judges

d. Judicial support staff

In a number of commonwealth countries, training is offered to magistrates. In Canada and United Kingdom, training is generally offered for all judicial officers. Aspirant or pre-appointment training is generally rare, although it is offered in England and Wales to part-time judges. In England and Wales, part-time work forms part of the criteria for appointment to judicial office. In Italy, Germany, Portugal, and Spain, pre-appointment training is the norm. In Uganda, a statutory body called the Law Development Centre is in charge of judicial training. It is chaired by a Supreme Court justice and gives a 9 months diploma course on the basis of substantive, procedural, evidentiary law and ethics. In Kenya, they have the Judicial Training Institute that is headed by a judge of the High court.

To achieve the objective of the judiciary attracting public confidence, it is much better to target all judicial officers – not just the magistracy or new judges. This is so because even judges at the highest tier of the judiciary can benefit from judicial training. For instance, in the area of HIV and the Law, judges as agents of justice need to be constantly capacitated with up-to-date knowledge and understanding of the science of HIV transmission, prevention, treatment, care and support. They need to be constantly updated with epidemio-logical developments; and the evolving roles of the law and the judiciary in HIV responses. This is equally true of many other disciplines.

At all times, the goals of continuous judicial education should be to maintain and improve the professional competency of all persons performing judicial functions, thereby enhancing the performance of the judicial system as a whole.

Continuous Judicial Education Needs Assessment

It is important that continuing judicial education should not be organized in a haphazard fashion. It is crucial that it must be preceded by vigorous needs assessment or situational analysis involving key stakeholders. A needs assessment will reveal the gaps/deficiencies in various levels of the judiciary that needs to be plagued. A needs assessment exercise may reveal varying gaps in the following areas:

a. Knowledge of relevant substantive law

b. Knowledge of rules of procedure

c. Knowledge of rules of evidence

d. Factual analysis ability.

e. Legal reasoning ability

f. Judgment writing

g. Ethics – Basic computer skills such as word processing and using computer as research tool.

h. Rendering rulings and decisions without undue delay.

i. Maintaining appropriate control over proceedings.

j. Even handed treatment of litigants and counsels

k. Absence of bias/prejudice based on gender, race, etc.

Compulsory Judicial Education and Mentorship Programme

Some authorities have suggested that continuing judicial education must be improved, by ensuring that it is State sponsored and mandatory. It has been suggested, for instance, that all new judicial officers must be trained in certain key aspects of judicial behaviour and temperament in the conduct of court proceedings. Examples that come to mind are courtesy to litigants, their lawyers and staff, patience, dignity and absence of arrogance to name but a few.

Conclusion

Having joined the bench from the academia, where research and continuous learning are highly valued and encouraged and having served the bench for over 10 years, I readily recommend and endorse continuous judicial education. It is an imperative.

To be effective, it must be scientifically organized. It must be compulsory and State sponsored. Regular, well structural seminars are important. In countries with no mentorship programmes, they can fill the void. A combination of a scientifically organized judicial education and mentorship programme is what is needed to achieve delivery of quality justice.

It also appears to me that training or mentorship may take the form of exchange programmes in the SADC region where judges are regularly attached to other courts in the region. We already have SADC Chief Justices Forum and operationalizing this idea should not be difficult.

The judiciary as a protector of human rights plays an important role in the lives of our people and in promoting the rule of law and access to justice. Historically, jurisprudence has had positive transformative effect on the lives of many people especially the marginalized. In a modern society, courts, literally everywhere in the world, find themselves grappling with difficult questions of human rights, insurance, finance and other branches of the law. For the judges to be ahead of their game, so to speak, they need to be regularly capacitated about cutting edge jurisprudence in their areas of jurisdiction. The simple truth that is incontrovertible is that judging, the analysis and conclusions a judge reaches are a function of knowledge. A country that pays lips service to continuously training its judicial officers will over time experience progressive decline of quality judgments to a point where the public will lose confidence in it. This is already happening in some countries where litigants on account of little confidence in the courts are increasingly using private arbitration to resolve disputes.

Chapter 14

Sexual Diversity and Gender Identity

A Speech delivered to African Parliamentarians (virtually) On the 26th of August 2021.

Director of Proceedings, honourable members of parliament, officials from the United Nations Development Programme (UNDP), it gives me great pleasure to engage with law makers from across the mighty continent of Africa on a very important matter that lies at the heart of the right to human dignity and equality before the law.

It is a rare honour for me, today, to address you in my capacity as President of the Africa Regional Judges Forum (ARJF) convened under the auspices of the UNDP. I wish to thank UNDP, Parliamentarians for Global Action and partners for opportunity to speak at this exciting inception meeting of the African Parliamentarians' Forum on Gender and Sexual Diversity, on behalf of the ARJF. I hope to share experiences and some thoughts of the value of being part of regional network of judges across Africa, on HIV, human rights and the law, since 2014.

Before delving into the essence of my address, Madam Director of Proceedings, permit me to make general remarks that connect our constitutional mandates.

Quite often our constitutional mandates and the doctrine of separation of powers keep us apart from each other and whenever an opportunity arises to talk to each other, we often tend to talk past each other. The truth of the matter though is that the legislatures and judiciaries as co-equal arms of government need to work together to promote and defend the human rights of all persons.

Members of Parliament have a constitutional obligation to provide oversight. This is a core function of all democratic parliaments, alongside representation, law making and control of the budget process.

The judiciary on the other hand is the guardian of the constitution with the final authority to say what the law is. Unlike you we have no control over the purse – only our learning and moral authority underpinned by public confidence that ensures that we fulfil our constitutional mandate, without fear, favour or ill-will.

In my mind the fundamental objectives of parliamentary oversight are to promote people's freedom and well-being (including sexual and gender diversity). As part of their oversight roles parliaments have a duty to promote inclusiveness – which is at the core of SDG 16 (peace, justice and strong institutions).

People who are sex and gender diverse have the same human rights as any other person, in particular, all human beings have the right to define and express their sex and gender diversity without being subjected to ridicule, stigma or discrimination.

We, the parliamentarians and judges, have a common responsibility to strengthen the legal protections relating to discrimination against people who are sex and gender diverse. The right to human dignity demands no less.

Our meeting today reminded me of this time seven years ago, when myself and a group of 10 other like-minded senior judges from 8 African countries held the inception meeting of the ARJF, in Johannesburg. It was shortly after the worldwide dialogues and landmark report by the Global Commission on HIV and the Law, an independent body convened by UNDP which examined links between legal environments and HIV responses.

The report clearly showed how bad laws exacerbated stigma, discrimination and violence against marginalized populations, making them vulnerable to HIV and AIDS – and the importance of solid, rights-based laws, applied with reason, and backed by medical and scientific evidence.

After reading the report it became clear to us, as judges – perhaps like yourselves as parliamentarians, meeting here today – of the critical role we had to play in supporting rights- based laws, seeking to protect those most marginalised in our societies. And so we determined to create a forum that reached across our respective borders, hoping to share with and learn from each other in our efforts to sustain judicial excellence on HIV, human rights and the law in our respective countries, and across the region as a whole.

We held a lively first meeting, opened by Justice Edwin Cameron, that luminary par excellence of the South African bench, then of South Africa's Constitutional Court, exploring HIV, law and human rights issues, discussing the challenges in our respective countries and our ambitions for the forum, which set the scene for the years ahead. With the kind support of UNDP we continued to hold annual in-person forums where we set the agenda and led the discussions, and also managed to keep in touch, sharing resources and discussing issues, between meetings. UNDP also supported us with the development of an online repository of resources, where we were able to access jurisprudence discussed during meetings. In our last forum, we discussed ways to turn this into an ongoing, online community of practice, with UNDP's help.

I have no hesitation whatsoever in testifying today, before you, the continental members of parliament, that the Forum Meetings themselves have been invaluable – although only once a year, they've been a safe space for us, removed from the constraints of our national environments, to share our triumphs and frustrations, to learn from each other's experiences in different countries and contexts, to listen to updated evidence from other experts in the field and, importantly, to hear directly from those who were most affected and the activists who support them, talking about the lived experiences of laws, policies and practices that limit their rights.

Over the past 8 years of the Forum, we've had heated discussions about cases, laws, policies and government actions affecting some of the most marginalised and discriminated populations in our societies - people living with HIV, people with TB, women and girls, young people, LGBTI people, sex workers, people who use drugs, and prisoners. The Forum has emphasised this cross-country learning, so that even where we've disagreed, our discussions have provided critical support to each other, in our daily work facing these challenging issues and contexts.

We have had the privilege of seeing our Forum grow in strength and numbers, reaching out across Francophone, Lusophone and Anglophone Africa, with over 60 members from 18 countries, and seeing our influence reach across regions, inspiring regional judges' forums in Eastern Europe, Central Asia and the Caribbean. Despite numerous challenges, we have also enjoyed celebrating in the successes of our peers and the extraordinary advances in laws and rights-based jurisprudence seen across the region in matters before our courts, from which we all benefit.

The highlights of our collaboration, joint learning and continuous capacitation include, for instance, the recent Botswana High Court ordering the decriminalisation of adult same-sex conduct; forum members were part of important judgements in the High Court of Kenya, that ruled that the overbroad criminalization of HIV transmission was unconstitutional and that the imprisonment of patients with TB was unlawful and beyond the parameters of public health legislation.

In Malawi, Forum members presided over a High Court judgement overturning the conviction of an HIV-positive woman for unintentionally exposing a child to HIV through breastfeeding (where HIV was not transmitted); and a decision in Botswana to provide HIV treatment to foreign prisoners with HIV.

Over the years we have worked hard to grow and sustain the Forum, but the benefits have been substantial not only to ourselves at personal and professional levels, but also towards advancing the rights of marginalised persons in our countries and regions. This has taken concerted efforts challenging ourselves to tackle new and evolving issues, networking with our peers, keeping in touch between forums and also working with Judicial Training Institutes to embed training on HIV, law, human rights and gender equality into the training of judiciary in our respective countries.

The commitment of initial core group from day one in Abuja, where the idea was initially mooted, and the support of UNDP as our Secretariat, has played a critical part.

In conclusion I would like to wish you well in your deliberations and express my sincere hope that the resolutions emanating from today's meeting will give urgency to the need to overhaul many of our colonial laws that hold so many of our people in bondage.

I am truly excited and gratified by what looks to be an exciting opportunity to share learning and support each other, as law-makers committed to advancing rights around equally challenging and sensitive issues of gender and sexual diversity. We at ARJF hope to have the opportunity to share in your successes and collaborate with your Forum in the years ahead to make this, our planet, a better place to live for every person.

Chapter 15

Tributes

A Tribute to Julian Mukwesu Nganunu – A great Jurist and Distinguished Chief Justice.

On Sunday the 3rd of August, 2014, whilst driving from Durban and filling up at Harrismith, I received an avalanche of text messages from a number of friends that our former Chief Justice Julian Nganunu has departed this troubled world to meet his creator. My heart froze and a sense of intense sadness engulfed me. The Nganunu family has lost a loving father, brother and relative. The nation has lost a great jurist and a reformer of note.

I convey my heartfelt condolences to the Nganunu family and besiege the almighty to guard and protect them. They should accept that Chief Justice Nganunu ran his race and that he completed his task in this world. His time had come.

Since his retirement from the bench, we tended to meet a lot and had time to catch up on a number of issues of mutual concern. Both of us were part of the regional team that was constituted by the International Commission of Jurists to go on a fact-finding mission concerning some turbulence in the Lesotho's judiciary a year or so ago. Although I eventually could not make it to Lesotho, we used to discuss at length the role of an independent judiciary in a democratic dispensation of which he was a strong proponent.

Chief Justice Nganunu recruited me to the High Court bench. It was sometime in 2005, shortly after Radio Botswana had announced that Molokomme J (as she then was) had left the bench to become the Attorney General of the Republic, that I received a call from the then Chief Justice. He said to me: "You know Keeth, these chaps, took your friend, the academic judge, I want to replace her with one like her, so may you please send over your CV this afternoon." The rest as they say is history.

Once at the High Court, we forged a very strong professional and personal bond and his confidence in me grew in leaps and bounds. I found myself, on more than one occasion, sitting as acting justice of the Court of Appeal and representing him at SADC Chief Justices Forum and the most memorable being the one that took us to Venice in Italy and to the European Court of Human Rights in Strasbourg. It was no wonder therefore that I was also entrusted to organize his farewell party at Phakalane when he left the bench and he was to subsequently launch my book, "Constitutionalism and the Rule of Law in Botswana" at the University of Botswana.

I have lost a mentor, father, and a friend. He had a habit of summoning me to his chambers just for a chat on diverse matters. He taught me that in the administration of justice, I must respect only the Constitution and the laws of the republic, but no persons, whatever their title; that whatever I do, I must do it correctly and resolutely; that in the execution of judgment, I must lay aside my personal preferences and that I must maintain an open mind until the matter is fully argued; that I be not biased with compassion to the poor or favour to the rich, in point of justice, that popular applause or vicious condemnation should not have any influence on what I do as a judge; he taught me that although he was my "boss" judges actually have no "boss", save for the Constitution and that he was just the first amongst equals.

I come from a school of thought that asserts that an account of the life of a judge would be incomplete without reference to notable judgments of his and to his extra-curial writings and speeches. It is common cause that some of his judgments have received both praise and criticism simultaneously. This notwithstanding, it must be conceded that Nganunu CJ is one of the few judges who clearly deserves an extensive intellectual biography.

In what follows below, I attempt to sketch his contribution to our jurisprudence. The major difficulty is to achieve balance in what was certainly an illustrious and wholesome judicial career. The other difficulty or limitation is the inhibitions and constraints which necessarily attach to my office – as a sitting judge. It is in that context that this piece must be read.

As some of his judgments would reveal, Nganunu CJ (as he then was) was very strong on the rule of law and legality. He read law in 1966 at the London School of Economics and Political Science, a constituent college of the University of London, (incidentally where I also did my postgraduate studies in 1992) and served both government and the corporate sector at the highest levels. He was a product of those times and the environments he worked in. And because no judge ascends to the bench as an ideological virgin, the circumstances that produced him are reflected in the orientation and legal reasoning he adopted.

Jurisprudentially, the conventional theory about judging, espoused by many positivists scholars and their counter-parts in the bench is that judges are simply neutral arbiters who apply the law to the facts in a somewhat detached and mechanical fashion.

Legal realists, especially those of the critical legal studies mould contend to the contrary. If judges make new law – even positivists now concede this reality – they couch it in sophisticated language. Lord Reid, one of the luminaries of the British bench thought it inconceivable that judges do not make law.

Reading Nganunu's judgments, you could place him somewhere in between the positivists and legal realists. He believed that judges have a role to play in advancing the values of a democratic society. His tenure as Chief Justice has been used to forge the High Court as the true guardian of the rights of the people.

Chief Justice Nganunu has produced judgments which the liberals and conservatives would celebrate in equal measure. The language he employed was always judicious, balanced, and courteous. Some of his passages in terms of lucidity and prose compare favourably with the best that English literature can offer. His cautious approach to interpretation of statutes was in many ways similar to that of Lord Simmonds – that sparring partner of Lord Denning – the two differed markedly in content and approach. Whilst Lord Simmonds was cautious, Lord denning believed that it is the duty of the courts to "iron out the creases" in legislative provisions.

In the area of constitutional law, one of the former Chief Justice's celebrated decisions is the case of Kamanakao v The Attorney General. At the heart of this case was the complaint by the applicant that Section 2 of the chieftainship Act in so far as it defined "tribe" and "chief" in a manner that excluded the Wayeyi and other tribes and/or ethnic groups offended against Section 3 (a) of the Constitution which deals with equal treatment and equal protection of the law. The court led by Chief Justice Nganunu agreed with the applicants and directed that Section 2 of the Chieftainship Act (Cap 41:01) be amended to afford equal treatment and equal protection by that law to the applicants.

The court refused to declare Sections 77 to 79 of the Constitution unconstitutional – a subject matter that receives some attention from the German constitutional court jurisprudence, yielding contrary conclusions.

In the case of Motswaledi (incidentally a case in which it is wrongly believed the Chief Justice removed me from presiding – the facts are a bit more complicated) the Chief Justice together with his other brethrens held that our Constitution prohibits private civil proceedings against the President of the Republic. It is often forgotten that law is not a pure science and that there is no such thing as the only "correct" answer. In this case, the court made a determination it did on the basis of its understanding of the applicable law and the Italian constitutional court dealing, more or less with a similar matter, came to a different conclusion soon after the Motswaledi case was decided.

In Kanane, the Chief Justice was among those of his brethren's who upheld the constitutionality of sodomy laws. The court held that there was no evidence that the approach and attitude of society in Botswana to the question of homosexuality and to homosexual practices by gay men and women required a decriminalization of those practices, even to the extent of consensual acts by adult males in private.

The above decision has been criticised in some quarters for having subordinated human rights to moral considerations. It may well be that when circumstances permit future generations of jurists would revisit this case and determine whether society suffers any prejudice by affording minorities outside the mainstream equal treatment under the law. It is true that the court must keep in touch with the thinking and mores of society, but in aiming for a proper balance, it must not subordinate justice to expediency. On occasions, and where the Constitution permits, it must nudge society forward.

It may well be that if the notion of human dignity is thrown into the mix and properly interrogated, the results may be different. Suffice also to say that the South African Constitutional Court faced with a similar question in the case of National Coalition for Gay and Lesbian Equality came to a different conclusion. It is plain, therefore, that human rights, though supposedly universal and indivisible remains fiercely contested.

On administrative law, he was an ardent believer of the audi rule (listen to the other side). The rule has ancient origins. When Nicodemus, the Pharisee, asked: "Does our law permit us to pass judgment on a man unless we have first given him a hearing and learned the facts?" He was of course asking a rhetorical question that in a way captures the logic of the law. The answer of course is in the negative.

Chief Justice Nganunu insisted on accountability of statutory bodies. He was of the view that creatures of statute must generally comply with the rules of natural justice before taking any adverse decision against any person or entity.

In the case of A V Communications v AG in which an order was sought to restrain the Government of Botswana, in particular the Government's

Central Tender Board, from issuing General Purchase Orders, pursuant to an award of two tenders and after emphasizing that it is impermissible for a statutory body to depart from important provisions of statute, he nullified the tender awards. Under his leadership, the High Court has exhibited greater willingness to scrutinize administrative actions, including the acts and omissions of Ministers and other top governmental officials, by the application of the principles of natural justice and judicial review.

Although, the courts under the leadership of Chief Justice Nganunu, have shown considerable enthusiasm for extending the boundaries of judicial review of administrative action, they have not lost sight of the importance of the balance between the need to control abuses of power and the need to allow public bodies to perform their duties without watching over their shoulders!

Chief Justice Nganunu would be remembered for a number of reforms that he brought to the judiciary besides the massive infrastructural developments that are littered all over the country.

Other than his jurisprudential output, Chief Justice Nganunu was a reformer of note. He introduced Judicial Case Management system in the operations of the courts, to ensure that litigation is conducted speedily and cheaply. Prior to the introduction of Judicial Case Management, the pace of litigation was largely in the hands of lawyers. Judicial Case Management shifts the control of cases from lawyers of the parties to a judge. On registration of a case, the case is immediately assigned to a judge, who, together with the attorney involved, will make a schedule for the conduct of the case to date of trial. This innovation has almost eliminated any backlog that was there and speeded up the pace of litigation.

Chief Justice Nganunu also introduced Computer Record Management system (CRMS). In terms of this system, all cases that exist in the courts are recorded in the system according to their age and type so that at the end of the day the judiciary becomes accurately aware of what workload it has.

It was also under the stewardship of Chief Justice Nganunu that the hitherto opaque appointment process was made more transparent by requiring that vacancies to the High Court bench be advertised and candidates interviewed. No doubt, opaque appointment processes are now generally frowned upon in most democratic societies.

Chief Justice Nganunu, in countless of his speeches has emphasized the importance of the independence of the judiciary. He understood that an independent judiciary is an indispensable component of a democratic society. He also emphasized this point at countless meeting of judges, including the one critical meeting that most judges would remember very well.

As a person, the Chief Justice was conscientious and a hard worker. It was not uncommon for him to knock off very late in the day - having started very early in the morning. O ne a rata letsela – ever well dressed and his colour scheme faultless. He was self-effacing and modest to a fault.

The Chief Justice has played his part with his innate dignity and dedication. And although he has gone to sleep his legacy is the wisdom, he bequeathed us, as captured clearly in countless of his reported judgments. Botswana has been blessed to have a Chief Justice of the quality and presence of Julian Mukwesu Nganunu.

May his soul rest in eternal peace.

A Tribute to a Towering Judicial Mind – Former Judge Marumo

1. Programme Director, the Hon. Chief Justice, Honourable Ministers, the Judge President of the Court of Appeal, Justices of the Court of Appeal, High Court, and the Industrial Court, members of the legal fraternity, fellow mourners, I greet you.

2. Words are not enough to capture the loss to the family and the nation occasioned by the passing of Mr. Marumo, former Judge of the High Court. I convey to the Marumo family our heartfelt condolences. Together with the entire nation, we share in the grief of the passing of this monumental legal mind, a loving and caring father, husband, friend, relative, a jurisprudential pathfinder of note, an embodiment of wisdom, courage, humility, and justice.

3. Moatlhodi Marumo is first and foremost my cousin. The blood that ran through him, is the same blood that shaped and defined my being. And even though he has gone to sleep, Marumo still lives amongst us his blood relatives. I am proud to say that his life was a blessing to his family and the nation at large. Professionally, our paths have tended to cross. He was appointed acting Judge of the Industrial Court in 1994. A few years later, I was appointed an acting Judge of the same court.

In 2001, he was appointed Judge of the High Court. In the same year, I was appointed Judge of the Industrial Court. He left the High Court bench in 2006. I was appointed Judge of the High

Court in 2005 and were neighbours at Lobatse. As Judge of the High Court, he was designated the Chairperson of the Law Reporting Committee – a committee that grades judgments of the higher courts for reportability. When his term as Chair of the Committee expired, I took over as the Chair.

4. The above more than qualifies me to speak about his professional life.

5. Mr. Marumo cut his teeth as a Judicial Officer at the Industrial Court. It was there that his talent as a jurist par excellence was revealed. One of the memorable decisions he delivered at the Industrial Court, of which I was Counsel for the applicant, concerned the Botswana Diamond Sorters' and Valuators' Union v Botswana Diamond Valuing Company.

6. In the above case the question that fell for determination was whether an employer, who, in terms of its conditions of service is granted the right "to vary its conditions of service at any time, at its own discretion", could do so unilaterally, without negotiating with the Union, alternatively to consult with it.

7. Marumo J (as he then was) held that the relationship between an employer and an employee should not be considered purely on contractual basis, but rather on the basis of fairness and reasonableness, because of the inherent imbalance in power relationship between the two contracting parties, the employer, in most cases being the dominant partner.

8. In so holding, he entrenched further the equitable jurisdiction of the Industrial Court and buried, once and for all the law of master servant. The Botswana Diamond Sorters and Valuators' Union case demonstrates that he had a liberal streak. Where the opportunity presents itself, he looks for ways to expand law to protect the weak, just as his mentor, Collins J (as he then was) would do, as illustrated by the latter's decision in the case of Macharia v The

Law Society of Botswana. Although both of them were blessed with a razor-sharp mind, the student was more circumspect and the teacher bolder. Both of them were cut out of the same cloth. In public law, they were always willing to expedite change when such change has clear beneficial effect.

9. Lord Denning that luminary of the British bench; some say the greatest Judge of the 20th century, once opined that there are two types of Judges: timorous souls and bold spirits.

10. Marumo was not a timorous soul. Just, like Lord Denning, Marumo believed that the progressive development of the law is to be credited to judicial creativity and courage of bold spirits. He disapproved of timorous souls who showed blind allegiance to old precedent even if it does not serve the ends of justice.

11. Marumo was of the view that if the powerful in society abuse their powers without restraint, it is essentially because of the dominant influence of timorous souls and those who Lord Atkin, in the celebrated case of Liversidge v Anderson, said were more executive minded than the executive.

12. Marumo believed that judicial officers, in interpreting the law, should never lose sight of the fact that, as Justice Benjamin Cardazo, would say, the final cause of law is the welfare of society.

13. When he joined the High Court in 2004, the values of fairness and justice had found a place of pride in his mind and his philosophy that law must serve the ends of justice was reflected in his judgments. A Judge's philosophy is important. It is his compass. It determines the interpretation he/she must place on words or textual provisions. By this, I do not mean that a Judge is at liberty to decide cases according to his personal predilections. He is not. Philosophy just guides him/her.

14. Not long after joining the bench, he presided over the first phase of Professor Good v The Attorney General case. Professor Good

had been declared a prohibited immigrant by the President of the Republic.

15. He approached the court challenging the presidential directive. Marumo J (as he then was) issued an interim order halting the deportation. The rest as they say is for future historians to grapple with – but whatever historians' final verdict will be, I am certain that history will absolve him.

16. Sitting in the High Court's exalted offices, what one often needs, is more than a law degree, but plenty of courage, intellectual depth and conviction. Marumo had all this in abundance.

17. The law has been called "the place where order and freedom meet". That is where Marumo lived. Blackstone called the law "the principal and most perfect branch of ethics". That too was Marumo's belief.

18. The Good decision demonstrates that he was not possessed of fear. He believed in justice for all. He administered justice without fear or favour. Before him the rich and poor, the old and the young, knew that fair implementation of the laws of the land and even handed resolution of disputes is guaranteed.

19. On criminal law and procedure, he was outspoken on the right of the accused to remain silent; to be free from unreasonable searches and seizures; to be represented by counsel; to be afforded adequate facilities for his defense. He insisted that those found guilty and sent to prison must be treated fairly and decently and to be afforded dignity that resides in all human beings. This approach gave recognition to the fact that these rights do not belong to government, but were carved by the people, for themselves, when they created government.

20. Marumo was opposed to the view that the abridgement of freedom was a proper response to high levels of crime and violence. He never forgot that our Constitution is but a promissory note, whose

promise - fundamental rights for all – can only be effected by an independent and impartial judiciary.

21.   The above is amply illustrated by the case of Muzila v The Attorney General, where after bemoaning the tendency of some lawyers not to embark on thorough and comprehensive research to assist the Court, his own research led him to conclude that the applicant was denied equal protection of the law decreed by the Constitution. After so declaring, he directed that the prosecution of the applicant must be proceeded with, without undue delay.

22.   It is plain from reading the case of Muzila that as a Judge, Marumo was opposed to mediocrity from both the bar and bench.

23.   On family law, he showed informed impatience with parents, especially men, who had to be dragged to Court to be reminded of their responsibility to maintain their children.

24.   For many who read his judgments, one golden thread is self-evident. His judgments are a model of lucidity. He was blessed with a sharp and nimble mind, a gift of simplicity and eloquent language. To read his judgments is to experience the joy of the intercourse between linguistic elegance and logical reasoning. His judgment writing skills and compelling logic earned him the affection of the legal fraternity and beyond.

25.   Marumo never shied away from engaging in open and robust debate. In a recent interview with one of the local newspapers, Marumo sought to challenge all of us to critically reflect on the appointment process of the bench, making it clear that a transparent and merit based process is in public interest.

26.   Often controversial, Marumo never rose beyond Judge of the High Court. But every lawyer who read his judgments and those who worked with him at the High Court, would testify that he was well-suited to grace the highest bench of the land. This notwithstanding, his impact on the law cannot be ignored. His

judgments cited with approval across our borders, speak volumes of his knowledge of the law.

27.   As I draw to the end, I wonder, aloud, what would Marumo ask of their Lordships and Ladyships still alive and busy at work today?

28.   To the above question, we can only hazard a guess, but I doubt whether those who knew him would be far off the mark. I think, among many other things, he would probably say, please, use your intellect, creativity and powers to end all forms of unfair discrimination, in all those areas of national life where discrimination still exists.

29.   If I were to paint a canvass of this towering judicial mind, I would paint him head bowed, writing a judgment, the rays of his intellect dispersing archaic principles of the law and commanding justice to take centre stage in his judgment. It would be a portrait of a man who despite the uncertainty and turbulence of the times, his personal safety, would not compromise on a matter of principle; would not abandon the standard of what is right; would not reject what he believes to be true. It would be a portrait of a man protecting his nation. The scales of justice evenly balanced on his table.

30.   In summation, I would say he was a man of courage, humility, energy, and vision. He was I think a more complex person than some have suggested. In him, there was an inter-mixture of the pragmatic and the idealistic. In him, there was a blending of compassion and strength of faith and reason, of hope and concern. He was gentle, yet firm; candid, yet cautious; flexible, yet decisive.

31.   A tribute to Marumo would not be complete without a mention of what he was like as a person. I cannot imagine any kinder, more generous person. He had a big heart. In the time I have known him I have never heard him say anything bad about any person. He treated everyone, young and old, rich and poor with respect.

A total gentleman; he honoured every commitment he made. He was a private person. He treasured the right to privacy for himself, his family and for everyone. He deplored eavesdropping in all its forms and considered it wrongful and intrusive.

32. Marumo was a reverent worshipper in the Catholic Church. He was a Christian in the true sense, believed in the gospel and practiced its tenets. On this he differed with his two cousins who hardly went to church.

33. I would like to end on a personal note. I respected and admired my cousin, my brother and my friend. But I come from his passing challenged and inspired to carry on in some small way his great work. I hope all of us here would say the same thing. We are the keepers of the republic now. He bequeathed to us the gift of courage and intellectual honesty. The rest is up to us.

34. May his soul rest in eternal peace.

A Tribute to Justice Legwaila – A Humble Servant of The Law

I was devastated beyond measure. A day earlier I had gone to Bokamoso to check on him, but on account of his apparent deterioration, I was not able to see him. Two weeks before his passing, on the 15th of July 2016, to be exact, I met my good friend A.T at the airport and we had occasion to reminisce about our relationship with our "old man" as we called him. We called his wife and promised to stay in touch. At the time, we did not and could not have known that he would be gone so soon. Our country and our people have lost one of the most beloved sons – a Justice who was the very personification of integrity and fairness.

Our sincere condolences go to his family, relatives, his sisters and brothers at the bench and friends. Justice Legwaila was a scion of Mr and Mrs Legwaila in Mathathane in the Bobirwa Sub-district. His parents irked a living from farming. His father Madome John Legwaila was a London Missionary Society (LMS) Deacon and Evangelist. To this day, the LMS Church in the village is associated with him. I have it on good authority that the Legwailas' were amongst the first to indulge in the luxury of tea-drinking in Mathathane and to send their children to school. They understood the value of education as the greatest equaliser.

Justice Legwaila started his primary school at the advanced age of 13 years. He completed his Form Five in 1966 at Moeding College. Thereafter, he was admitted at the University of Botswana Lesotho and Swaziland (UBLS) to do the degree of Bachelor of Laws (LLB), which he completed in 1972. He holds a Master's Degree (LLM) from the renowned Harvard University in the United States of America. In 1976 he married the love of his life Marty Isabelle Legwaila nee Makhuba. They are blessed with two children, Karabo (son) and Morongwa (daughter). As a student at the University of Botswana I had known Justice Legwaila as a public figure; then the Permanent Secretary to the President. I had personally taken pride in this achievement by one of our own. My first face to face meeting with him must have been in the year 1999, at the Industrial Court, in his chambers.

We had a pleasant encounter. I referred to him as "PSP" (even though he was a judge then); and he simply called me "moratho" meaning "my younger brother" in Sebirwa. Our meeting marked the beginning of a long-lasting relationship at law and beyond. It is a relationship that challenged my thinking, nourished, enriched my approach to law, even as we would often differ sharply on the jurisprudential direction of the Industrial Court. This much is clear from the two judgements we simultaneously penned, involving more or less the same facts; but coming to different conclusions, in the cases of Jimson and Diau - both involving a tale of two security guards employed by BBS.

The task of judges is not easy at all. As it is often said, dispensation of justice is an attribute of God. Blessed are those few who have been bestowed with the honour and privilege to pass judgement over the affairs of their fellow human beings. Even God, who has created the human being, does not sit in judgement over our deeds until after he has recalled us; whence only he determines whether we deserve to be sent to heaven or hell. Judges have immense powers, including the power to take away a human being's life. No other living mortal has this power. It is therefore important that they be humble, wise and learned. Justice Legwaila had all the above attributes.

No Judge Ascends To The Bench As An Ideological Virgin

It is often said that no judge ascends to the bench as an ideological virgin. Every judge is partly a product of his upbringing and foundational values. Justice Legwaila was no exception. He was a deeply thoughtful and devoted practitioner of his faith from whose teachings he drew many of the central concepts of social justice which animated his life at the bench. As Judge President of the Industrial Court he understood that he was only the first amongst equals and an intellectual leader of his colleagues and that his core function was to craft and weave a jurisprudential tapestry that was consistent with our constitutional values.

For a long time, prior to him joining the Industrial Court, the court held the positon that illegal contracts are unenforceable at law. The result of this logic was that many illegal immigrants who were employed by unscrupulous employers well knowing their status, upon dismissal, were simply ejected without any benefits or payment. However, soon after he joined the Industrial Court he redirected the jurisprudence of the court so that those employees cannot be exploited. He crafted a remedy for them, based on the concept of unjust enrichment (see Olena Melefi v Blue Blends Investments PTY Ltd)

John D. Voelker J, said the following about judges: "Judges,… may be divided roughly into four classes; judges with neither head nor heart-they are to be avoided at all costs; judges with the head, but no heart- they are almost as bad; then judges with the heart but no head- risky but better than the first two; and finally, those judges who possess both a head and a heart." I can say without fear of contradiction; that Justice Legwaila fell into the last group.

The Ultimate Objective of Law Is The Welfare of Society

In the case of Rovos v Global Resorts Justice Legwaila quoting extensively from one of the foremost American jurist, by the name of Justice Benjamin Cardozo said that "the final course of law is the welfare of society. The rule that misses its aim cannot permanently justify its existence."

Later on in the case of Charabanguwa v Falcon Investments 2007 (3 BLR) Legwaila JP (as he then was) expressed himself with characteristic clarity when he said: "the law has outgrown its primitive stage of formalism when the precise word was the sovereign talisman, and every slip was fatal… we are thinking of the end of which the law serves, and fitting its rules to the task of service".

Unequal power relationships between

Employers and employees

Justice Legwaila was ever conscious of the importance of labour law. He understood that labour law is an extremely sensitive subject; based upon a political and economic compromise between organised labour; a very powerful socio-economic force on the one hand and the employers of labour an equally powerful socio-economic force on the other hand. He was always alive to the unequal power relations between the employers and employees and was committed to using law to redress this imbalance in order to achieve justice. In the case of Kenosi he stated that: "…this case was a glaring example of that inequality. While the respondent (employer) handed over the conduct of its case to one of the most powerful firms of attorneys, the applicant (employee) did not have the luxury of representation by a counsel (lawyer)".

In the above case, the lawyer for the employer had raised a technical point relating to how the matter ended up in court. When the employee was asked to reply, she asked the court not to be distracted by technical issues but to attend to her complaints; as it turned out, the lawyer was dealing with a point that had nothing to do with her complaint. Legwaila JP agreed with the employee and proceeded to hear the merits of the case.

Justice Legwaila firmly believed that custom and history should not retard the growth of the law. He reasoned that custom and history have their place but they are subordinate to the ultimate purpose of law, being the welfare of society. Being a man of faith he constantly reminded us of an old legend that on occasion God prayed and his prayer was: "Be it my will that may justice be ruled by mercy", adding that, this is the prayer that we, judges, need to utter at times "when the demon of formalism tempts the intellect with the lure of scientific order".

Justice Legwaila upon being elevated to the Court of Appeal, the Apex Court of the land continued his quest for justice. This is clearly illustrated by his judgement in the case of Kealeboga and another v Kehumile and another which dealt with the rights of children to inherit under customary law. In that case Justice Legwaila held that children born out of wedlock are entitled to inherit from any of their parents.

It may be argued with some measure of credibility that Justice Legwaila's legacy is in the area of employment law (illegal contracts of employees and customary law and inheritance). In 100 years from today, scholars will still talk about his contribution in the cases referred to above. In both cases he rewrote settled law. His decisions were breath-taking in their boldness. They challenged fundamentals to the core. He did so in an area traditionally resistant to change: employment and customary law. In the above cases, Legwaila JP rewrote the major premise and the terra nullius – was cast aside – a new chapter that recognises the legal rights of illegal immigrants and children born out of wedlock to inherit under customary law was rewritten.

One justice, I will not reveal her identity, upon reading the cases referred to above informed me that the judgements "were momentous" and that she is not sure she would have gone that far.

Legwaila JA understood, very well, that law, particularly customary law, in a developing country cannot remain static, but it shouldn't be routinely and unnecessarily destabilised. He understood, perfectly, that if law is to be a living force, it must be dynamic and accommodating to change. It must adapt itself to fluid social norms and values and the ever-changing perceptions of justice. This must be so because if the law is inflexible and lags behind social changes and the judges who interpret it also remain inflexible, wedded to the norms of the yesteryear, the people impatient that it no longer serves their needs, will inevitably cast it aside; and they may not do it in an orderly and dignified manner progressive judges would do.

Lessons of life

As we reflect upon his remarkable career at law, we have to ask, why would such a gifted lawyer who had reached the position of number one civil servant with all the attendant connections decide to join the bench, instead of making money in the commercial world? The answer is simple: material vanity never appealed to him – justice did. Justice Legwaila was a different breed of a judge. His heart and mind were in gear. He had a rare capacity to bring warring parties together – to smoke a peace pipe. He would smile wryly when lawyers threw thunderbolts at each other that seemed not to advance their case in any way, if you knew him and mastered his body language you would see that he had no interest in legal gymnastics as he would be searching for the justice of the case.

Virtues of a judge

From the above narrative on the life of Justice Legwaila, I've learnt a few virtues or qualities of a judge. The first quality is humility. Anyone who knew him would testify that he was humble to a fault. He was a perfect gentleman. This reminds me of the remarks of one Chief Justice who once said he wants his judges to be gentlemen and that if they knew a little law the better. Justice Legwaila was not just a perfect gentleman; he was wise and knowledgeable in the law. Speaking for myself, if I were the Chief

Justice I would, in addition to the traditional requirements, want them humble, knowledgeable in the law, imbued with integrity, and have hearts and plenty of courage.

It was a Greek Philosopher Socrates, writing way back in the 4th Century, who said there are four qualities required in a judge- "to hear courteously, to answer wisely, to consider soberly and to decide impartially." Judge Legwaila epitomised these values. To answer wisely is particularly important. To be able to answer wisely the judge must have fact finding skills and be analytical. To answer wisely he must not be too quick to enter the arena. He must be gifted in the art of listening. He must keep an open mind to the very end; having considered every argument and its implications. Only then can he answer wisely.

Patrick Devlin says; "I put impartiality before appearance of it simply because without the reality the appearance would not endure." In truth however, appearance of impartiality is equally important, if not more, because, as it is often said; "The judge who gives the right judgement while appearing not to do so may be thrice blessed in heaven but on earth he is of no use at all."

Personal reminisces

I will miss Justice Legwaila sorely. He was a man of many virtues. He believed in punctuality, invariably turning up at work at 7:30 a.m. On occasions, I would arrive at the office after 7:30 a.m. and my secretary would inform me that the JP called and he said you must call him back. Effectively, that meant I was to call to confirm that I was late. Over time as a result of this practice of calling me whenever he arrived at his office, I learned to arrive earlier so that I would be available when he called. He would often be very informal with me, calling me "Monna Key" whenever he wanted to start a conversation with me. Interestingly, all my previous Chief Justices often connected to me informally, the current CJ would say, "Monna Dingake" and former Chief Justice Nganunu would call me "Keith", he could not say "Key".

Legwaila JP would spot me riding in my official car, seated at the front passenger's seat and the following day he would call me to order and say you are supposed to be seated at the back not at the front. Since then I always sit at the back. He had issues with my almost permanently clean-shaven head suggesting that it may be inappropriate for a judge to keep no hair.

As far as I may recall he was not fond of flying. On a number of occasions whenever he had to fly to Maun for circuit sessions, we would debate the transport logistics and he would insist that he prefers to drive because should anything happen he may just find a way to escape possible fatality. We used to chat about his stint as Deputy Attorney General. He had glowing admiration for Attorney General Mokama. He informed me that during Mokama's tenure the executive knew that only he could give them a legal opinion which they were not at liberty to second guess and change.

Legwaila JP had a sense of humour. Once we attended a funeral in my native village of Bobonong and one tribesman, my relative, who spotted us together, got quite excited and later told me: "I am told Monnamogolo (referring to the JP) has anointed you to take over from him". When I told him he laughed, and said: "You must have told him I am not God, I don't anoint"! The country has lost its finest and humble son. You have run your race Mokgomomg. May your soul rest in eternal peace and God give the family the strength to bear this unbearable pain. To all the people who loved and admired him, it may be as well to begin everyday with this prayer:

"Oh God, give me the courage, to change the things I can change, grant me the serenity to accept the things I cannot change; and the wisdom to know the difference."

So long my brother. So long, Mokgalabye…

A Tribute to Michael Kitso Dingake ('MK')

"Since apartheid affects humanity, as a whole, because of its inhuman character, it must be fought by all mankind and eradicated root and branch from all elements of society… The major weapon will neither be the AK-47 nor the grenade, all these must form ingredients of the arsenal. The critical weapon will be maximum unity of the oppressed."

"Africa cannot be free until all Africans are free. It is not yet uhuru. Not yet". (241)

Source: Michael Dingake, "My Fight Against Apartheid"London: Klipton Books(1987)

Michael Kitso Dingake, otherwise called MK, my revered and iconic brother, turned 95 years on the 11th of February 2023. My people hosted a party at "Go Rra Dingake", somewhere in the bush, in the outskirts of Thamaga, where the young Dingake (Martin) resides, in his honour. Unfortunately, I could not attend the party because I remain trapped in the bowels of the mighty Pacific, in a country called PNG. The event was an emotional roller coaster for me as I watched a series of video clips – one of them showing my daughter, Lesedi, usher the legend to the top table. The legend was in high spirits and occasionally engaged in rhythmic movements. He was so animated that at one stage I feared he will throw away his walking stick and start twisting and turning! What a man!

MK's 95th birthday came a few months after the University of Botswana conferred on him the degree of doctor of letters. A man of letters indeed. He is now Dr Michael Kitso Dingake. Whilst in prison he effortlessly obtained three degrees in administration, economics, and commerce. Those who have read his books and occasional thought pieces in the media – or his occasional face book postings, parring blows from youngsters, can testify that he deserved this honour. The Bible teaches that those in power should not withhold good from those to whom it is due. We live in this society, and we fully understand the dynamics that dictated its timing. The family is grateful for the honour.

Seated on a couch in the courtyard of my apartment, overlooking the rolling hills of Port Moresby, thousands of kilometers away from home, and flipping through the video clips, I was overcome by emotion and shed a tear. My mind took me back to the events of 1981, soon after he was released from Robben Island, during his home coming, riding a friend's blue beetle automobile. Our people lined up along the streets to welcome him; old women wrapped in blankets and old men holding firmly on their walking sticks. As the convoy entered our humble homestead women and men cried, loudly, and some rolled on the ground crying. Some people prayed quietly as they battled to contain their tears. As our people swamped our yard, some signing, a biblical hymn: kena le modisa (The Lord is my Sheperd), I saw my father – who taught me that "a man never cries" – shed a tear. Overwhelmed by emotion my old man hugged his son and said: "Ah, Knowledge!" – a Setswana translation of Kitso. And at that stage Mom was drowning in her own tears! He was 53 then! The parallels were striking!

MK as I shall call him hence forth, out of deep fondness, is a native of Bobonong, not Diepkloof as some have suggested! He is the first in a family of 13 siblings. I am the 13th. I wag the tail as he is fond of saying. As a result of this ordering, I call him "Senior" and he calls me "Junior". Of recent we just call each other, "Sejiye" – our clan's name! He is by tradition the head of our family now that our parents are no more. In Gaborone and its environs there is a pervasive belief that he is my father, which I never contest, because, in many ways he is also my father. On occasions there is confusion as to who between us is Mike or Key! I have also heard people call him Dr or Professor Dingake, long before the recent conferment of Doctor of Letters on him by the University of Botswana. During his tenure as a Member of Parliament for Gaborone Central some people referred to me as "Honorable MP"!

Some people say we look alike, which I often dispute, save that the lips may give it away! MK is in many ways a striking resemblance of dad; and took after my dad's work ethic and temperament. Many who have not seen him angry must count their blessings!! For some inexplicable way, these days, he does look like dad, especially, when he clears his throat and starts talking. He talks slowly, almost reluctantly, and so did my dad.

When I grew up in our village, MK loomed large. His life was wrapped in mythology. He was a living legend. All sorts of stories were told about him. Some quite hilarious. I once heard someone point to an occasional sight of an aircraft in the sky, and suggest that it is being piloted by him, apparently in some surveillance mission against the boers.

I never knew until later in my life that he is alive. There were times my parents were not quite sure their son was amongst the living. He was the stuff of regular animated conversations. According to my dad he is super intelligent and courageous as shown by his involvement in the South African struggle. Well, dad thought he was meddling in matters that do not concern him and warned me not to follow in his footsteps.

At school he is reported to have been extremely brilliant - always emerging at the top of his class. On occasions, as I understand, our late cousin, Professor Serara Khupe, would topple him from his usual number one spot! Because of his academic record, dad thought I had no reason to perform below the standards he set. So, I was expected to do the same. Coming second was acceptable, but not good enough; and coming third, which was the case with me on a few occasions, was risking being withdrawn from school completely, because it meant, I was not serious about school.

In 1978 I sat for my Standard Seven Examinations and obtained First Class. Somehow the good news reached MK, in Robben Island, and I received a congratulatory card from him – the first hard evidence that indeed my brother was alive! I do not know who shared the good news, although I suspect it was Mmaagwe Ish, my loving sister! On the day I received the card I was super excited. I had afternoon classes that day! Turbo charged, I decided to skip classes and dash to Mosalakwane to share the good news with my parents that yes, Mike is alive. So, I took off and ran non-stop from Matshekge Hill School to Mosalakwane, about 15 kilometers, to deliver the good news. My parents received the good news with mixed feelings, not sure whether I was hallucinating, or it was for real. My mother ululated and did a jig. Dad was clearly the doubting Thomas. Hardly five minutes after delivering the good news dad wasted no time in reminding me that it is getting late; and I needed to make my way back. I had thought dad would go easy on me this time around, on account of being the bearer of good news and allow me to miss classes the next day. I was not that lucky. I was sent back. That was dad, true to character. Always a disciplinarian!

We kept in touch after receipt of that historic congratulatory card, bearing Robben Island Stamp!

In one of our communications, I asked him to advise me about the salaries of Judges and the President of Botswana, as I was eyeing those positions. In my naive mind, then, I thought that to be President, and therefore entitled to be the most highly paid person in the country, one must be the most educated of the lot. In 2013, after I was appointed to the Residual Special Court of Sierra Leone, by the Secretary General of the United Nations, and Letsweletse and Dikeledi had hosted a party for me; MK brought the letter I wrote him then. I regret deeply that I have misplaced the letter!

A few years after he was released from Robben Island, I went to stay with him at the Village suburb in Gaborone. He was working for the University, and I had just completed my Form Five and working at Bank of

Botswana whilst awaiting my admission at the University. Whilst at Bank of Botswana my supervisor had persuaded me to ditch my law ambitions and to do chartered accountancy instead. I was sold to the idea. When I broached the idea with MK, he shot it down mercilessly. So it came to pass that in 1984 I enrolled for Law Degree at the University of Botswana. I am what I am because of him! My dad was not amused that I enrolled at the University to study law. In disbelief he asked MK: "Are o ya go dira eng ko UB, monnao" (what is your brother going to study at UB)?. When MK answered that I enrolled to study law, he was dismissive: "Owaii, o raya motho a ya go ithuta maaka." (You mean he is going to study to be a liar)?

Dad had conceptualized law to include his commands. So, a year into my Law studies he had ordered me to wake up early to undertake some chores, which I failed to do. Not amused he confronted MK: "O dira molao ofe monnao, if he can not comply with my orders"!

MK is a prolific writer. We often argue with each other as who is more prolific between the two of us. A month ago in Johannesburg, I heard him tell Wally Serote, the celebrated South African poet that I am more prolific than him. Whoever may be more prolific than the other doesn't really matter. What is plain is that we are cut of the same cloth. The blood that runs through his veins is the same that runs through mine. Our lives have converged in interesting ways. We both like writing, save that he writes far much better than I do.

A few years ago, when Exclusive Books was at River Walk, our books used to be displayed along each other's, as if by design!

In 2018 at my farewell party to celebrate my pending departure to PNG, he had described me as "Botswana's crown jewel in her international image" and as, "Botswana's most precious commodity exceeding Lucra Diamond in the global market". MK waxing lyrical about his brother! Ironically, I do think those same words are more fitting for him than me! Well, it may well be that the Senior and Junior have a mutual admiration for each other and are given to exaggerating each other's strength!

In my previous life as High Court Judge in Botswana, some mischief makers thought he had some influence on my judgements. Some status quo disruptive judgements I delivered were suspected to be a result of his influence. Not once have we ever discussed any judgement of mine! Besides I wouldn't trade my independence as a judge for anything. Without independence one cannot claim to be a judge. After the contentious Motswaledi case in which it was alleged that I was removed to pave way for conformist judges to sit, MK penned a piece, suggesting that the law is an ass, but judges perhaps more! Because of this unfounded belief that he had influence on my work, some within our ranks wanted me to account for the article and even suggested that I must ask him to retract his statement. I did no such thing.

MK has dedicated his entire life to fighting for freedom and justice in Botswana, South Africa and globally. He is part of the leading personalities of the South African struggle such as Moses Kotane, Oliver Reginald Tambo, Nelson Mandela, Walter Sisulu, Chief Albert Luthuli, Anton Lembede, JB Marks, Yusuf Dadoo, Govern Mbeki, Bram Fischer, Mike Harmel and many other stalwarts of the South African struggle.

Somehow circumstances collided and colluded to deliver him to the furnace that was the South African liberation struggle. He played a historic role in helping the ANC to dislodge the apartheid regime. He was in the trenches at many key moments in the history of the ANC such as the adoption of the Freedom Charter. In 1965 he was arrested, tortured and imprisoned on Robben Island, alongside Nelson Mandela, for 15 years.

MK is a product of the circumstances under which he was born and brought up. As I often say he did not grow under self-selected circumstances. Completely selfless, he was a soldier with complete integrity. MK has never considered himself as an individual detached from the broader society. Significantly he considers himself as a member of the oppressed with ties and responsibilities to other members of society. He was propelled by his society's values to immense himself in the struggle for freedom. His life is better seen as a general manifesto for freedom. He worked hard in the long historic march to Canaan. And even though he and the people he led never landed in Canaan the foundation to finally reach Canaan has been laid.

Many people have asked me: how did your brother end up being entangled in the South African struggle? It was MK's pursuit of education that resulted in him being captured by the raging revolutionary war of liberation that was led by the African National Congress in South Africa (ANC). It was whilst attending a Catholic mission school in Roodepoort, outside Johannesburg, that the political bug struck, and he never looked back. He experienced the worst of the living conditions of the black people in South Africa whilst living in such overcrowded places as Alexandra and Sophiatown.

He was deeply involved in in the ANC Programme of Action of 1949, which ushered in a new era of militant forms of struggle that bid farewell to ineffectual protests. He was involved in the resistance campaigns of the 1950's leading to the Sharpville Masacre. In the trenches he learnt to sleep for a few hours, even minutes, with one eye half closed and the other fully open, to survey enemy movements. He was a key member of the ANC underground activities and would occasionally cross the boarder to brief the leadership of OR Tambo about the balance of forces and tempo of the struggle in the country.

In prison the regime sought to de-personalize him by identifying him not as Michael Dingake as such, but prisoner 277/66 and later 130/67. MK is part of that rare breed of revolutionaries who immersed themselves in the struggle without any expectation of personal gain. He played no less a role in the independence movement that birthed the Republic of Botswana. After he was released from prison in 1981, he refused to be co-opted by the status quo preferring instead to join the opposition and pursue his vision of a better Botswana. To date he remains steady fast in that vision and his loyalty to the cause of freedom. At the University of Botswana where he once worked as a purchasing head, he had negotiated himself a porta-camp located conveniently in the easterly corner of the University; and whose broader purpose we would rather leave future researchers to write about.

After leaving the University he pursued his lifelong passion of being an advocate of a better Botswana. This culminated in him being a Member of Parliament for Gaborone Central after a bruising primary election. He later rose to be a Leader of the Opposition in Parliament. In terms of the Westminster conventions any person occupying the position of Leader of Opposition is a shadow, President.

Dad suspected that MK had presidential ambitions but could not understand how a commoner can do that! He once asked me: "if your brother succeeds to be President where will he get money to build schools and roads"? According to dad, MK should not have compared himself to Seretse Khama, the first President of Botswana, because Seretse Khama was an in- law in England, and he would easily get assistance from his in- laws, to supplement money sourced from taxes!

I conclude by addressing MK directly: We love you Sejiye! And as I always say the family will honour your legacy. For us, your family, to whom you did so much, in your quiet humility, we vow never to dishonour your name and what you stood for. We will continuously drink in the massive reservoir of your wisdom and knowledge – and how you conducted yourself during the dark days of apartheid, your selflessness and commitment to justice will continue to be a mirror before which we look at ourselves, in order to advance the cause, you stood for.

As a husband, father, grandfather, brother, you are a role model, always full of love. You have taught us that it is better to die on one's feet fighting against injustice. You have taught us to live our lives serving highest good for all. I thank you my Grand Chief for your legacy and lessons that you have left with us. We applaud you for sacrificing your life so that humanity can be free. I sign off this piece by assuring you of my highest respect and admiration for all that you have done for humanity.

Long live MK! Long live Sejiye

Tribute to Gobe Matenge

Over the years, since GW commissioned me to write his biography: "Unearthing the Hidden Treasure: The Untold Story of Gobe Matenge" my relationship with him and his family deepened. We became one family – his children my sisters and brothers. I wrote the book in close collaboration with Tsompie – the special emissary of GW on the project. This is how I earned my tittle: "Boss".

I deeply regret that due to my being trapped in the bowels of the Pacific I could not make it to Botswana to pay my last respects to my mentor, friend and father. However, with modern technology I followed the proceedings every step of the way and I was deeply touched by the outpouring of grief and love from hundreds of our people, young and old; people of diverse religious denominations and political affiliations. A fitting tribute to a man who respected every person without any distinction whatsoever.

At this juncture it is proper that I must express my sincere condolences to his family and say to them that as much as I understand the loss they have suffered, they must take heart that he has rested. He seemed to be in great pain when I last visited him at Gaborone Private Hospital in March, 2018. What was remarkable though was that GW was ready to meet his Maker. He was not afraid to die. He was fearless to the end.

GW's passing was not only a loss to his family, friends and relatives, but it is a great loss to the country too. A larger than life figure has fallen. The mighty tree that sheltered the young and old, the poor and rich has fallen. The aftermath of this loss shall be felt in many parts of our republic, not least in Matenge where GW used to pay for uniforms of school going pupils.

Death may have succeeded to physically separate us from this iconic son of the soil, but it cannot succeed to kill his name and deeds in this, our earthly world. Although GW did not play any visible and prominent part in the nationalist movement that ushered republican politics in our country he was instrumental in building certain aspects of our identity as a people and nation. For instance, he contributed in ensuring that the song " Fatshe leno larona" is chosen as our national anthem. As GW explained to me, "Fatshe leno larona" composed by Tumediso Motsete was more appropriate than other competing songs because it was unique and exuded national pride. The preferred song, according to GW, captured the pulse of the nation and expressed the joy and patriotic mood of the people at having taken control of their affairs.

Our country has lost an exceptional human being whose kind we may not see again. He was extra-ordinary in many respects. He was a snappy dresser, with a passion for a white shirt. His children say they often lost count how many times in a day he would brush his teeth. His brother Robert once told me that GW exhibited propensity for being clean at all times during his early days. According to his brother: "Gobe o ne a rata metsi. Ha a tsene mo metsing ko nokeng o ne a sa tswe; a ikgotha dinao jaaka mosetsana"

GW is well known for his punctuality. He doesn't like people who don't respect time and he was hardly sympathetic to any excuse proffered for not keeping time. His contemporaries say that he was not a great fan for quorum in meetings because he firmly believed that having quorum should not stand on the way of delivery.

All those who knew him well would testify that he was a man of unbending principle. It is in the class character of the middle class to blink and equivocate in the face of injustice. No so GW. On principle he never equivocated. At the time he permanently fell asleep he remained committed to a fairer and better society for all. He was famous for being even handed. As a District Commissioner in Kanye he used to reprimand the Special Branch Police who were mandated for reporting on party political meetings for filing reports only on the opposition, telling them in no uncertain terms that they must file reports of all political meetings.

From humble beginnings, in Matenge, a small village tucked away in the North East of Botswana, he achieved so much and touched so many hearts with his regal posture, dignity and sharp intellect.

He is one of the Elders of our nation that had a profound impact on our democracy. He was principled, warm, loving, empathetic, thoughtful and kind. He was humble in the way he treated everybody, no matter how they ranked on the social ladder in this class divided society of ours.

GW was humble and wise. He would listen very intently to a debate; nod if in agreement, but maintain stony dignified silence when not in agreement and on occasions he would quietly shake his head in disagreement, and once the speaker is finished, he would clear his throat, chuckle and engage. He respected everyone's opinion, no matter how humble their station in life and treated them with respect and dignity. He commanded without issuing commands and he would offer his path breaking wisdom. He had an unmistakable sense of purpose and justice especially for the poor and the marginalised.

Somewhere in the book of Luke it is reported that Jesus spoke about preaching the gospel to the poor, about healing the broken hearted and proclaiming liberty to the captives. GW was not a religious man, but his mission in life was to uplift the poor; to end the indignity brought by poverty and to fight against discrimination based on ethnic, gender and other irrational grounds. GW had hoped that the Balopi Commission set up to address the issue of equality of all segments of our society would finally lay to rest complaints of ethnic inequality; and was disappointed that this was not so.

This tribute is not the place to give a full account of who GW is. What I hope to do is to sketch, in broad strokes, his remarkable life journey, just to give a sense why he was so much loved and respected. My hope is that young people will learn something positive from his life experience. At the end of this sketch, I will outline in summary form what I think the valuable lessons of his life are to the youth of our country.

GW believed in political pluralism. This is a man whose political home was in the Opposition, but some of his best friends came from the other side of the political divide. He counted amongst his best friends His Excellency former President Mogae and David Magang, amongst others. This generation of leaders represent who we are as a people – a trait that unfortunately appears to be on the wane. In the contemporary Botswana, one can pay a crippling price for holding a different point of view. We should refuse to go in this direction. It is alien to who we are as a people. It is a deadly seed to cultivate.

GW may have been critical of his government, but not once did he doubt the patriotism of its functionaries. He was tolerant and decent in his politics. He did not believe in the politics of abuse and insults. He was dignified and civil and made politics seem so natural like breathing oxygen. He always insisted that critiques of the establishment must articulate robust policy positions that can drive the country forward.

GW was a product of his own circumstances - a scion of Wilinani and Goitsemang Matenge. He was born on February 28, 1926, in Matenge Ward near Makaleng Village in the North East District. The name, Gobe, means " Mpho" in Setswana and in English it simply means, " Gift" – and what a gift he was to this nation.

According to some sources the Matenges originated from West Central Africa. Their Totem is Ngama (hartebeest). The Matenge men, like most Nswazi men share the honour of being addressed as Bo-Ntombo – a revered salutation of his people. He is the eldest of the three brothers, (GW, Robert and Tjiga. In 1950 GW married Daisy Matenge, daughter of Motshobi and Gertrude Sebina of Tonota. They were blessed with six children: Kutlwano, Tjakazwagwa(Bandu) Nkwebi, Goitsemang(Chibi), Nlebeleki (Matsi) and Tsompie (Selloane).

GW lived his life to the full. He did not scale the heights of formal education but he could debate any scholar on major issues of the day. He rose from being a messenger/interpreter at the office of the District Commissioner (DC) in Francistown to being a Permanent Secretary in the Ministry of Home Affairs. As a public officer he knew that he was a servant of the people and a trustee of people's property and funds.

GW's rise to the top echelons of the civil service did not surprise those who knew his passion for delivery. His sense of fairness. In terms of service delivery and in conducting himself as a public figure GW had no rivals. If all our civil servants could emulate GW's sense of duty our country will develop in leaps and bounds and would be corrupt free.

As a District Commissioner and Permanent Secretary he was guided by the law in carrying out his mandate and feared no one. An encounter with the then Vice President Masire when he was a District Commissioner in Kanye illustrates his principled and fearless nature. GW had received communication that Vice President Masire who was also the MP for Kanye was going to be touring the area and that the office of the DC was expected to arrange for the tour. GW demanded to know in what capacity the Vice President would be touring the District. He got no response. On the appointed day for the tour the Vice President did not come to his office, instead he went to the office of the Police Station Commander. And as fate would have it, towards the end of his tour the Vice President's vehicle needed petrol which could only be authorised by the District Commissioner. The VP drove to the office of the DC. GW was advised that the President was outside and asked if he cared meeting him. He requested that the Vice President come to his office so that they can discuss whatever assistance his office may render. The VP went to meet GW but was livid at the apparent insubordination of the DC. GW refused to bend. He put it to the VP that he takes instructions from his Minister not the VP.

The duo engaged in heated exchange. At the end of the exchange Vice President Masire was willing to make peace. He offered a handshake. GW was not impressed, asking: "Why do you want to shake my hand"?. Such was the unbending nature of GW on matters of principle.

Then is the much told story of a government vehicle. The story is told how once when GW was having a chat with President Seretse Khama's private secretary, he saw the President's daughter driving a government vehicle to which he took exception openly. He was reprimanded by his Minister but later exonerated by the President.

His colleagues in the opposition said he had a rare courage of talking truth to power. A source reports that once at a heated meeting of his party he told his revered and highly respected leader that despite the obvious love and adoration of the masses, he must remember he is not God, but a mere mortal with faults and flows.

GW's life is an inspiring lesson to all young people. His life teaches that with hard work anything is possible; that success is not an accident; that failure is not final and that no one is born a failure. We were all born to succeed if only we could learn to focus on what has to be done. Yes, his life teaches that dreams don't give up on us, but we give up on our dreams, more often than not prematurely. GW's life teaches that we may come from hardship circumstances yet we can still cast aside our circumstances and succeed. The principle remains the same for every struggle – that if we have stubborn determination to succeed, we will.

GW served our country with distinction, more pre-eminently as a District Commissioner and Permanent Secretary. He was once tasked with the organisation of the 10th Anniversary of Independence Celebrations a task he discharged with pride and distinction. As his friends would testify, he made sure that everything was "tip tops".

I end this tribute with a humble call to those who have power to make things happen. As a nation we need to honour every Motswana who deserves to be honoured because there is verifiable evidence that supports such an honour. I think there is sufficient evidence to support a plea that GW must be honoured in some form. Perhaps, we as a nation could name some street, space or building after him so that future generations can read about him and be inspired.

Farewell Ntombo. You were a cut above the rest. All is well with my soul. I have accepted it was your time to go. You ran your race and completed your tasks in this world as a servant of the people. I have accepted that as they say, there is a time for every matter under heaven. A time to be born and a time to die. Parting is always hellish. My consolation is that good men never really die, they sleep. God bless the memory of GW. May His Soul Rest in Eternal Peace.

The Brilliant Conservatism of The Is Kirby Court – Reflections on Justice Kirby's Contribution To Botswana's Jurisprudence

Justice Kirby hanged his judicial robes at the end of November 2021 after many years of distinguished service. Born in 1945, the content of his jurisprudence, was in many respects generational. Like the late Justice Scalia of the Supreme Court in the United States of America, history will confirm Justice Kirby as a brilliant conservative judge, occasionally prone to progressive impulses as his last judgment delivered on the 29th of November 2021, a day before his last day in office shows. Unlike any other decision he has ever delivered his last judgement dramatically expanded rights – and judicial power in a manner that is unprecedented – and it seems the timing was perfect.

In the philosophy of law there are certain markers that point to the philosophical inclination of a judge. Elements of conservatism include willingness to limit individual rights where they conflict with government authority, preference and respect for private property; deference to governmental decisions and reluctance to upset same; concern for law and order, often over liberty and equality, less enthusiasm to embrace international law; deciding cases on narrowest of grounds, avoidance (if that is possible) to decide cases on constitutional grounds, respect of precedent (even in circumstances where the march of time dictates otherwise) and preference for textual provisions on constitutional matters and not paying much attention to the spirit thereof.

It needs to be stated that conservative judges often deliver liberal and progressive decisions, just as liberal and progressive judges may occasionally deliver conservative judgments. It is the general tendency that is a marker of the philosophical inclination of a judge. Most judges go about their work without caring about which philosophical school of thought they belong to. In any event in ordinary run of the mill cases this hardly matters. It does however matter in high stake cases of constitutional importance.

In the literature on law few books qualify to be called classics. However, Benjamin N. Cardozo's The Nature of the Judicial Process is such a classic. If it were left for me to dictate it would be mandatory reading for every law student and every judge. Some of Cardozo's probing reflections needs to be recalled in order to give context to this piece. In his book referred to above he ponders the following questions (which I personally find I usually confront in a number of cases of national importance):

"What is it that I do when I decide a case? To what sources of information do I appeal for guidance? In what proportion do I permit them to contribute to the result? In what proportion ought they to contribute? If a precedent is applicable, when do I refuse to allow it? If no precedent is applicable, how do I reach a rule that will make a precedent for the future? If I am seeking logical consistency, the symmetry of the legal structure, how far shall I seek it? At what point shall the quest be halted by some discrepant custom, by some consideration of social welfare, by my own or the common standards of justice and morals"?

The above summarises questions that often crop up in a judge's mind when deciding a verdict of a matter and provides a context of my interrogation of justice Kirby's contribution to our law through an assessment of a cross section of some of his defining cases. This is so because the best way of paying tribute to a judge is through a consideration and assessment of his jurisprudential trajectory that lays bare his contribution to law and reveals his legacy. Justice Kirby's contribution to our law is undeniable.

Our law reports are littered with many of his decisions. However, the following easily stand out for their jurisprudential brilliance or lack thereof: These are: Attorney General v Motshediemang; Attorney v Peter Ogbal Paul, Attorney General v Mothusi, Kajabanga v Attorney General v Kajabanga, Attorney General v BOPEU, Hands-up Case (involving the Speakership of the National Assembly) Attorney General v Tapela and Others, Attorney General v Rammoge and Others, Mzwinila v Attorney General, Patson v Attorney General and Boko and others v IEC. I will discuss a few of these cases below.

It is of course true that no judge ascends to the bench as an ideological virgin. We all come to the bench from different backgrounds that often has a bearing on how we engage with the law. Justice Kirby is no exception. His world out look that was mirrored in his judgements may have been at variance with those who grew up in circumstances different from his.

In his days as a practicing lawyer he ran a successful law firm with significant corporate clientele. He was also the legal advisor of choice by those at the top echelons of power and their associates for a very long time. He later rose to become the Attorney General of the Republic – and then judge of the High Court, before being elevated to head the Court of appeal, by President Khama.

In our constitutional arrangement the President of the Court of appeal and Chief Justice are gifts to the nation from a sitting President. Botswana remains one of the few countries were appointment of Chief Justice and President of Court of Appeal is the sole prerogative of the President. The Judicial Service Commission is not involved and so is Parliament and Civil Society.

Critics have bemoaned political considerations that often inform such appointments. In South Africa there is scholarly literature that suggests that the ANC appointments of heads of the judiciary and other members of the bench, are often intended to secure hegemonic control of all levers of power in society.

As an Attorney General justice Kirby came to know what drove the passage of certain laws and the general executive policy of which he was an integral part. As Deputy Attorney General, justice Kirby was the lead counsel for government in the seminal case of Dow v the Attorney General. In that case he argued against the expansion of rights, asking the court to uphold the Citizenship Act that discriminated on the basis of sex. He passionately argued that were the court to strike down the Citizenship Act, the judgment would be at odds with the patriarchal values upon the nation was built.

His arguments in the Dow case set him apart as an originalist. Originalism is a strand of conservatism that says words in a constitution should be interpreted as they were understood at the time they were written – in accordance with the thinking of those who drafted the constitution. The majority of the justices repudiated his submissions, holding that a constitution is a living organism, one that evolves, changes over time, and adapts to new circumstances, without being formally amended.

It is pleasing that in Motshediemang Kirby P in his last day at the bench clearly came to terms with this realization – thereby conceding by parity of reasoning – that indeed through their interpretative power judges do make law – something that positivist judges often consider blasphemous. It may well be that the jury is still out whether justice Kirby now embraces the logic of the Dow case wholeheartedly or not. Some progressive elements of the bar and the bench are relieved that he never tossed it out of the window, when he could have, was he so inclined.

In his days in legal practice human rights litigation was not one of his main assignments. As those familiar with the law – in particular human rights discourse, may well know, rights claims and rights rhetoric in the struggle of the oppressed and the poor – entails elements of both possibility as well as limits when considered in the light of emancipation and freedom projects.

The Law as written is not always clear. I know it is the weakness of many of us in the legal fraternity to speak of law as a set of neutral rules – something that in truth is pure fiction – in most cases, if not in all. Sometimes we speak of law as a self- contained subject – something to be examined like a laboratory specimen in a test tube – yet the law as is and the law as it ought to be is a complex phenomenon. It is this complexity, (also explained by the background of the judge) that may explain why judges may not agree with each other on a matter, including on whether to embrace or discard technicalities in any matter.

When the law' intention is unclear it behoves the judges to give meaning to the words employed by legislation to advance justice – this being the ideal. Too often owing to many factors, we the judges, can occasion injustice in our interpretation of the law. As I often say in the hands of men and women of good will and learning the law can be a force for good, but in some hands law can be a force for bad things. It can be an instrument of oppression. It can be used to suffocate democracy and supress rights. The latter explains why progressive judges are always alert to ensure that law does not result in injustice. Unjust laws are not consistent with constitutionalism and the rule of law.

Overall the Kirby court was restrained and brilliant in its genre of conservatism. The case of Motshediemang is evidence of the latter. In a stroke of a pen, he ended the long and tortuous road to equality of gay people. I was reminded of this long and tortuous road by a piece written by, Zackie Achmat, that indefatigable human right defender, recently, when he reflected on a union of gay men, one Khoi and the other a Dutch sailor, way back in 1735, who for their love for each other were brutally murdered.

In truth our constitution never denied the right to equality for gay men. It was society and the judges who did – some arguing that the time is not right to extend equality rights to gay persons – forgetting the self-evident truth that we are all born equal and that rights are not negotiable – not even with judges.

It ought to be remembered that the Motshediemang case was similar to the case of Kanane that preceded it. Justice Kirby was part of the panel that sat in Kanane. In Kanane he agreed with the other justices and refused to strike down the offensive legislation. The same legislation he struck down in

Motshediemang. There is no doubt in my mind that Kanane was wrongly decided at the time, as several of my writings thereafter contended, having regard to the legal injunction to always interpret constitutional rights liberally and to treat the constitution as a living organism. In Kanane the Court of Appeal held back our march to freedom for more than a decade – and perpetuated the suffering of gay persons as their being was criminalized based on an inaccurate and narrow reading of the constitution.

The truth of the matter is that our constitution never denied gay persons the rights to equality and the right not to be discriminated against. Some sections of society (may be the majority) and the bench did so. The bench did so because of the choices they exercised. They chose to interpret the constitution restrictively, which is not permissible; they chose to be blown away by "public opinion", which was not right, and they chose not read: "sexual orientation", into section 15 of the constitution, which they could have done.

Our constitution commands that it be interpreted in a manner that saves humanity from the scourge of indignity – and with a sense of the future – and to secure the rights of generations yet to be born. It is always the duty of judges to breathe life into the constitution – and to effect the promise of the constitution – by among other things rejecting the tyranny of the majority.

Section 3, the principal section conferring fundamental human rights in Botswana has always been there. It was ignored in Kanane, and thankfully given effect to in Motshediemang. A big lesson here is the often overlooked fact: judges matter! Who the judge is may be life changing in any given matter. When one considers the decision in Kanane and Motshediemang, based on similar facts and the diametrically opposed conclusions, one may be given to think that may be: "the constitution is what the judges say it is", at any given time, as that brilliant luminary judge and scholar, Charles Evans Hughes (1862 -1948) LLD, once ruminated. A similar case to Motshediemang in Kenya may also underscore the observations of Charles Hughes.

In Kenya despite having a transformative constitution that demands transformative jurisprudence the right to equality of gay persons was denied. This was at a time when Leburu J working only with rudimentary judicial tools - a retrogressive and time barred constitution was able to carve out of its terms and spirit a brilliant jurisprudential masterpiece, laced with scholarly permutations.

Leburu's piece was not only searching and thorough; it was erudite and scholarly. He remains the judicial midwife of what is now the law in Botswana. His place in history is secured. The justices of appeal gave him credit for his rendition; which he deserved. He made their task much easier.

The Court of Appeal decision is to be celebrated for many other reasons, including that it seemed to be more receptive to comparative constitutional law and scholarly work than before – a positive development for the future of the country's jurisprudential development. This gives me hope that the next generation of jurists – and there are many now languishing in the periphery – will one day take up their rightful places and take the country's jurisprudence to another level.

As indicated earlier, it may not be unfair to suggest that when it came to expanding rights the Kirby Court was largely cautious, calculating, reluctant and occasionally brilliant.

It constrained the rights of the accused as the case of Kajabanga would show; and was hesitant to hold the executive to account and at times exhibited breath-taking "unconscious bias" towards the executive as the Bopeu judgment discussed below may suggest. On the whole his judgements were carefully crafted and closely reasoned. Often his intention and sense of future direction would lie in between the lines.

In a number of cases, his nimble forensic footwork, would be on full display to marvel and cherish. He would even seek to –pre-empt an anticipated future argument and bury it. He used simple language to capture complex legal reasoning.

Amongst the most memorable judgements to come out of Kirby P's pen are the Hands –up case, (on election of the Speaker), Tiro v the Attorney General, on the proper approach to interpreting the rules of the High Court and the case of Attorney v Peter Ogbal Paul. The latter case concerned a judicial review of a presidential deportation order which he correctly set aside. In that case he sought to distinguish it from the case of Good, suggesting, by implication, if not explicitly, that Good was correctly decided, a position which I do not share. I am certain that one day the jurisprudence of Good will be peacefully buried and laid to rest on account of its intrinsic jurisprudential deficiency.

By and large his record in public law was a mixed one. In public law some lawyers tended to think he would fit the category of the judges that Lord Atkin considered executive minded - and perhaps even more than the executive. Jurisprudentially a close academic scrutiny of his judgements; how he elected to exercise the options before him in any case reveal him as being inclined to legal positivism. In many high stake cases of national importance his deference to the executive was often undisguised.

The case in point was the case of Bopeu v the Attorney General. At issue was whether the dismissal of the public sector employees who embarked on a strike to press home their demands for better working conditions were lawfully dismissed. They had contended before the High Court and the Court of Appeal that their dismissal was unlawful because it was not preceded by a hearing.

The Court of Appeal, in a judgment penned by Kirby P, held that the dismissals were lawful in that the requirement to hear the other side before an adverse decision was taken was not breached. Justice Kirby stressed that the strike posed a danger to the life and health of patients and that the pressing urgency of the situation occasioned by the strike and the danger it posed to life and property required that decisive action be taken to protect the public. In order to cast doubt on the reasonableness of the workers' demands, he cited issues of recession – and also offered his view that strikes in the public service should be a rare occurrence.

In the cause of his rendition in the Bopeu matter he would make statements to the effect that Botswana has enjoyed peace and stability for more than forty-five years since independence – a common self -praise line by members of the executive over the years – and perhaps a tagline appropriate to be issued by an Attorney General. If ever there was a case that opened Kirby P to accusations of executive mindedness this would be the one. The judgement as one Senior Advocate in South Africa, once pointed out, was littered with too many political statements – so many that had there been a higher court to appeal to, the possibility of the Court of Appeal being reversed existed.

In Oatile v the Attorney General, a case in which the state appealed against an order of the High Court ordering the state to pay compensation to the accused whose right to trial within reasonable time was breached he reluctantly embraced the novel idea, in Botswana's jurisprudence, of the need to hold the state accountable for wrong doing through ordering constitutional damages as a remedy. The reluctance manifested itself in the low quantum odf damages the court issued.

Before then, our courts had relied on the law of delict to remedy any wrong doing by the state and were reluctant to embrace the possibilities offered by public law – in the form of constitutional damages as an alternative. Oatile explored two related but distinct themes: the need to hold the state accountable for its wrong doing and the need to hold it liable to pay a monetary sum to a victim of its wrong doing. It boldly posited that in an appropriate case, an award of constitutional damages, may be a better means to hold the state accountable for the performance of its distinctive obligations.

In 2019 Botswana held elections that were marred by allegations of irregularity. On the merits petitioners averred, amongst other things, instances of alleged corrupt and/ or illegal practices. These included assertions that several companies were used to launder money to pay IEC officials, that IEC officials issued more than one voters registration cards in order to circumvent the requirement of one man one vote; that there was double registration of voters, that voters were paid money to vote more than once; and that voters rolls were falsified to favour some candidate. Several petitions were registered challenging the undue return of members of parliament.

The allegations were grave. They called into question the integrity of the elections. The High court dismissed the petitions on technicalities. The majority of the judges dismissed the petitions on the basis that the petitions were presented to the Registrar of the High Court, outside the requisite 30 days set by Section 17 (b) of the Electoral Act, on the main, including that the petitions were not accompanied by a written notice of the presentation of the petition as envisaged by Section 118 of the Electoral Act.

An appeal to the Court of Appeal in the case of Duma Gideon Boko and Others v Independent Electoral Commission and Others was not successful. The Court of Appeal, in a judgement penned by Kirby P held it had no jurisdiction to entertain the appeal. Surprisingly, the court then proceeded to give a 70 page or so rendition that appeared to veer into the merits of the dispute. Surprisingly, a court without jurisdiction, went so far as to make it clear that it disagrees with the dissenting judgments in the three sets of petitions delivered by the High Court.

This is one case in which finding my own position with respect to the conclusion of the court that it had no jurisdiction was difficult. I found myself overruling my previous day' conclusions adinfinitum. I confessed this recently to one judge after engaging in the across –the oceans midnight debate on the matter. Could it be (I asked myself) that the case of Gideon Boko would in future be remembered as a case that held back the tectonic plates of power from shifting.?

This was not an easy case. The force and weight of section 106 of the constitution was unmistakable. Perhaps the potential of section 7 of the Court of Appeal Act as a logjam breaking mechanism was not fully and exhaustively interrogated. The dismembering of the section and assigning adverse meaning to the first limb of the section and not interrogating the potential of the second limb may explain the conclusion reached by the court. And my rumination continues: could it be that even a full interrogation of section could have cum to a judicial cul- de- sac.? Without the benefit of full argument on the point, I cannot adequately proffer an informed opinion on same.

It may well be true that although we may never know with complete certainty the winner of the 2019 general elections, because the merits were never traversed and the Court of Appeal denied jurisdiction, the identity of the loser is clear: it is the people's confidence in an electoral regulatory framework that denies aggrieved parties access to the apex court and in the ability of the rule of the law and the judges to hear them out - to listen to what it is they say happened.

In the discipline of criminal law, Kirby P tended to embrace restrictive approach as in public law. Two examples would suffice: In Lyndon Mothusi v the Attorney General, he suggested that the right to speedy and expeditious trial did not include an appeal. And in Attorney General v Kajabanga he diluted the time frames that were more favourable to the accused as to when the cloak starts ticking, set out in the famous case of Sejammitlwa, when determining an application for permanent stay of prosecution.

Justice Kirby had a deep influence on the development of the law in our country. He was a remarkable man of the law in many respects; but more significantly he was a product of his generation and the circumstances under which he grew. All those influences found their way into our law in one form or another – because the truth of the matter is that no judge ascends to the bench as a virgin.

He had the power during his tenure to live the true values of the judiciary by reforming the process of appointment to the court of appeal to ensure that appointments to the apex court, out of respect of the people who delegated judicial power to the court ("we the people") and the litigants were done transparently and based on merit. He failed to do so. He opened himself to accusations of privatization of the judiciary and that he had turned the judiciary into a "private spaza". These accusations stigmatized the Court of Appeal and would hurt his legacy badly.

It is important to remember that the court exercises delegated judicial power from the people. Secrecy can never be in public interest. It is imperative that the leadership of the judiciary must conduct themselves in a manner that promotes the respect and dignity of the court. The dignity of the court is maintained better by being transparent, fair and appointments merit based.

As an administrator justice Kirby was efficient. In my experience he executed all tasks assigned to him in time. I was privileged to work closely with Kirby P on many occasions, twice or so as an acting justice of appeal at the instance of Nganunu and Dibotelo CJ. I chuckle, on reflection, recalling what both Chief Justice Dibotelo and Nganunu said to justify enrolling me to sit together with justice Kirby, in the Court of Appeal, in the few cases we did. That they all had same reasons was to my mind interesting and revealing.

Chief Justice Dibotelo also appointed me to a committee which Kirby J (as he then was) chaired. The other member was Phumaphi J. He is a hard worker who executed assignments on time as agreed; and excellent at drafting whatever the committee may have agreed upon. It appeared drafting was second nature to him.

Fare thee well my brother. You worked hard for the republic over the years. You deserve to rest. Some elements in the bar and academia liked portraying us as ideological opposites. I do not know how true that is. History shall be the ultimate judge. I have read many of your judgements with profit. Find time to write and let us compare notes.

Tribute To George Bizos- A Larger Than Life Crusader For Justice

On the 9th of September 2020 George Bizos, that unrelenting crusader for justice, succumbed to death at a ripe age of 92. His passing hit close to home. It left my brother, Mike (a former client of Bizos) heart-broken. I was similarly deeply saddened. He impacted on our lives in different ways. Mike wrote me soon after he learnt of his passing: "My intimates are falling in quick succession. Beginning to feel like I am in the queue". Not long time ago he lost another close friend – Andrew Mlangeni, an anti-apartheid campaigner, who, along with my brother and Nelson Mandela were imprisoned for furthering the aims of the African National Congress (ANC) and were sentenced to serve in Robben Island.

George Bizos was a legend. He was an unmatched champion of human rights and unquestionably committed to the cause of humanity especially the oppressed and downtrodden. The record speaks for itself: he played a pivotal role in many major human rights trials, among them the Treason Trial, the Rivonia Trial, the Nusas Five Trial, the Delmas Treason Trial. He was also involved in the inquests into the deaths of activists Ahmed Timol and Steve Biko and more recently, the commission of inquiry into the Marikana massacre. He also represented a host of ANC leaders such as Winnie Mandela, Albertina Sisulu and Barbara Hogan in numerous political trials.

When still a young boy Bizos, in the company of his father, set off on a journey that ended in South Africa. They had to leave because they had helped Allied soldiers to hide from the Nazis, and were expecting imminent reprisals.

Years later, as a lawyer and judge, he impacted directly on my life and that of my brother as I shall briefly explain.

Bizos was particularly famous the world over for having been part of the legal team that represented Nelson Mandela, Walter Sisulu and other stalwarts of the South Africa liberation struggle during the Rivonia Trial. It was during the trial that his formidable cross examination skills came to the fore. He had this rare skill of asking a witness deceptively simple questions that at the end of the day would prove fatal for the opposing side. In many respects his style, courtesy and focus reminded me of my soft –spoken friend, Dick Bayford, whose cross-examination skills are legendary. On a few occasions when we locked horns, I emerged bloody nosed! He is in fact our own George Bizos!

I have read a few of his works, including his monumental biography, Odyssey to Freedom. Though it is packed with wisdom, the book also shows him as an admirable human being. For example, we read how he used to bring home-grown salad, cheese and other goodies to his clients, the Rivonia trialists!

Bizos rescued my brother from the gallows. He was Mike's lawyer back in the 1960's, in the case where he was charged with Issy Heymann for being a member of banned organizations, namely the ANC and the South African Communist Party (SACP), and for recruiting young people for military training outside South Africa. His friend Issy was only found guilty of one count: being a member of the SACP. My brother was found guilty of the balance of the counts and was sentenced to 15 years imprisonment on Robben Island. He informs me that it was difficult to find lawyers to represent them as most lawyers were scared to represent, "terrorists". They were lucky that the underground leadership of the movement managed to secure Bizos to represent them. He tells me that Bizos represented them with skill and conviction, despite the fact that they were eventually found guilty as charged, a verdict that reflected badly on the apartheid court, not on Bizos, the lawyer. Mike was very impressed that Bizos was not afraid of whatever evil the fascists might unleash on him for taking on the case.

Many years later, as a justice of our highly respected Court of Appeal, Bizos contributed to the decision of the Court of Appeal in the famous case of Unity Dow v The Attorney General. He later told me that during argument in the matter he had difficulty appreciating the point being made to the court, namely that the founders of our constitution deliberately intended to discriminate against women, and that public opinion was opposed to equality between men and women because Botswana is patriarchal society. To my surprise, the latter part of the argument was again advanced, decades later, before me, but with no success.

On a personal note, however, the case that stands out is that of the Student Representative Council v The University of Botswana. It is this case that saved me and many of my colleagues from guaranteed poverty and suffering, consistent with the law of uneven development that governs the global economic system. Bizos literally made me who I am today, by using law as a tool for justice and in order to promote the right to education. Law in the wrong hands can be an unmitigated disaster while in good hands it can be a liberating tool - especially if it is understood that the ultimate objective of law is the welfare of society. At the end of the day justice is the ultimate aim of law.

In 1989, following a prolonged boycott of classes, the University of Botswana was closed. This was to enable management to sift out ringleaders and ensure they did not return when the university opened. I was looking forward to graduating that same year but unfortunately, Dick Bayford and I were targeted for expulsion because we were considered the leaders of the boycott. Before the axe could fall, however, we got a whisper of this from a member of the university council, someone who is now a leading banker of unparalleled distinction and brilliance in Botswana. He later told me that the injustice and irrationality of the decision was such that he felt he had to warn us. The news came as a shock to me and my family. On hearing of it, one of my sisters broke down and cried. She kept asking me: "How can you, Nnaka, (my young brother) when you are about to graduate and our parents expect you to start supporting them, after they toiled for so long?".

She was so traumatized that she even called the then Vice Chancellor, Thomas Tlou, our cousin, to find out whether it was true that I would not be allowed to return when the university re-opened.

Terrified, Dick and I managed to convince the Student Representative Council (SRC) to challenge the closure in court. We petitioned the High Court and lost. We appealed. The matter landed in the lap of Bizos who wrote the judgment for the court. In a landmark decision, etched in my mind as Civil Appeal no 1 of 1989, the court ruled that the closure of the university was illegal and that the university council could not close a university for the purposes of sifting out ringleaders with a view to excluding them. Such a purpose ran counter to the mandate of the university which was to promote higher education.

Bizos JA (as he then was) added that education was too important a right to be left to the bureaucrats alone. I have always thought this line was wrong in the context of the Botswana constitution, but it didn't matter because, as the lawyers would say, it was obiter, meaning that it was not the real basis for the judgment. Apart from that, I loved the polemic and ring of the line. Overall, his superior reasoning shone through the entire judgment. His clarity of reasoning could only be matched by his clarity of expression. Had it not been for his judgement it is probable that Dick and I would be languishing in the streets unemployed and without any degree or other means to do anything useful for ourselves and humanity.

I digress. Back to Bizos. Many years later our paths would cross, especially at conferences organized by Section 27 in South Africa and the International Commission of Jurists. On many occasions we shared the podium, the student and the teacher, as speakers. In one such occasion I walked towards him and teasingly said: "My Lord, may I approach the bench". He looked puzzled. Enjoying the awkward moment, I persisted:

"Afternoon, judge". He may not have been on the bench then, but in my mind he was a judge. Once judge, always a judge. He chuckled and responded "Key, call me George". He was humble to a fault, with that rare combination - humility, humanity and brilliance. His modesty and politeness were disarming, a rare quality since members of the legal profession are known to throw their weight around.

I last met him in 2015 at a meeting organized by the International Commission of Jurists (ICJ) in Johannesburg to celebrate the release from prison of my dear friend, Swaziland human rights campaigner, Thulani Maseko. Arnold Tsunga, that indefatigable defender of human rights, had made it possible for the meeting to take place, as he always does, so that proper lessons could be drawn. Thulani was a victim of a judicial officer who was drunk on power and found himself languishing in prison for no reason. In different ways, both the Swazi Constitution and the judiciary had failed him. But that is a chapter for another day.

At this meeting, Bizos took me aside and, his voice almost failing and with deep concern showing all over his face, asked me: "What is the state of jurisprudence now in Botswana? Is there still reluctance by the judges to use the constitution?" He was referring to what I once, in an unguarded moment in a judgment, termed constitutional phobia. In the minds of many traditional judges, whenever there is a dispute before court it should only be resolved by invoking the constitution if there are no other grounds that can be utilized. It is a problematic reasoning that pays only lip service to the notion that every law is shaped by the constitution that is the Supreme law.

I say to George: farewell, champion of champions. You were a fine human being. You were respected and loved by many. Thank you for the impact you had in our lives. It is truly amazing that although you was born so far away in Greece you could impact so positively on the lives of sons of peasant parents from Mosalakwane, a sparsely inhabited and denuded oasis of peace, in the outskirts of Bobonong, hardly recognizable by GPS. You were a blessing on our lives. Your commitment to the rule of law is unsurpassed by anyone. You were a living proof that integrity and deep moral compass are not opposites but complementary. We are poorer without you in our midst! Fare thee well George! Robala ka kagiso motho wa batho!

by GPS. You were a blessing on our lives. Your commitment to the rule of law is unsurpassed by anyone. You were a living proof that integrity and deep moral compass are not opposites but complementary. We are poorer without you in our midst! Fare thee well George! Robala ka kagiso motho wa batho!

Tribute To Thulani Maseko- An Advocate For The Rule of Law and Champion of Human Rights

"So, I do believe that the dignity and humanity of the people of Swaziland, across Africa and the world, can only be restored with the full enjoyment of all human rights, fundamental freedoms, and civil liberties without distinction. We must stand up for dignity and justice for all. Africa must rise from the darkness of repression and walk forthrightly to the bright sunshine of human rights." – Thulani Maseko

I wish to begin this tribute by expressing my heartfelt condolences to Mr Maseko's dear wife Tanele, their children, the extended family, friends, and relatives. I know there are no words to take away the pain and anguish caused by this senseless murder, but I want to assure Mr Maseko's family that we feel their pain. Their pain is ours too. I pray for their strength and wisdom in this difficult time and ask them to accept that which they can't change. I pray that Mr Maseko's soul rests in eternal peace and that the blood he shed will nourish the seeds of a truly democratic dispensation in Swaziland.

I am certain that history will ensure, in the fullness of time, that his death was not in vain. I am also certain that history will absolve this unflinching torch bearer of democracy in Swaziland, Africa, and the Globe.

Mr Thulani Maseko, was brutally murdered by forces of darkness and repression on January 21, 2023, perhaps falsely believing he was plotting or campaigning to overthrow the monarchy, which was never his intention.

In 2014 in his statement from the dock, Mr Maseko was crystal clear that the struggle for democracy in Swaziland was not about the overthrow of the monarchy. He emphasised that the demand was for a system of government where democratic governance can co-exist with the monarchy whose powers would be limited by law, so that nobody is above the law, but the law is the ruler.

Thulani Maseko was a human rights lawyer. As a lawyer he had on many occasions tried to use law to open and expand democratic space in Swaziland, so that the country can transition to a society that truly embraces political pluralism and democracy. Mr Maseko conceptualised law as the locus of political contestation. He was critical of the use of law as an instrument of oppression. He litigated before the courts in Swaziland to vindicate his constitutional rights and those of his clients. He understood the value of strategic litigation, which includes, educating the public and engaging in a dignified and informed debate with the judges on matters of human rights. He also appreciated that even a losing case may have far reaching educative value. Mr Maseko understood that the symbol of justice is best seen as a "turbulent cascading river". He believed that the essential precondition of the effectiveness of the law is that it must be legitimate and fair and not prone to manipulation.

Mr Thulani Maseko was born on the 1st of March 1970, in KaLuhleko in Bhunya, in the Manzini region of the Kingdom of Swaziland. He was the scion of Mr Sam Mbanana Maseko and Mrs Beauty Vilakati. He was the last of the eight children. His father worked for a while in Plantations under the section which was referred to as A3; and his mother was a housewife.

Mr Maseko obtained his Bachelor of Laws Degree from the University of Swaziland; and his master's in law from the University of Pretoria (specialising in human rights and democratisation in Africa); and through the Hubert H. Humphrey Fellowship Programme, he studied Law and Human Rights at the American University, Washington College of Law, USA. Mr Maseko was a decorated human rights champion. In 2011 the

University of Pretoria awarded him the Vera Chirwa Award for the pursuit of human rights and democratisation in Africa, especially in Swaziland. Mr Maseko has written several articles on the rule of law and human rights in several academic journals. At the time of his death, he was a registered doctoral student at the University of Pretoria.

Mr Maseko was a renowned champion of human rights, democracy, and the rule of law in Swaziland and globally. At the time of his brutal murder, he was the Chairperson of Multi- Stakeholders Forum - a convergence of civil society organisations, business, trade unions, political parties. The objective of this Forum was to collectively campaign for a democratic order in Swaziland. Mr Maseko believed in an organised, active, and informed civil society. He understood that even a progressive constitution could be a toothless tiger – a mere piece of paper if its promises are not implemented – and there is no active civil society to enforce accountability.

In 2014 Mr Maseko and his colleague Mr Bheki Makhubu, editor of the Nation Magazine were convicted of contempt of court for comments that they made in two articles that were published in the Magazine, in which they raised concerns about the country's judicial system, including the lack of judicial independence and impartiality. Mr Maseko regarded himself as a prisoner of conscience and his prison numbers were: 353, 438 and 579/2014. Following his arrest, I was part of the fact-finding mission set up by the international commission of jurists (ICJ) to gather facts about circumstances leading to his arrest. It was during this assignment that I learnt more about Thulani as an untiring champion of human rights. Our fact-finding mission revealed that Thulani and his colleague Mr Bheki Makhubu were needlessly incarcerated at the instance of a judicial officer who had mistook himself as some demi-God immune to criticism. This judicial officer was a very quisquous character.

Let's put the issue of contempt of court in sharp perspective. Judges are not above criticism. We are not sacred cows. How can servants of the constitution be above genuine criticism? The criticism against the judiciary and judges can be sharp and robust - and if it is genuinely held, even though misinformed should not be punishable. It would be a dark day if the judiciary or judges in a constitutional democracy use the offence of "contempt of court" to muzzle criticism.

After his release we would communicate now and then about what needs to be done to deepen the independence of the judiciary in Africa. I shared the piece I wrote on the independence of the judiciary in Africa published in the University of South Illinois Law Journal in the United States of America (USA). This thought piece was to act as a basis of occasional animated debate on the subject of the independence of the judiciary. During our debates, it became very clear to me that the issue of the independence of the judiciary was very close to his heart. He held the view that politicians should not dominate bodies that are constitutionally charged with the responsibility to appoint judges and that only a transparent and merit-based system can deliver a judiciary that is trusted by the people. We both agreed that an independent judiciary; that was not beholden to vested interests was the bedrock of a constitutional democracy. Regarding the independence of the judiciary, we both noted a trend where, on some occasions, the judges, chief justices would undermine the independence of the judiciary by giving lip service to the oath of office -or simply lacking courage to resist influence or direction by the executive. The issue of judges undermining the judiciary was a sore point to Mr Maseko.

We both bemoaned the jurisprudence of deficiency that is manifest in some of our law reports that often gave restrictive interpretation to the bill of rights provisions instead of embracing a generous and expansive interpretation that is required when interpreting a constitution.

We met again in Johannesburg at an event organised by the ICJ to celebrate his release in 2015 and we spent time discussing the role of the law in a democratic society. Thulani believed that the ultimate objective of law was the welfare of society but cautioned against excessive belief in the law as a panacea of all ills. He was of the view that in the hands of men and women of goodwill the law can be a force for good, but in the hands of bad people it can be an instrument of oppression and subjugation. We agreed with Justice Cameron, formerly of the constitutional court of South Africa who once stated that: "the law, when used properly, even in times of great injustice, can produce outcomes that are just."

Thulani believed that good laws produce good governments and that bad laws are the worst form of tyranny. He readily acknowledged that law is not written in stone; that it is dynamic and always evolving as it seeks to answer complex societal problems. He was ever ready to explore and interrogate the thinking behind the thinking that resulted in a particular law, or in a particular judgement.

Maseko was a proponent of the rule of law, along the lines of Greek philosophers who influenced many of his writings on the rule of law. Early Greek philosophers, Aristotle, Plato and Dicey wrote of the supremacy of the law as the central pillar of a truly democratic society and posited that men should not be governed by men but by law; that everyone is equal before the law; including those that made the law and those in power.

Maseko did not believe in the existence of just any law, but good laws – which is what constitutionalism is about. He believed that the authority of government should be derived from the people who choose their leaders in periodic free and fair elections. These values were dear to Mr Maseko's heart and many times he indicated to me and many of his friends that he was ready to die for these ideals, if need be.

Sadly, notwithstanding his efforts and indeed of many other human rights advocates, the rule of law in some countries in our region is in the intensive care unit. The march to a fully-fledged democracy has been slow. Human rights in our region are not fully embraced. The rule of law is perpetually under threat. The threat to the rule of law may be due to many factors, including greed – greed for power, possessions, and fame. The most loyal disciples of greed are found amongst the most powerful – the political elites – and to them greed and denial of rights and equal citizenry appears never ending. In the process the political elites easily become the enemies of the rule of law.

In one of our exchanges in 2020, after he wrote a piece on me in the Swazi Nation, entitled: " Can a judge of virtue, called to "priesthood" Rise in our Judiciary", we started debating threats to the rule of law generally. He had so many fascinating insights, which I summarise below. According to Mr Maseko one of the threats to the rule of law comes from law making itself. He argued that those whose responsibility it is to make laws must make laws that are good for the people. Often this is not the case as laws are made to serve self-interest. These include laws that are made to confer absolute power on certain persons without responsibility or accountability; laws that entrench government power on those not elected by the people; laws that do not sufficiently protect human rights and independent institutions.

Put simply, Mr Maseko believed that the good of the people is the chief law.

He pointed out that good laws are important, but the problem arises where those laws are not implemented, or are by design or ignorance, not applied. Of concern, may also be the rigid, mechanical application of law without regard to intrinsic values of human rights.

Mr Maseko was a highly principled and fearless human rights crusader, who, during his life journey, adopted a disposition which is biassed in favour of the less fortunate in society, the wretched of the earth as Frantz Fanon posited. It seems to me to be true as Fanon once argued that : "each generation must discover its mission, fulfil it or betray it…". History will record that Mr Maseko was one of the foremost human rights champions of his generation. The oppressive status quo feared his brilliance and courage. Being the cowards they are, instead of debating with him, they decided to kill him. Mr Maseko chose not to betray the mission of his generation, for he understood that in the struggle against injustice indifference amounts to acquiescence.

Mr Maseko did not appear from nowhere. He was a product of the circumstances he lived in. He did not grow under self-selected circumstances. He grew under circumstances existing at the time, which circumstances shaped who he was. I am of the considered view that every historical epoch in oppressive societies produces leaders whose historical mission is to end the injustice of the time. Many of these leaders are often killed by the oppressive status quo or imprisoned. The South African struggle produced Steve Biko and Nelson Mandela, among many other heroes and heroines, and the Swaziland situation produced Thulani Maseko.

Swaziland, Africa, and the world has lost a human rights champion whose kind we may never see again. On principle he did not waiver. It is the class character of lawyers (a privileged layer of the middle class) to equivocate and collaborate with the oppressors. Not so with Mr Maseko.

It has been an interesting discovery for me that some of the Biblical verses resonate so much with the work that Mr Maseko was doing. Somewhere in the book of Luke it is reported that Jesus spoke about preaching the gospel to the poor, about healing the broken hearted and proclaiming liberty to the captives. In Swaziland Mr Maseko did not pursue objectives dissimilar to the above. He sought through peaceful means to end both political and economic oppression. As my revered brother Masuku J eloquently pointed out in his touching tribute to our departed brother, Mr Maseko believed in negotiations. He was a man of peace. Like Sir Winston Churchill, the wartime British leader he believed, "jaw-jaw is better than war-war."

I also came to know Thulani as a committed family man. His love for his wife and children was plain and deep. He was also committed to his friends, and he had time for all those he loved. His friendship ran across many divides, politics, age, and social standing. As a person he was humble to a fault. He was one of those rare combinations – a confluence of humility, humanity, and brilliance. His modesty was disarming – a rare attribute of a member of the legal profession. Mr Maseko was a kind man of uncommon compassion and goodness of heart. He was also an unflinching idealist.

As I draw to the end, I wish with respect and humility to plead with our SADC and African Union leaders to join civil society in condemning the brutal murder of Mr Maseko and then making sure that the perpetrators are found and punished. We need an independent judicial inquest into the murder of Maseko. Civil society must be involved in every stage of setting up the judicial enquiry, including the terms of reference.

Thulani my friend let me conclude by addressing you directly. You were a cut above the rest. My soul is restless. It will never know peace until there is justice for your family and the broader human rights community. All is not well, but I can assure you that history will absolve you and one day the Swaziland of your dreams will be achieved through lawful means. History will avenge your death! I have accepted you are no more. I was lucky to know you and call you, my friend. I will miss you sorely. I can assure you though, that we, your friends in the legal fraternity, (I have talked to many in Africa and in the diaspora) who are committed to the rule of law and constitutionalism and inspired by your thoughts and deeds will never dishonour the cause of freedom. Fare well champion of champions!

PART 2

Published Articles

Chapter 16

Constitutional-Building and Safeguarding The Integrity of Elections In Afrcia

South African Journal of International Studies Volume 30, 2023, Issue 3

Introduction

The main preoccupation of this article is to explore the nexus between constitution-building and electoral integrity in either abetting or forestalling democratic recession in Africa. It acknowledges the impact of democratic recession in many African countries, most of which have had to overcome layers of racial discrimination and colonialism. The article further highlights the importance of constitution-building and the pivotal role it plays in safeguarding electoral integrity and its potential to contribute to the reversal of democratic recession, thereby revitalising democracy on the African continent.

Following this introduction, the article is divided into three sections. The first section, immediately below, introduces the concepts of electoral integrity and democracy, the importance of constitutional protection of electoral rights, constitution-building and best practices. The second section provides the barometer of free and fair elections. It discusses the importance of an electoral justice system in African countries and highlights key areas and elements for strengthening electoral integrity through constitutional reforms. The last section closes the discussion by highlighting key observations.

Electoral Integrity and Democracy

Electoral integrity refers to the 'agreed upon international conventions and universal standards about elections reflecting global norms applying to all countries worldwide throughout the electoral cycle, including during the pre-electoral period, the campaign, on polling day, and its aftermath. It is an important element of democratic procedures.

Democracy as a concept and/or idea denotes a state that is led by its people, with their will and desires manifested through free and fair elections. Undoubtedly, democracy has evolved through ages and centuries taking many shapes and forms. At one point the concept was used by authoritarians to gain legitimacy and at another point it was used to overrule the very same authoritarians. Further, the idea of democracy is context-specific given that it differs from one society to another and from one generation to the next. One cannot succeed at an attempt to pin down a universal definition of the term. Nonetheless, in modern times there are universally accepted tenets that make up democracy. In their simplest form these include, inter alia, citizen participation, holding free and fair elections, respect for fundamental freedoms, the rule of law and political tolerance.

Conversely, the notion of democracy can also be explicated by what it is not. There is often confusion in both policy and academic discourses whereby elections tend to be equated with democracy and vice-versa. That is not correct. Elections, though a key component of democracy, are not, in themselves, tantamount to democracy. Aptly put, 'democracy, it is true, cannot be judged solely by looking at the ability of citizens to vote at elections and exercise their civil and political rights'. For a society to be democratic, the electoral process, itself, must be free and fair, the citizens must have access to accurate political, economic, and social information, and the rule of law must always be respected.

For decades, countries have been applauded for holding regular elections and that has, for many, been equated to democracy. This has come at a cost as sight was lost on what democracy is and has led to systematic relapse in democracy birthing a crisis now widely known as democratic recession. In particular, over the yester decade democratic recession has become prevalent at an alarming rate. According to Khabele Matlosa, the key contributors to democratic recession can be classified as 'structural' and 'super structural. These include the high levels of capitalism and globalisation during the 1997/1998, 2007/2008 financial crises, underdevelopment, poverty, unemployment, and inequality. There is a prevalence of populism, war, unconstitutional change of government and mismanagement of diversity. These factors combined have contributed to the decreasing confidence in elections which is evidenced by lower voter turnout rates and increasing trends of public mistrust in governance institutions.

The root causes of democratic recession have been aptly canvassed by other scholars. Therefore, these should not detain us for purposes of this article. This article, however, acknowledges the impact of democratic recession in many African countries. The article highlights the importance of constitution-building and the pivotal role it plays in safeguarding electoral integrity and its potential to contribute to the reversal of democratic recession, thereby revitalising democracy.

Importance of constitutional protection of electoral rights

The level of protection and enforceability of electoral rights is highly dependent on where and how they are provided for. Electoral rights may be protected in the constitution, primary and secondary legislation, and codes of conduct. This article argues that constitutional protection of electoral rights is the highest form of legal protection. Nevertheless, complementary legislation (primary and subsidiary legislation) and codes of conduct still play an important role in enhancing electoral integrity. The effective protection of electoral rights is not only dependent on their inclusion in the constitution but also on the commitment of the government, political parties, civil society, and citizens to uphold and implement them. This commitment, by various stakeholders, is what distinguishes a constitution from constitutionalism. In recognition of this intricate nexus, some scholars have observed a trend of constitutions without constitutionalism in several African countries.

A constitution is commonly defined as a: document, written, or unwritten, which governs and allocates power, functions and duties amongst different agencies within the state and between the governed and government. The main purpose of a constitution is to limit the use of government power in a manner that will prevent the twin dangers of anarchy and authoritarianism.

Constitutions can come in many forms. The classic distinction that is commonly made is between majoritarian and consociationalism constitutions. Majoritarian constitutions involve institutions such as a winner-take all electoral system, a single legislature, and an executive with more power than the legislature and thus more likely to bring single-party government. Consociationalism constitutions involve institutions such as a proportional voting system, a federal and decentralised state, and a bicameral legislature; such systems are thus more likely to bring about power-sharing situations.

Constitutionalism is a much broader and complex concept in both form and content than that of 'constitution'. As with the idea of a constitution, the concept of constitutionalism denotes limited government. But it also entails protection of citizens against arbitrary rule. It is about the existence of clearly defined mechanisms for ensuring that the limitations on state power are legally enforceable. The core elements of constitutionalism include the recognition and protection of fundamental rights and freedoms, the separation of powers, an independent judiciary, the review of the constitutionality of laws, the control of the amendment of the constitution, and institutions supporting constitutional democracy and accountability.

Generally, the main functions of a constitution are to establish a state or nation, create a government framework with the necessary powers and institutions to manage public affairs, limit the powers of the government for the protection of individual rights and freedoms and declare and reflect the ideals of the nation and the responsibilities of the state towards its subjects. Constitutional protection of electoral rights outweighs the safeguards in primary or secondary legislation and even codes of conduct. The constitution holds the highest legal authority in the legal system; thus, all other laws must conform to the provisions of the constitution. This ensures that electoral rights are protected even when there are conflicting laws or codes of conduct. The procedure for amending constitutions is more difficult than that for primary and secondary legislation and codes of conduct.

The role of constitution-building in safeguarding electoral integrity

Constitution-building refers to the process of negotiating, drafting, and implementing constitutions. It is a long-term process that is constantly ongoing and includes 'establishing institutions, procedures and rules for constitution making or drafting, giving legal effect to the constitution, and implementation.' Indeed, this process requires judicial creativity and innovation, as may be necessary, in the judicial system through the courts and public discussions. It requires jurisprudential analysis of the constitutional provisions to give effect to the rights contained therein by the judicial officers who are tasked with ensuring adherence to the constitution. In most African countries the constitution is often referred to as a means of last resort and not a point of contact. This has led to a situation where the constitution remains untested for a long time.

Previously, the process of establishing and later reviewing and revising a constitution did not involve members of the public and was only led by experts.16 However, in recent years public participation in the process has increased and is now recognised as a basic democratic right, affirmed by the United Nations Human Rights Council through Article 25 of the International Covenant on Civil and Political Rights. Mechanisms that have been identified as employable in this pursuit include civic education, public consultations, citizen participation via lobby and advocacy by civil society including minority groups, expert groups and referenda. Most African countries do not adequately provide for citizen participation in constitution-building processes. For instance, the 2005 constitutional amendment in Eswatini was not considered inclusive of citizen participation and was therefore widely rejected. This led to skirmishes between the security forces and the labour and political activists who objected to the Tinkhundla (individual merit) electoral system prohibiting political parties from contesting elections. In 2007, a series of attacks on public buildings involving petrol bombs occurred in some parts of the country, leading to arrests and treason charges against members of the People's United Democratic Movement (PUDEMO).17 PUDEMO is the largest opposition party in Eswatini.

Constitutional amendments should not be avoided or delayed as countries continue to pursue democratic goals, particularly with regard to electoral laws. One of the best practices is presented by the Kenyan Constitution which welcomes initiatives for its amendment by extra parliamentary means. While these provisions safeguard constitutional electoral democracy, there remains the risk of well-organised political interests and groups taking over the process in a way that may put constitutional stability and overall institutional development in jeopardy. The case of Kenya sheds light on the risks involved in advancing popular amendment initiatives. If not well monitored, politicians can easily take advantage of these amendment provisions which would have adverse implications on governmental bodies and on democratic development and stability of the country at large.

International IDEA suggests a two-step process of constitution-building that: (i) uses an interim or transitional constitutional plan, specifically addressing stability and concluding the peace process; and (ii) allows final constitutions to emerge with a stronger focus on a long-term vision of institutional design. Furthermore, IDEA proposes that the process should identify whether constitutional solutions that may succeed in preventing or stopping violence also effectively address other constitutional issues, such as corruption, accountable government, and the mass abuse of human rights.

Constitution-building must be designed to safeguard electoral integrity by regulating private funding of political parties and ensuring a level playing field in electoral contests. Where political funding is not regulated it can be a means to destroy a fair electoral process and it may jeopardise the ethical integrity of the leaders in government. Political party funding that is fair and transparent guarantees equal access by political parties and candidates to state or public media, and can help in levelling the electoral playing field. All these requirements are often lacking in African democracies – in part because of democratic recession. In addition, constitutions must provide for the regulation (including public disclosure) of private funding of political parties and candidates to avoid state capture and financing by criminal networks and terrorists.

Constitution-building must further be utilised to secure the independence of the judiciary, which is key for the electoral processes, complementing the role of electoral management bodies (EMBs). Judicial independence refers to the capacity of the courts to perform their constitutional functions free from actual or apparent interference by – and to the extent that it is constitutionally possible, free from actual or apparent dependence upon – any persons or institutions including the executive arm of government.

Judiciaries in most African countries also rely on the executive to provide them with the equipment, tools, and enforcement mechanisms of their orders. This has subjected the quality of work of the judiciary to the executive, thereby limiting their independence, especially when there are crucial election petitions involving the ruling elite. Indeed, some unexpected breakthroughs have occurred, such as the 2019 Supreme Court decision in Malawi, nullifying an earlier election that was marred by widespread electoral malpractices. This was the first time in Africa where an election petition that was successful resulted in the re-run of a flawed election leading to the defeat of an incumbent president. By and large, many countries in Africa still face problems of political polarisation, institutional dysfunction, and threats to civil liberties.

Constitution-building must ensure the independence of the media for credible free, and fair election reporting. Despite playing a critical role in the dissemination of information before, during and after elections, the media is often left unprotected with no safeguards on their security and independence. There is increased persecution of journalists and reporters that has limited the ability of the media to provide accurate information to citizens and consequently the public remains largely uninformed about key electoral processes. The constitution must outline safeguards to protect the media and make it a matter of national interest and security when there arise any threats to the media reporting on elections and electoral processes.

It is important to highlight that constitution-building must be conscious of providing independent enforcement mechanisms and not restrict constitutions to substantive provisions only. It is one thing to have a right and another to have the enforcement of that right. Similarly, it is one thing to have the desired independence of EMBs and autonomy of the judiciary, and to declare media freedom, but it is another thing to enforce these principles. This, therefore, requires constitutions to provide for effective and efficient mechanisms that stakeholders can use to assert their autonomy.

Free and fair elections in the context of Africa

One key pillar of sound constitution-building is the electoral justice system (EJS). This is an essential instrument that protects the rule of law and guarantees compliance with the democratic principle of free and fair elections. The EJS in African countries has become important as a foundation of democracy and a catalyst for change, as a mechanism for measuring a country's political stability and a government's legitimacy, as well as for garnering domestic and international support. The main objective of an EJS is to prevent and identify irregularities in elections and to provide the means and mechanisms to correct those irregularities and punish the wrongdoers.

On 26 March 1994, the Inter-Parliamentary Council adopted the Declaration on the Criteria for Free and Fair Elections during its 154th session held in Paris, France. Building on the 1948 Universal Declaration for Human Rights and the 1966 International Covenant on Civil and Political Rights, this declaration stipulated that the authority of government draws from the will of the people as expressed in genuine, free and fair elections held at regular intervals on the basis of universal, equal and secret suffrage. The declaration covers a wide gamut of various aspects that contribute to electoral integrity including (a) voting and elections rights, (b) candidacy, party and campaign rights and responsibilities, and (c) rights and responsibilities of states.

The notion of 'free and fair elections' became popular following the above declaration, especially in the 1990s. For instance, in 1997, Jorgen Elklit and Palle Svensson penned an interesting article that proposed a checklist for assessing the 'freeness and fairness' of elections.24 This article proposed a comprehensive barometer covering the entire electoral cycle (pre-polling, polling day and post-polling stages). Despite the criticism that the notion of free and fair elections received later on, such as the one advanced by Chigudu, this article adopts its overall framework as the standard to adjudge Africa's performance in respect of safeguarding electoral integrity. It cannot be overemphasised that there needs to be infrastructure proposed to drive independent electoral administration with a mandate to preserve its professionalism, resources, and credibility. It is also important to protect stakeholders such as independent media, their ability to function without hindrance or fear of government intervention and other private players who may want to silence the media.

Both the Declaration on Criteria for Free and Fair Elections and the scholarly works by Elklit and Svensson are unanimous that every adult citizen must be afforded the right to vote on a non-discriminatory basis; that there is an effective, impartial, and non-discriminatory procedure for the registration of voters; and that every candidate must have the right to move freely within the country to campaign for election and to campaign on an equal basis with other political parties, including the party forming the existing government.

Strengthening electoral integrity: Key areas and elements for constitutional reforms

To safeguard electoral integrity and mitigate the impact of democratic recession, constitutions must provide for an independent electoral process, independent judiciary, independent media function and respect for the rule of law and the mechanisms of enforcement. Most of the elements required for strengthening electoral integrity are drawn from those of a democratic constitution.29

Establishment of independent electoral management bodies (EMBs)

EMBs must be seen to be effective and illustrate the highest level of 'independence and impartiality to promote justice, transparency, accessibility, inclusiveness and equality.' There must be no threat or allegations discrediting the system, causing voters to second guess their participation in the electoral system or, worse, to reject the outcome of an election. It is therefore important that the system is effective and offers timely electoral justice to maintain its credibility and confidence among the people.

Constitutions should establish independent and impartial EMBs with the authority to conduct free and fair electoral processes. Constitutions should provide for the composition of EMB members, procedures for their appointment to office and removal from office, the administrative and financial independence of the EMBs and the functions of the EMBs. Constitutions granting the EMB statutory de jure independence create even greater de facto independence.

Problematically, in many African countries, chairpersons and secretaries of EMBs and other top officials are appointed by the government and at times by the head of state, who naturally has an interest in the outcome of the work and functions of the EMB. The appointing authority ordinarily also has the power to remove EMB officials from office. This, therefore, places the officials under the scrutiny of the governing power and puts them in a compromised position where they may have to meet the demands of the governing power for fear of their job security. Constitution-building must ensure that the appointment is by independent bodies that have no interest in the outcome of the election, and the appointment process must be transparent.

Another problem for African EMBs is a lack of sufficient resources. Most African countries fail to meet the criteria set for free and fair elections by failing to provide for independent and sufficiently resourced EMBs. Funding is important in the conduct of elections, and it should be adequately provided to allow EMBs to engage in citizen education campaigns to keep the public informed of their electoral rights, and to ensure that there is proper registration of voters, one of the basic tenets for free and fair elections.

Inadequately resourced EMBs are prone to reliance on funding by the government, a situation that allows the government to have an undue influence on the running of EMBs, with possible adverse effects on electoral integrity. In instances where governments have unfettered discretion over the funding of EMBs, opportunities for real or perceived election rigging abound.

Recognition and protection of electoral rights and interrelated rights

Constitutions should explicitly guarantee the protection of electoral rights and interrelated rights according to the appropriate and justifiable limitations required of a democratic nation.

Constitutions should guarantee the right to vote to all eligible persons. There should be provisions to ensure regular democratic elections, term limits and presidential powers to enhance democratic competition. Regrettably, Africa has recorded a decline in free and fair elections as most countries fail to meet the minimum criteria set for free and fair elections. In some countries, elections are not held at regular intervals and in fact some countries have not held a single election. For example, the State of Eritrea has not held a single election, notwithstanding that it attained its independence in 1993 and has since then been a member of the United Nations. Presidents who have attempted to extend their stay in office are often successful; since 1990, 80% of presidents who have attempted to bypass the limitations in their constitutions with regards to their tenure have done so successfully.

Most countries in Africa adopted their constitutions after gaining independence from colonial rule. This process was largely controlled by the colonial governments and they in some cases implemented their own constitutions into their former colonies. As a result not only did that erode the cultural concept of democracy, but it also provided African countries with constitutions that are devoid of their African values and principles and were in many ways in conflict with their traditional approaches of organising their societies. In consequence, these constitutions failed to find genuine legitimacy among the Africans.

Further, a notable feature of African countries' constitutions is that they were reactionary. Most African constitutions adopted their constitutions following the decolonisation, liberation and independence struggles. Some constitutions were adopted after attainment of freedom from apartheid and racial discrimination. As a result, these constitutions were heavily influenced by the need to deal with social injustices and in the process failed to make adequate provisions for transparent governance, democratic rule, and respect for the rule of law. In some instances, the constitution has no provisions on the socio-economic-political factors that affect democracy and electoral integrity.

This inadequacy in Africa's constitutions has provided loopholes for manipulation by leaders who wished to extend their presidential terms and alter the election process in contravention of the 2007 African Charter on Democracy, Elections and Governance. In response to this scourge of power grabs by incumbents, in 2022, the African Union (AU) adopted the Declaration on Unconstitutional Changes of Government in Africa. The declaration emphasises the AU's zero-tolerance for the overthrow of constitutionally elected governments, including manipulation of constitutions by incumbents and all other forms of unconstitutional changes of government. Further, it underscores that countries must respect their respective constitutions, especially adherence to presidential term limits; respect for the outcomes of elections; the creation of governance structures that allow smooth transition processes; and inclusivity in national engagements to address lack of fidelity to transitional justice in the community.

Governance systems that do not have any presidential term limits go against democratic ideals for two main reasons. The first reason is that by virtue of their being in office, presidents typically enjoy great advantages as compared to their challengers. They control the implementation of budgets and laws, and they have the power to manipulate them to meet their own political agendas. Because of weak legislative frameworks, there is limited accountability, which perpetuates these advantages and basically renders presidents invincible. Many African states are faced with this challenge, and this explains why it is of utmost importance for constitutions to provide term limits in support of ongoing consolidation of competitive electoral democracy on the continent.

The second reason is that, in the absence of term limits, power is vested in the hands of one individual or a small group of people for an extended period of time, and yet it is known that the essence of democracy is the division and also the limitation of power through constitutional checks and balances. The longer a person is in power, the more likely interest groups are to stop investing in institutions and rather focus on the individual that holds power, which ultimately leads to 'institutional decay'. Limiting terms is therefore important in ensuring that power does not sit in the hands of one or a few individuals for an unreasonably long time, which, in turn, will encourage investment in governance institutions rather than individuals.

Constitutions should also protect all interrelated rights, including the freedom of expression, access to information on all electoral processes, freedom of the media, freedom of association and assembly for all eligible persons. Weak protection of these rights is problematic for electoral integrity in Africa. The problems faced during electoral processes in Africa relate to the broad restrictions to these rights that often hinder the free flow of information and participation in the making of electoral laws and in electoral processes.

Constitutions should provide guidelines on the application of international law and instruments on electoral rights and integrity in the country. International law and instruments encourage international election observation and regular and transparent electoral audits in democratic states. This can ensure the application of well-established best practices to enhance electoral integrity during law-making processes and even enforcement of laws.

Electoral laws and regulation

Although an electoral justice system does not alone absolutely guarantee that elections will be free, fair, and genuine, without it the reality is that conflicts would be worsened. If elections are held without a comprehensive and agreed upon legal framework that is aimed at enforcing democratic principles and values, the electoral process may well worsen frictions or even lead to outbreaks of war or revolts against the outcomes. The violence that erupted in Kenya after the 2007 elections proves the above assertion and it may well be attributed to the lack of a credible and impartial court which is focused on resolving electoral disputes.

Level the playing field for political parties

Africa has reported numerous instances of political harassment of election candidates by other candidates, especially the candidates of the ruling parties. This occurs through threats to the lives of opposition candidates, as well as economic harassment through the imposition of unreasonable tax and other money demands from candidates. In some instances, the violence has extended to voters. Studies show that parties have resorted to intimidation and violence directed at voters during electoral campaigns. Violence against voters has frequently been initiated by members of the ruling parties who utilise official security forces bound to obey their instructions. On another note, the African political landscape is largely influenced by social factors of ethnicity, tribalism, and social class. In this way, ethnic and tribal hatred often trigger political violence.

Constitutions should address the influence of money in the electoral process by establishing state funding for political parties and elections. Most opposition parties in Africa lack resources to push their political agenda and run their parties.48 Incorporating provisions that require transparency in the funding of political parties, in expenditure reporting, and in the announcement of election results can help maintain public trust in the electoral process.

Equality and non-discrimination

Inclusiveness is a core value of democratic governance and electoral integrity. Constitutions should guarantee maximum participation for all sectors of the population and minority groups in electoral processes. Minority groups include vulnerable and marginalised groups like women, persons with disabilities, youth, and ethnic, cultural and religious minorities.

Electoral dispute resolution

Electoral justice involves the means and mechanisms available in a specific state, local community or on a regional or international level for (a) ensuring that each action, process and decision related to the electoral process complies with the legal framework; (b) protecting or restoring electoral rights; and (c) giving people who believe their electoral rights have been violated the ability to file a dispute, have their case heard and receive a fair ruling.

The wider electoral justice system includes a variety of specific mechanisms to ensure credible electoral dispute resolution. This includes preventative measures as well as both formal and informal means of resolving electoral disputes. A strong view suggested by International IDEA is that an increasing respect for the rule of law will lead to a decrease in the number of electoral disputes that require resolution. Once a state has nurtured a culture that promotes lawful behaviour and civic respect for democratic norms, this will help to decrease the likelihood of electoral disputes. It is also important to involve the main political parties and key sectors of civil society when developing electoral legal frameworks in preventing the likelihood of disputes.

Allow for constitution-building and review of electoral laws

One of the ways to ensure the efficacy of an electoral justice system is to review it periodically and ensure that it fulfils its objectives of safeguarding electoral integrity predicated upon free, fair, credible and genuine elections conducted within the confines of the law. This may occur through constitution-building or amendment of electoral laws that are contrary to the constitution. The study of electoral justice systems has shown that there is no perfect or best system per se, and it is advisable to assess the strengths and weaknesses of different systems, identify ongoing trends and offer other elements of analysis, noting the successful experiences or practices that have led to the best outcomes.

Africa has done little by way of constitution-building that would entrench institutions that support democracy and ensure that the voice of the people as expressed at regular elections would not be subverted for narrow partisan ends. Most of the continent's constitutions remain deficient in aiding democratic consolidation even when the societies have drastically changed. The challenges to the constitution-building process in South Sudan is one case in point. A constitution-building process is a sovereign process that must not only promote inclusive participation from citizens, political parties, and civil society, but also requires an environment free from violence and intimidation. The environment in South Sudan in non-conducive for this process.

The South Sudanese are more divided in recent times than even before they attained self-rule in 2011. Barely three years following the declaration of its independence from Sudan, South Sudan was engulfed in a protracted and violent conflict that persists to date. To find a sustainable solution to this conflict, a diligent and transparent reconciliation process is a major imperative. Only thereafter can the state purport to undertake the process of constitution-building. Observers have opined that 'South Sudan might be rushing to adopt a permanent constitution, yet it has not addressed serious underlying contentious issues such as land' and that 'South Sudan should slow the constitution-building process and embrace processual solution.' It goes without saying then that the process can only be undertaken successfully in a harmonious environment that is conducive to negotiated outcomes and encourages inclusive national dialogue and exchange between the state and its people.

Conclusion

This article has proposed that constitution-building is key in safeguarding electoral integrity. By extension, constitution-making is one of the mechanisms to combating democratic recession and revitalising democracy. For this to happen, at the heart of constitution-building should rest the imperative to secure the independence of the EMB, provide for free and fair elections, and ensure judicial independence, media freedom and respect for the rule of law. This will rely upon inculcating a culture of constitutionalism overall. This paper has set a clear guide on the removal of undue influence by the executive on the electoral process and the judicial system to remove compromises that hinder free decision making.

The article has shown that free and fair elections are a key cornerstone for electoral integrity. Regular constitutional reforms have a huge potential to anchor the integrity of elections as free and fair. The article has also highlighted the significance of electoral justice systems. It has pointed out that although an electoral justice system does not, in and of itself, absolutely guarantee that elections will be free, fair, and genuine, its absence has a potential to worsen violent election-related conflicts. If elections are held without a comprehensive and agreed upon legal framework that is aimed at enforcing democratic principles and values, the electoral process may in fact exacerbate existing frictions or lead to revolts or even outbreaks of war against the outcomes of an election.

Chapter 17

The Role of The Courts In Stregnthening Electoral Justice In The Southern African Development Community(Sadc) Region

Source: Electoral Commission Forum of SADC- A Regional Policy Dialogue Compendium on Democracy & Elections in the SADC Region (2022)

Introduction

Regular elections constitute a key element of the democratization process and therefore, are essential ingredients for good governance, the rule of law, the maintenance and promotion of peace, security, stability and development. Thus far, the Southern Africa Development Community (SADC) region has made significant progress in institutionalising electoral democracy over the course of the past decades. This is reflected in a number of multiparty elections in most member states. Notwithstanding these achievements, however, major challenges remain. These include an increasing number of electoral challenges alleging that the elections were rigged and even suggestions that the courts entrusted with presiding over electoral disputes are not independent and impartial. This paper examines the role that the courts play in strengthening electoral justice in the SADC region.

The data for this paper was based on literature review that included applicable case law in the SADC region and interviewing lawyers and judges – many of whom were involved in the litigation – either representing parties to the litigation or presiding over the electoral disputes.

In Africa, electoral governance has been situated within a landscape of civil and political rights as guaranteed by international, regional and national law. The African Union (AU) member states have committed themselves to certain rights and obligations under which democratic elections are conducted, including the right to challenge the election results according to the law. Indeed, article 17(2) of the African Charter on Democracy, Elections and Governance (2007), obliges member states to establish and strengthen national mechanisms that redress election-related disputes in a timely manner.

It is generally accepted that the judiciary plays a pivotal role in ensuring free, fair and credible elections by upholding the rule of law, the right to vote, and equality before the law. It is often contended that electoral disputes lie at the intersection of law and politics, and once framed as legal disputes catapult the judiciary into the status of a political actor. Petitions against election results represent one of the most intriguing instances of the system of checks and balances between the three branches of government.

The judicial branch is simultaneously taking stock of the work of other branches of government, and all of this plays out against the backdrop fraught with political tension. Electoral disputes being essentially political in nature, the courts are often compelled to consider which approach may be appropriate between a restrained and a proactive approach, having regard to the nature the judiciary as a third arm of the state.

Azu suggests that the low success rate of elections petitions across the continent can be explained by judicial mindfulness of their positions as the "unelected minority arm of government and so it must tread cautiously on any path that would easily be construed as a usurpation of the right of the electorate to determine their political leadership through the ballot."

Constitutionalism, Democracy and Elections in Africa

A number of African states, especially in the SADC region, largely work with adopted and imported constitutional models. These independence constitutions were the outcome of an "agreement" between a colonial power and representatives of the colonised peoples. There was no broad participation in this model of constitution making.

Although most of these constitution's guarantee regular elections, they do not necessarily guarantee a level playing field – just elections.

Regular elections are a critical element of a democracy yet they are not on their own a guarantee of sustainable democracy. What is clear is that electoral governance in the immediate post-election period forms an integral part of consolidating democracy. Writing about 'garrison' elections in Nigeria, Omotola emphasizes that "The greatest threats to the consolidation of democracy in the aftermath of the garrisoned elections relate to the handling of post-election issues, especially election petitions, tribunals and court processes, by all stakeholders in the democratisation process."

Omotola further suggests that "The future of Nigerian democracy is clearly dependent on how well, and on how timely, post-election issues, particularly allegations and counter-allegations at the tribunals and courts, are handled. In handling these cases, it is important that the judiciary is independent, courageous, fearless, meticulous and objective."

Azu examined two decisions on presidential election petitions – one from Ghana and another from Kenya, in both cases the issue was whether the non-compliance was "substantial enough to have adversely impacted on the results." The body of electoral laws across the continent largely recognise that "things can go wrong with elections and provide for the possibility of redress. This is because election wrongs or allegations of wrongs often have a bearing on the legitimacy of the electoral process." Elections are complex systems designed and run by fallible human beings who commit errors and wrongs in the course of running the said elections. These wrongs can be redressed by a credible and transparent system.

Writing about credibility and transparency in election disputes, Hatchard opines that: Disputes as to whether a presidential or parliamentary election was "free and fair" can inevitably raise considerable

tensions with the losing candidates often alleging vote-rigging, corruption, bribery and other electoral malpractices by their opponents... It is therefore essential to have in place a credible and transparent system to address allegations of

electoral malpractice. Whilst electoral commissions often have general responsibility for the settlement of disputes prior to the election itself, the traditional approach in common law countries is for post-election challenges to be brought to the appropriate court by way of an election petition.

These election courts are generally empowered to examine the validity of the election such that they can even annul it, requiring a new one to be called. "There are broadly three grounds for annulling an election: first, a breach of electoral administration law, secondly, corrupt or illegal practice by the winning candidate, and thirdly, disqualification of the winning candidate." In this manner, the court can correct the outcome of the election by deciding which votes should lawfully be counted, and consequently who ought to have been returned as the winning candidate.

"A fair and transparent redress mechanism, which commands the respect of the people, lends legitimacy and credibility to the election and 'serves as a peaceful alternative to violent post-election responses. On the other hand, a failure to put in place an effective electoral dispute mechanism 'can seriously undermine the legitimacy of an entire electoral process'." This is relevant but also hanging.

The Jurisprudence of Election Petitions In Sadc Countries

The above contextual consideration lays a basis for a brief overview of the jurisprudence of electoral disputes in the SADC region through a discussion of case law from selected countries in the region. This section, on the main, examines selected cases on electoral disputes in Botswana, Malawi and Zimbabwe. The Malawi Presidential election petition is the only that succeeded, and the rest failed. However, reference is also made to other cases bearing on adjudication of electoral disputes in other jurisdictions in Africa to enrich the discussion.

When assessing a case, the courts examine whether electoral malpractice has occurred, either deliberately by a candidate and his/her campaign team, or by the electoral management body (EMB) overseeing the electoral process.

The position of the law is that the person who asserts must prove. The burden of proof in an election petition rests with the petitioner, to prove to the satisfaction of the court. The petitioner is required to prove, not only non-compliance with the electoral law but also how non-compliance affected the results of the elections.

This is an important backdrop to understand the case law discussed hereunder.

In Zimbabwe, the harmonised Presidential, Parliamentary and Local Government Elections were held on the 30th July 2018. The decision of the Independent Electoral Commission to declare President Mnangagwa duly elected President was challenged, unsuccessfully, in court, in the case of Chamisa v Mnangagwa and 24 Others 42/18 [2018] ZWCC 42 (24 August 2018). The court found that the applicant, Nelson Chamisa, had failed to place before the court, clear, sufficient, direct and credible evidence that the alleged irregularities marred the election process materially.

The nub of the applicant's petition was that the recorded number of votes had been doctored to hand President Mnangagwa victory.

However, the court dismissed the allegations as unsubstantiated, and concluded that it would be unnecessary in the circumstances to ask and answer the question whether irregularities materially affected the result of the election. The court also added that it is an internationally accepted principle of election disputes that an election is not set aside merely on the basis that an irregularity occurred. According to the court, there is a presumption of validity of an election. The court held that an election conducted substantially in accordance with the constitution cannot be nullified because it is not the business of the courts to decide elections; it is the people who do so. The court concluded that it is the duty of the courts to strive in the public interest to sustain the will of the people.

In 2019, Botswana held national elections that were marred by allegations of irregularity. In turn, several petitions were registered challenging the undue return of members of parliament, and the judges disagreed on the appropriate verdict.

In the case of Duma Gideon Boko v The Independent Electoral Commission and Others (MAHGB-000877-19) (Unreported) the majority of the judges dismissed the petitions on the basis that the petitions had been presented to the Registrar of the High Court, outside the requisite 30 days set by Section 117(b) of the Electoral Act, on the main, including that the petitions were not accompanied by a written notice of the presentation of the petition as envisaged by Section 118 of the Electoral Act. In a nutshell, the petition was decided on a procedural irregularity, and the complaint was not tried on the merits as pleaded by the petitioners.

On the merits, the petitioners averred, among other things, of instances of alleged corrupt and/or illegal practices. These included assertions that several companies were used to launder money to pay IEC Officials, that IEC officials issued more than one voter registration cards in order to circumvent the requirement of one man, one vote; that there were double registration of voters, that voters were paid money to register and vote more than once and that the election rolls were falsely manipulated to favour some candidates. Unfortunately, these allegations could not be tested in a trial as the petitions were dismissed on account of procedural technicalities.

The petitioners who were aggrieved by the decisions of the High Court that dismissed the petitions on technical procedural grounds appealed to the Court of Appeal without success, which in turn held, in the case of Duma Gideon Boko and Others v The Independent Electoral Commission and Others – Court of Appeal Case No: CACGB-002-20 (Unreported) that it had no jurisdiction in the matter. In other jurisdictions the court would not permit a petitioner to be driven from the judgment seat without considering his or her right to be heard, except in situations where the petition is frivolous or amounts to harassing the other party. Consequently, on the 29th January 2020 the court struck out the appeals of the fourteen unsuccessful National Assembly candidates as impermissible.

In a land mark judgment, in the case of Saulos Klaus Chilima and Lazarus McCarthy Chakwera v Arthur Peter Mutharika and Electoral Commission, a unanimous decision of the Constitutional Court of Malawi nullified the country's May 2019 elections and ordered that fresh elections be held within 150 days, citing widespread polling irregularities, that included the unlawful use of correction fluid on ballot papers. The court also found that only about a quarter of the results sheets were verified, and concluded that such conduct amounted to "serious malpractice that undermined the elections".

On appeal, the Supreme Court of Malawi, in the case of Professor Mutharika and Others v Chakwera MSCA

Constitutional Appeal no 1 of 2020 upheld the decision of the Constitutional Court, and consistent with the court order the elections were held, and President Mutharika was defeated. Both the decision and the implementation of the orders of the court must count as a triumph of democracy in a continent where quite often the might of the sword triumphs over that of the pen. As a result of that decision, Malawi became the first country in Africa that an election re-run led to the defeat of an incumbent. It would seem from a reading of the Supreme Court decision that the Electoral Commission (EC) appeared to have taken liberties on the requirement that it strictly follow procedures set by law in conducting elections.

The law required that result tally sheets, once compiled at a polling station, must mandatorily be signed by the returning officer and polling staff. The court found that the EC in tallying the national result, inter alia, used tally sheets that had not been so signed. When this result tally sheets leave a polling station they are supposed to be guarded against any form of tampering or interference. They are supposed to go to the District Commissioner's office for a compilation of a District result before being sent, under conditions of security, to the National Tally Centre. The EC ignored this and without following procedure created Constituency Tally Centres where massive alterations where made to the tally sheets that were not to be tampered with.

The court also found that some original tally sheets were inexplicably replaced with duplicate tally sheets with the originals not being kept for verification. Other Tally sheets had Tippex used to hide what was originally written on them and then over written with new figures. The court further found that in some instances improper tally sheets and reserve tally sheets where instead used but they were all the same accepted and used by the EC in compiling the national result. All this was not permissible under law and was being done in the absence of those that had witnessed the vote counting and without verification from the counted ballots which were then sealed and only to be opened at the National Tally Centre.

At the National Tally Centre before compilation of the national results the EC was supposed to resolve all outstanding disputes, but it left a huge number unattended. It also came to light that for those it claimed it had resolved, the EC had largely abandoned its quasi-judicial functions by delegating that task to the Chief Elections Officer and Staff. The EC then proceeded to announce the national result before fully complying with all the precondition that must precede that step. The EC even signed the national result after they had already declared it. The Constitutional Court found the violations grave and as a clear demonstration of the EC's incompetence. The Supreme Court agreed with these findings and conclusions. Malawi's 1994 Constitution as subsequently amended has resulted in an expansion of the democratic space generally, and also created courts that are by design more independent than those inherited at independence.

The new Constitution, on a proper reading, of both its spirit and provisions, has created a judiciary that is bound to be interventionist in character. In Malawi, it seems the guardians of the constitution are independent and fearless – bold spirits as Lord Denning would describe them.

The "substantial effect" test The general test is that for an election petition to succeed the petitioner must show by cogent and credible evidence that the irregularities complained of substantially affected the results of the elections. For many years in Africa, the dominant test to succeed in an election petition has been that the aggrieved party had to establish how the alleged irregularity affected the result of the elections. Failure to prove that the irregularity affected the result of the election is usually fatal. This test is often called the quantitative test. It was established in the old British case of Morgan v Simpson 1975 OB 151.

In the above case Morgan and others contested election results as invalid after 44 ballot papers were not counted because they were not stamped by election officers. Had they been included the rival would have won by 7 votes. The Divisional Court held that the elections were conducted substantially in terms of the law and the errors committed by election officials were not sufficient to nullify the results. On appeal, the Court of Appeal said the error affected the results of the elections and nullified them.

The quantitative test is used as a measure in determining the accuracy of the results and the numbers that the winner got relative what the petitioner obtained, is critical, and measured against how many votes the irregularities could have cost the petitioner.

The contending test to the quantitative test, hitherto not embraced by African judiciaries until recently, is the qualitative test. The qualitative test looks at the integrity of the electoral process. If for instance, the electoral process was afflicted by violence, intimidation, improper influence and corruption, at a scale that renders the election a sham, viewed objectively, such an election may be invalidated; even if the margin between the winner and the loser may be huge. The requirement that an electoral process must be transparent and administered in an impartial, neutral and efficient manner represents a qualitative aspect of elections. Qualitative requirements evaluate whether an election is conducted in an environment that is free, fair and credible.

In the case of Raila Odinga and another v Independent Electoral Boundaries Commission and others, No 2 of 20th September 2017, a majority of the court agreed with the petitioners that the respondents did not organize the elections in accordance with the law and nullified the same. They applied the qualitative test.

The quantitative test is often considered relevant and applicable where numbers and figures are in question whereas the qualitative test is most suitable where the quality of the entire electoral process is in serious doubt – or its credibility and the court has to determine whether or not the election was free and fair.

In the case of Malawi, both the quantitative and qualitative test was used. However, it appears that the qualitative test had an upper hand because the court found that the EC fundamentally departed from the dictates of the Constitution and Electoral Laws governing the conduct and management of election, and that there was no way any quantity could have been seen as being other than a result of massive irregularities that were committed. The qualitative test remains a contested terrain. Although the increasing adoption of the qualitative test by our courts is a progressive development, it can be a problematic approach given the absence or difficulty of objective measurement of the test.

The above notwithstanding most courts in the region still subscribe to the "the substantial effect test." Kaaba provides the following succinct explanation of the substantial effect test and how it operates: "when courts are faced with an election petition, there is, therefore, the need for a legal device or mechanism whereby they will determine which irregularities are minor and inconsequential, and which are significant and in need of redress. The substantial effect rule does this. In many Anglophone African countries, this is an old rule inherited from the English legal system. The gist of the rule is that elections should not be nullified for minor irregularities or infractions of rules." Kaaba attests that

The substantial effect rule has worked in the most disingenuous way in Africa to uphold elections fraught with major irregularities and fraud. As will be seen from the following case examples, election petitions that manage to survive being thrown out on technicalities are usually decided and dismissed for want of satisfying the substantial effect rule.

As established by the jurisprudence detailed in the preceding section, the general test adopted by the courts is that "a breach will not invalidate the election if (a) the election was run "substantially in accordance with" electoral law and (b) the breach did not affect the result. While this provision appears plain, it has proved very difficult to apply and interpret." Thus, as pointed out by Arori, to succeed the petitioner needs to demonstrate "in addition to the irregularities, that such irregularities had a substantial impact on the result of the election, so that the result does not reflect the will of the electorate."

Usually, the courts will accede that there were proven irregularities in various aspects of the elections but rarely will these suffice to nullify the results. This is particularly common in presidential election petitions. In a study of post-elec- tion petitions in Uganda, Murison noted that "the Supreme Court, which hears presidential election petitions, acknowledged voting irregularities, yet was unwilling to rule against the president". This is so because the court found, in effect, that despite the irregularities, the will of the people was correctly reflected.

The Intent of the Voter

Elections, particularly presidential elections, are key to the franchise of the public. As such the interests and intent of the voting public are justifiably held in high esteem by courts when hearing election petitions. In many cases the courts often cite "public interest" as holding the courts back from readily reversing the outcomes of an election. Generally, the courts are ever mindful that the election of a President and or other representatives is the preserve of the voting citizenry and the court should not rush to tamper with the results which reflect the expression of the population's electoral intent. Non-compliance will always be held up to the standard of whether the breach was such as to affect the will of the majority. As shown in Cox J in Fitch v Stephenson and Others EWHC 501 (QB): "the Courts will strive to preserve an election as being in accordance with the law, even where there have been significant breaches of official duties and election rules, provided the result of the election was unaffected by those breaches". Put differently, the court must on the one hand avoid upholding an illegitimate election result, and on the other, it must avoid annulling an election result that reflects the free will of the majority of the electorate.

The "Burden" of Proof

As stated earlier, it is incumbent upon the petitioner to prove the case. In most jurisdictions the standard of proof is ona balance of probabilities. It is a basic principle of the law of evidence that the petitioner is required to produce sufficient evidence to satisfy the court of the facts in issue, in order to succeed, short of which the claim may fail.

Judicial challenges to presidential election results are hardly ever successful. As noted by Azu, "In all the instances where presidential election petitions have been unsuccessful, although the petitioners alleged non-compliance with electoral laws and adduced evidence in support, the courts declined to invalidate the election results on the basis that the alleged irregularities were not substantial enough to affect the validity of the results. This, therefore, raises questions about the threshold of proof applicable in presidential election disputes and how it is discharged." The explanation for this is that, based on the evidence, the court may come to the conclusion that the irregularities that have been proved are not enough to upset the elections. Where this is the conclusion, the standard of proof would not have been discharged.

The Importance of Context

Azu asks a critical question: "So, is it the case that most presidential election disputes are unsuccessful because the petitioners generally fail to discharge the burden and standard of proof, or is it because the judgments are sometimes influenced by extra-legal considerations?" 22 There is one extra-judicial consideration that should not be overlooked – this is the political context within which the decision is made.

Hatchard emphasises that when analysing such decisions, it is imperative to place them against the background of the significant pressures inevitably placed on judges dealing with presidential petitions "especially for those serving in small, ethnically divided and/or politically volatile countries." Murison identifies at least three features that impact upon a judgement and therefore the extent of judicial independence or interference: "the 'context', in terms of which level of court the case is heard, and the political environment at the time of judgements; the 'case itself', particularly if the case is highly political or involves elections; and the 'nature of the judge who took the decision', i.e. their background, citizenship, and contract."

The courts deliberate upon these politically charged cases in the equally charged post-election period.

Unsuccessful Petitions Still Matter

Focusing on presidential election petitions in Uganda, Murison's points out that despite the petitions being unsuccessful they still cast doubts on the quality of the elections and the realities of politics in Uganda:

"The political implications for Uganda's security would have been immense had the Supreme Court ruled against the president. An examination of the parliamentary election petitions during the same period shows that the High Court did rule against NRM members. Although the presidential election petitions were unsuccessful, they did show publicly, both in Uganda and internationally, that the presidential elections had been biased and unfair, and that in itself did focus attention on how the political game was being played." In a similar vein, Kwarteng concludes a review of the judicial challenge of Ghana's 2012 elections by pointing out that the election and "the tension that it generated, have enhanced the democratic dispensation of that country, through the testing and trial of institutions, such as Ghana's Electoral Commission and the Supreme Court." Omotola also notes that the emerging trend of challenging electoral fraud through the courts – suggests a sign of the consolidation of democratic processes and the strengthening of rule of law:

Lessons From the Malawi Case

The lessons from Malawi are that elections are an important pillar of democracy, and an independent judiciary was crucial to protect the right to vote, at all costs. The other lesson is that Electoral Management Bodies must be independent and conduct the elections according to law. The Elections Management Bodies being creations of the law, must comply with the law fully, and not make the law in the process of conducting the elections.

It is also instructive to note that the re-run was conducted by the Malawi Electoral Commission (MEC) under a new Chair, who came with unassailable independence and impartiality credentials. He is also credited with having persuaded the government to release funds to allow elections to go ahead and make sure that there were no more questions about "Tippex" being used in the tallying process.

What then are the implications of the judgement on Election Observer Missions which pronounced elections free and fair?

In the case of Raila v Uhuru cited earlier, the court seemed to cast doubt on the adequacy of the scrutiny by election observers. The court stated that: "In passing only, we must also state that whereas the role of observers and their interim reports were heavily relied upon by the respondents as evidence that the electoral process was free and fair, the evidence before us points to the fact that hardly any of the observers interrogated the process beyond counting and tallying at the polling stations. The interim reports cannot therefore be used to authenticate the transmission and eventual declaration of results."

In all the election petitions registered in Botswana, Malawi and Zimbabwe, the independence of electoral commissions was impugned. In some cases, it was alleged that the independent electoral commissions either participated in fraud or tolerated it. This is a serious indictment that brings the credibility of Election Management Bodies into grave doubt. It is important that Election Management Bodies must not only be independent but must be seen to be so.

In the Namibian case of Charmaine Tjirare and Another v the Chairperson of the Electoral Commission of Namibia Case No: EC 2/2020, the court questioned the fact that in an election dispute the independent electoral commission was represented by the Attorney General who would have been appointed by the governing party and took the view that in order to be seen to be independent it is desirable that the IEC should have been independently represented so that the opposition feel that it is free in its actions, reactions and involvement in litigation.

Conclusion

The recent developments in Malawi surrounding the 2019 elections demonstrate why it is often said that the independence of the judiciary is an indispensable element of democracy and the rule of law. Coming about two years after a similarly ground breaking Supreme Court of Kenya decision, in 2017, there is reason to be optimistic about Africa's future in so far as electoral justice is concerned.

Murison suggests that the challenges concerning election petitions are not the weakness of the judiciary per se, but rather the shortcomings of the laws. The legislature has to enact laws to enable the judiciary's engagement and the enforcement of awarding punitive damages or punishments.

Contrary to the views of Murison above, three judges interviewed virtually in March 2021 by the author in Botswana, Kenya, Zimbabwe and Uganda emphasise judicial courage in electoral adjudication and independence of judges as important factors in electoral adjudication.

Chapter 18

Community Violence Against Suspected Witches: Sorcery Accusation-Related Violence In Papua New Guinea

Source: Journal of the Commonwealth Magistrates' and Judges' Association Vol 26 No 3 June 2023

Introduction

This article discusses the phenomenon of community violence against suspected witches.

The author will use Papua New Guinea ('PNG'), the country where the author sits as a judge, as the context for his discussion of the phenomenon.

The beliefs and practices of witchcraft are embedded in many societies, including the author's home country of Botswana. The author's home village, Bobonong, is alleged to have residents who are deft at practising witchcraft, although he has never been able to tell whether the accusation is factual or fictious.

Certain sections of Ghanaian society are known or believed to practice witchcraft too. Papua New Guinea is no exception.

Definitions

Witchcraft is difficult to define with precision. In their Introduction to Henrietta L Moore and Todd Sanders (eds), Magical Interpretations and Material Realities: Modernity, Witchcraft and the Occult in Postcolonial Africa (Routledge 2001), scholars Sally F. Moore and Todd Sanders define witchcraft as: ...a set of discourses on morality, sociality and humanity. Far from being a set of irrational beliefs, they are a form of historical consciousness, a sort of social diagnostic.

In Zambia, the Witchcraft Act defines witchcraft in the following terms: 'Witchcraft' includes the throwing of bones, the use of charms or any other means, process or device used in the practice of witchcraft or sorcery.

The repealed Sorcery Act in PNG provided that: ...'sorcery' includes (without limiting the generality of that expression) what is known, in various languages and parts of the country as witchcraft, magic, enchantment... whether or not connected with or related to the supernatural.

The meaning and purpose of witchcraft varies across different PNG regions. Most link it to a 'supernatural force' used by witches to cause harm to others. Some regions like Milne Bay focus on 'good witchcraft', which is said to include witches healing pregnant women by providing knowledge of essential herbs or giving protection to the community via sorcery.

However, it is usually the former type of witchcraft—witchcraft that is associated with sorcery accusation-related violence ('SARV')— that is of greatest concern. SARV is thus the focus of this article.

Things can often take a turn for the worse when there is an unexplained calamity like sudden death, illness, or misfortune. Community members may be quick to associate a strange event with the doings of a witch because, according to their belief system, only a witch can create unusual harm via magic. It follows that in such circumstances the community's most vulnerable individuals can be blamed for practising witchcraft and consequently tortured, i.e., they become victims of SARV.

Witchcraft in Papua New Guinea

Currently, data show that currently, 12 people are killed, and 14 people suffer serious harm, due to SARV each month in PNG. The number is likely to be materially higher because many cases are not reported.

To put the issues of moment in sharp perspective, it is important to sketch, albeit briefly and in broad strokes, the profile of the country I refer to throughout this article by the acronym, PNG.

PNG is a constitutional democracy, located in the Southwestern Pacific. It has one of the most progressive constitutions in the world. It is a country of immense cultural and biological diversity. PNG is a developing country grappling with socio-economic challenges of unemployment and poverty, like many other developing countries. In PNG, low levels of literacy are a critical challenge for the country's development. According to some reports in 2016, about 37 percent of the population was considered illiterate, with the majority living in rural areas.

PNG is a predominantly Christian country and very diverse. (Its population speaks more than 800 languages.) Overall, there is much respect for traditional beliefs and the spiritual realm is very much part of PNG society. It may seem to many quite paradoxical that a Christian country such as PNG would have deeply embedded beliefs in witchcraft.

Hans Werner attempted to answer this paradox, in the context of Ghana, in his book Witchcraft in Ghana: A Study on the Belief in Destructive Witches and its Effects on the Akan Tribes (Presbyterian Book Depot 1961). According to Werner, although the Christian faith teaches against fear of evil spirits and immortality (since Christ sacrificed himself to conquer evil),

'...the simple truth is that superstition and fear of evil spirits is as strong as ever today amongst Christians, literates and illiterates alike.'. The same may indeed be said of PNG

The Jacob Luke Incident: An Illustration The recent Jacob Luke incident provides a helpful illustration of the persistence of SARV in PNG society and the havoc it can wreak.

According to media reports, the body of a prominent and successful businessman and chief, Jacob Luke, was discovered by workers on 21 July 2022. Luke had been bushwalking in Enga Province. His death was wholly unexpected. He had appeared fit and well up to the time of his disappearance. Luke's tribe's people attributed the death to witchcraft.

The following day, members of Luke's tribe at Lakalom village accused a group of nine women of secretly removing Luke's heart and eating it—a practice called 'kaikai lewa'.

Out of fear, one of the women 'admitted' the allegation. Petrol was splashed over the nine women, and they were set alight. From among the nine, five were selected for further torture that involved hot irons being applied to their genital areas whilst they were suspended naked between poles. While this was occurring, the local village men, families and children— including their own family members and children—looked on. The women were tortured from the morning through to midnight.

News of the torture spread through the province, and six policemen accompanied by a priest, headed to the village to rescue the women. On their first attempt to investigate and offer protection to the victims they were sent away by a crowd of hundreds of angry villagers. A second attempt to rescue the women the next day failed. Eventually the rescue party was able to retrieve the women, but by then only five of the original nine were still alive, and they were in a fearful state, having lost copious amounts of blood and body tissue.

This is just a recent event, and possibly not the last.

Given space limitations, this article will address two themes relating to community violence against suspected witches. These themes are:

(1) that SARV is a violation of human rights;

and (2) that SARV is a gendered phenomenon.

Following that, I will discuss challenges raised by the problem of SARV and some possible solutions for it.

SARV is a Violation of Human Rights

As indicated earlier, Papua New Guinea is a constitutional democracy with a constitution more progressive than many that have been lauded as progressive. Fundamental human rights, such as the right to life, dignity, security of the person and liberty are entrenched. The National Court, the equivalent of the High Courts in many Commonwealth jurisdictions, has a Human Rights track dedicated to addressing litigation on human rights violations.

Yet there is still the clear sense that sorcery accusations are like 'passing a death sentence' against those so accused; the subjects of the accusations are often stripped of all semblances of human dignity and any real constitutional protection. As the Jacob Luke case demonstrates, suspects— mostly women—

suffer physical violence of the worst kind, emotional trauma and mental distress. Rescue operations often fail. The taking of life in this way represents an abhorrent violation of human rights.

The level of brutality perpetuated on women infringes international human rights laws.

When a SARV victim is murdered, there is a breach of their fundamental right to 'life, liberty and security' (Article 3, UN Declaration on Human Rights). The extremely humiliating and undignified treatments like 'beatings, banishments, cutting off body parts, stoning and amputation of limbs' contravene the right to be free from 'cruel, inhuman or degrading treatment or punishment' (Article7, International Covenant on Civil and Political Rights). Public humiliation and accompanying social isolation after sorcery accusation without physical abuse may also constitute mental torture.

Sometimes, witch persecution may involve numerous sexual offences. The daughters of women accused of sorcery may be subjected to sex trafficking.

The question remains: how can such violations occur in a constitutional democracy with entrenched rights and a diverse community that ostensibly is sensitive to human rights violations.

To repeat, at the international level, SARV directly offends against the right to life,

liberty, security of the person entrenched in the Universal Declaration of Human Rights and the robust international protections specifically provided for women, as reflected in the Convention on the Elimination of All Forms of Discrimination ('CEDAW'), and its Optional Protocol, both of which have been ratified by many countries in which SARV is nevertheless prevalent.

SARV is a Gendered Phenomenon It is important to note that SARV is highly gendered. The prevalence of SARV is relatively much higher amongst women. For example, Amnesty International identified that PNG women are six times more likely to be suspected of sorcery than men. Some subgroups like girls, older women, women with disabilities and women with albinism are especially at risk of being made the subjects of witchcraft accusations. A UN Independent Expert has noted that sorcery accusations might also be made against the mothers of people with albinism.

In other situations, villagers may assign a 'witch' status to a household and transfer the accusation from one female to another within it. This occurred in the gruesome case of a six-year-old girl who was kidnapped, stripped naked and brutally tortured by removing skin from her buttocks and back. The girl was singled out because her mother had previously been accused of sorcery and inevitably burntalive some years earlier.

Such gender-based violence is further highlighted in recently reported SARV cases which showcase women as the accused and groups of males as the accusers:

- In April 2022, two women were accused of sorcery after a child unexpectedly fell ill and died. A mob bound them with ropes and they were physically beaten and abused with hot iron rods.

- In October 2021, a person was bedridden with symptoms like COVID-19. He stated that he saw a woman 'doing something' with sugarcane sprouts (implying sorcery). The woman was later beaten to death with a piece of timber.

- In October 2020, a dog attacked a child who later died. Seventeen women were suspected of witchcraft and were taken to an isolated place and tortured. They have still not been found.

- In August 2020, three women were blamed for performing magic on a person who fell unconscious. A group of men tortured the three women with iron rods and knives. Their belongings and houses were also burnt to ashes.

- Media reports after the Jacob Luke case accused the PNG government of having failed to end the evil SARV. All of this raises the question of how governments can end community violence against suspected witches.

Possible Solutions to the Problem of SARV in PNG SARV Attracts Widespread Condemnation by International Bodies

Numerous human rights organisations have recognised the importance of state-led intervention to deal with the persistence of witchcraft, and SARV in particular, in some states. For example, in 2010, the Committee on the Elimination of Discrimination against Women concluded that the PNG government must 'prosecute the perpetrators of such acts [to] prevent their recurrence in the future' and 'strengthen the enforcement of relevant legislation'. The UN's Human Rights Council's 2011 report added that PNG must 'accelerate its review of the law on sorcery and related killings'.

Similarly, NGOs like Amnesty International have highlighted the need for strong 'legal intervention and reform' in this area in PNG.

The international community perceives the state-led intervention as especially important because of SARV's disproportionate effect on women and their children. CEDAW imposes a positive duty on the PNG government to address discrimination against women. This includes protecting women from gender-based violence, defined as:

…any act which results in, or is likely to result in, physical, sexual or psychological harm or suffering to women, including threats of such acts, coercion or arbitrary deprivation of liberty, whether occurring in public or private life.

Similarly, the UN Convention on the Rights of the Child requires PNG to …take all appropriate legislative, administrative, social and educational measures to protect the child from all forms of physical or mental violence, injury or abuse, neglect or negligent treatment, maltreatment or exploitation, including sexual abuse, while in the care of parent(s), legal guardians or any other person who has the care of the child.

Steps Taken by the PNG Government in Attempting to End SARV The Repeal of the Sorcery Act 1971 The Sorcery Act 1971 attempted to reflect PNG society by legitimising beliefs in witchcraft.

It criminalised the use of sorcery, which was expressly defined as: including what is known in various languages and parts of the country as witchcraft, magic, enchantment, puripuri, muramuradikana, vada, meamea, sanguma, or malikra, whether or not connected with or related to the supernatural.

The Sorcery Act was repealed in 2013 after some graphic images of two women being tortured went viral. Many international organisations criticised PNG for not adequately addressing the SARV issue. They focused on the Sorcery Act, saying that it provided no effective deterrent because it excused the attackers from liability by giving effect to defences such as provocation.

Some Relevant Jurisprudence

In 2007, long before the repeal of the Sorcery Act, the Supreme Court—including my brother judge Kandakasi J (as he then was)—held that sorcery is not grounded in fact, but only in belief.

He noted that offenders claim belief in sorcery to evade the consequences of their actions. The court also held that acting on a belief in sorcery is repugnant to general principles of humanity and that only in exceptional circumstance can that belief be regarded as a mitigating factor for sentencing purposes—and even then, only in cases where the offender acted in the spur of the moment and without preplanning.

A mitigating factor reduces the severity of the sentence for a convicted person. Previously the PNG courts considered the belief in sorcery a 'special mitigating factor', which would reduce a sentence by one-third. Courts have now moved away from this position and are using it merely as a 'mitigating factor'. The degree to which a belief in sorcery may decrease a sentence depends on the facts of each case.

If a defendant was motivated by fear or self-preservation and acted quickly, then belief will likely reduce the sentence: State v Dokal [2018] PGNC 364. However, if facts show that the offender had alternative remedies to self-help and the knowledge that violence is unacceptable, then belief in sorcery is unlikely to influence the sentence: Dokal, supra. Relevant facts may be the defendant's educational level, availability of village councillors or courts, police, and other educational influences like radio, mobile phones and television.

It is important to note that in addition to such factors, courts must carefully examine the question of whether the defendant's belief is genuine or merely a pretext. In the latter situation, there is no justification for it to be treated as a mitigating factor; rather, it should be seen to be an aggravating factor—one which increases the sentence: see State v Uma [2019] PGNC 214.

Some scholars have questioned whether belief in sorcery should be accepted as a mitigating factor. One such prominent scholar is Prof Miranda Forsyth, author of a chapter entitled

'A Pluralist Response to the Regulation of Sorcery and Witchcraft in Melanesia' in her book, co-edited with Richard Eves, Talking it Through: Responses to Sorcery and Witchcraft

Beliefs and Practices in Melanesia (ANU Press 2015). Prof Forsyth contends that the law must disregard the belief for public policy reasons because it can be seen as encouraging 'vigilantism, payback killings, and giving a licence to attack suspected sorcerers' (p 231).

However, she acknowledges that other scholars have argued that if the belief is not considered, the criminal law would not properly reflect PNG societal values, raising the risk that the criminal law could being viewed as 'illegitimate and a foreign imposition' and overly harsh in individual cases (p 231). These two divergent arguments are difficult to reconcile.

The Criminal Code and the Criminal Justice System

The Criminal Code is legislation that defines and addresses the more severe criminal offences. It is not sorcery-specific legislation like the now-repealed Sorcery Act 1971. Instead, it includes many crimes relevant to SARV, such as wilful murder (s 299), murder (s 300), grievous bodily harm (s 319), wounding and similar act (s 322), common and serious assaults (s 335; s 340; s 341), rape (s 347), sexual assault (s 349), abduction (s 350) and threats to do any injury (s 359).

The Criminal Code was amended in February 2022 to include a provision that criminalises the activities of glasman/glasmeri and those who engage in their services in exchange for money. This is a crucial step because glasman/glasmeri—paid intermediaries who make accusations of sorcery and have been described as 'con artists who destroy the lives, communities and the reputation of [PNG communities]'—can propagate sorcery accusations and indirectly benefit from the torture of innocent victims such as mothers and their children.

The Time Taken by the Criminal Justice Process and the Hurdles it Faces Before a person is found guilty under any criminal code provision, he or she must go through the lengthy processes of PNG's criminal justice system. First, a SARV victim submits a complaint against the alleged perpetrator(s) to the police. The police then investigate all facts, and when there is sufficient evidence, they will arrest and charge the abusers under the relevant law. Next, the matter goes to the magistrates' court, which examines if there is enough evidence for the defendants to stand trial. If there is, then the issue goes to the Office of the Public Prosecutor (the 'OPP'), who will act as the prosecutor at the National Court.

Criminal matters can proceed through the National Court either by trial or via a guilty plea. If there is a trial, the prosecutors present all the evidence previously collected by the police in its initial investigations and any other relevant evidence. The defence may choose to call evidence and raise any counterargument it wishes to the claim. Then the court decides whether the defendant is guilty or not. If the accused is guilty, then the court prescribes a sentence. The court may take various aggravating and mitigating factors into account to increase or decrease the sentence.

The Foregoing Process Is Very Time-Consuming

In March 2022, PNG presented to the UN Human Rights Council its responses to recommendations from its Third Universal Periodic Review (UPR) during the 39th session of the UPR Working Group. One of the key responses by the PNG government was its general affirmation combatting gender-based violence and SARV remains a high priority. Many barriers prevent the criminal justice system in PNG from effectively dealing with SARV offenders. These are discussed below.

Particular Challenges Faced by PNG in its Efforts to Curtail SARV

Most SARV cases are not reported

Most SARV cases do not come to the attention of the police, the OPP or the courts, because victims do not report them. This is especially true if the victim is (as is usually the case) a woman. For example, the number of National Court cases on PACLii (the online legal database where PNG cases, among others, are published) showed that at the time of the 2022 CMJA Triennial Conference, 17 reported cases involve men as the victim, and three involve women as the victim. This implies that a matter will most likely go to court only if a male is a victim of SARV. In comparison, female deaths often go unnoticed or do not seem to warrant action against the preparator(s).

Most SARV cases never reach the National Court SARV cases are predominantly dealt with by village courts, particularly those in distant rural areas where the sorcery concerns are the highest and often part of daily discussions: Melissa Demian, 'Sorcery Cases in Papua New Guinea's Village Courts: Legal Innovation Part IV' [2015]

ANU College of Asia & the Pacific In Brief, The Village Courts Act 1989 provides that these courts have both civil and criminal jurisdiction in relation to specifically identified offences, including 'sorcery'. Magistrates instead deal with SARV under 'customary law' and have a great deal of discretion in SARV instances: Demian, supra, p 2. Police response rate to SARV allegations is low.

The Royal Papua New Guinea Constabulary (the 'RPNGC') must protect SARV victims and arrest alleged perpetrators. However, current reports show that RPNGC is not meeting its obligations. (See, for example, Part

I of the Inquiry into Gender Based Violence in Papua New Guinea—a report of a Special Parliamentary Committee on Gender Based Violence issued in August 2021). In many rural SARV cases, police officers cannot travel to the crime scene promptly because they simply do not have enough resources—that is, insufficient petrol and/or no available vehicle.

When the police do arrive, offenders go into hiding. Such slow response rate decreases the number of SARV prosecutions. It also affects the police's ability efficiently to obtain medical reports and material evidence used in courts to prove SARV against victims.

Furthermore, police are sometimes unwilling to cooperate with victims. Investigating officers may have similar sorcery suspicions regarding victims and encourage SARV rather than stop it. Police may also possess a lack of commitment to investigate violence cases against women and accordingly attempt to persuade victims to dismiss their claim or drop charges.

Police's lack of response to SARV allegations is a symptom of their limited knowledge and skills in arresting accused persons and investigating SARV cases—particularly those where women are the alleged victims. They must be educated on such issues. The RPNGC has a gender violence curriculum taught to cadets and existing police officers. That curriculum is being updated and will include robust policing procedures for SARV. The Special Parliamentary Committee on Gender- Based Violence noted in its Report mentioned supra that resources must be invested to ensure the curriculum's proper roll-out. Perhaps, even before this stage, each cadet should be vetted so that only cadets with good character join the RPNGC. An officer with integrity is likely to abide by the procedures outlined in the curriculum and, as a result, improve the investigation of SARV cases. It can also enhance public confidence and trust in policing in PNG.

Lack of Admissible Evidence In Sarv Cases

Any SARV victim requires evidence to provea particular cause of action or offence. The police do not specialise in such investigations and lack the forensic skills which are needed to obtain admissible evidence to prove physical assaults. Instead, the police rely on witness testimony to identify offenders. A surviving SARV woman victim can quickly identify her abusers because they are usually her family members. But, sometimes, victims may not speak up as there may be communal pressure or threats from offenders that secure their silence.

Other village members may fear repercussions from the abusers or be unwilling to help the SARV victim because they also believe she is a sorcerer who harmed someone.

The situation becomes even more difficult when a SARV victim has died.

Concluding Reflections

In conclusion, it may be apposite to indicate that belief in witchcraft is protected under the rubric of the freedom of conscience entrenched in the constitutions of many countries. As we all know, freedom of conscience entails the freedom of an individual to hold or consider a fact, viewpoint or thought, independent of other viewpoints. The belief is not the problem; it is the violence that can accompany the holding of a belief that is the problem.

The law and the courts of PNG have a role in addressing SARV. As for the law, it must manifest zero tolerance for any form of harmful violence and the courts are duty bound to enforce such law. Perhaps the bar might be set somewhat higher for judges, having regard to their role as leaders of society, so that they might play a more educative role through their judgments and in suggesting necessary reforms.

Law cannot be a panacea tasked to resolve all social ills. Even in countries that have criminalised witchcraft, the fact that alleged witches continue to face violence indicates that the problems associated with witchcraft may not be resolved solely by legal solutions.

Of course, law properly formulated and implemented can help to control SARV. We need to reform the criminal justice system to make it easy for victims of SARV to report instances of it to the police and ensure that the police are properly trained and are available to assist.

Governments, lawyers and civil society groups need to formulate sustainable strategies that can address the root causes of SARV. Amongst the key strategies should be an appropriate public educational programme that acknowledges belief systems and their consequences and the ways those belief systems and consequences intersect with factors such as poverty, disability and gender.

The state as a duty bearer has a duty to do all it can to end SARV. This duty may include criminalisation of the practice of witchcraft.

The state must establish effective witness protection schemes so that people are able to testify about the horrors they have seen or experienced. We need restorative justice in PNG to help offenders understand that SARV is wrong and to engage restored and reformed offenders to talk to members of the public

about SARV. Measures must be put in place to work with victims of SARV to enable them to have a voice that can bring about essential change

Chapter 19

Appointment of Judges and The Threat To Judicial Independence: Case Studies From Botswana, Swaziland, South Africa, and Kenya

Source: South Illinois University Law Journal Volume 44

Introduction

At the end of the eighteenth century, English philosopher John Locke, who strongly influenced the 1688 English Revolution and the 1776 American Revolution, wrote that societies lacking established laws with the right of appeal to independent judges are still "in a state of nature" because such rights are essential to a civilized society. Consistent with Locke's philosophy, modern constitutional law theories often emphasize the importance of an independent judiciary as an indispensable element of the separation of powers.

The rule of law as a constitutional concept can only have meaning in a society which has an independent judiciary. The manner in which judges are appointed affects the independence of the judiciary. Judges who have been appointed on the basis of membership in political parties and/or political connections may not be perceived as impartial and independent by society. Indeed, history has proven that when politicians are permitted unfettered powers in judicial selection, the whole administration of justice is more likely to be put into disrepute.

An assessment of whether a judicial selection process promotes an independent judiciary turns on two important considerations: first, the criteria for judicial selection, and second, transparency and openness in selection processes. The process of appointing judges is one of the major indicators that signifies whether a country subscribes to the rule of law and democracy.

A political appointment process that pays lip service to merit will inevitably produce judges only chosen by their name and will continue to impact the judiciary years after. Constitutionally entrenched criteria for judicial selection is an important safeguard against appointments motivated by political considerations. The appointment process should ensure that persons selected have the necessary qualifications and experience. Generally, the prospects for an independent judiciary are enhanced when the judicial selection mechanisms are transparent.4 Making judicial selections with openness and transparency allows principled public debate about the suitability of the judge. Transparency is often manifested by publicly

advertising judicial vacancies, disseminating the criteria for selection, and conducting public interviews.

This Article discusses and compares the judicial appointment process in Botswana, Swaziland, South Africa, and Kenya, stressing the importance of fair, transparent, and merit-based judicial processes which enjoy public confidence.

I. Background Information

Solid institutions that enjoy public confidence are an essential feature of any successful democracy. Several studies have shown that countries with strong rule of law credentials tend to be more economically stable.6 Most theories of judicial independence highlight the significance of judicial selection systems as a key and indispensable element of judicial independence.

Therefore, it is extremely important to design judicial selection mechanisms that produce judges whose independence, integrity, and impartiality are not in doubt. Judicial independence is enshrined in several international and regional human rights documents, as well as in most national constitutions. The Commonwealth Principles on Promoting Good Governance and Combating Corruption (The Commonwealth Principles) emphasized that "an independent and competent judiciary, which is impartial, efficient, and reliable, is of utmost importance" to any democratic state. There are debates within the sphere of judicial appointments about how the selection process can be made more transparent and better able to identify talent and enhance gender parity from a diverse pool of candidates.11

Further, there is much debate over how to design an appointment system that strengthens judiciary principles of judicial independence, public confidence in the administration of justice, and the rule of law, generally.

In an effort to integrate these principles, many African countries have implemented Judicial Service Commissions or Judicial Service Committees (JSC). Using the JSC model to appoint judges is significantly less confrontational than other methods, such as the "tap on the shoulder" process used in the United States and England. A model JSC is made up of judges, lawyers, and others outside the legal profession,15 making this non-traditional composition successful. According to the Bingham Research Centre, by 2015 more than 80% of Commonwealth member states utilized Judicial Services Commissions.

In the United States, the judicial election processes have been negatively impacted by so-called "dark money." "Dark" refers to the underlying donors being undisclosed. In response to concerns that executive and legislative officials were undermining judicial objectivity, the United States established judicial elections as a means of reformation. A number of U.S. states elect judges, raising serious concerns over the influence of money in the election of judges and whether judicial independence will be undermined as a result. It is argued that the election provides an opportunity for conflicts of interest that may undermine the fair distribution of justice. It is further argued that it is unacceptable to raise money from lawyers and parties who would at one point appear before the judge they endorsed. Additionally, there are those who are opposed to the appointment process. This opposition argues that appointment is like anointment and is therefore not good for society. Supporters of the election method argue that the appointment process is characterized by "behind the scenes" influences. In contrast, elections are not as subject to deal making because they take place in the public sphere. The American Bar Association, in an attempt to alleviate dark money's influence, included Rule2.1n the Model Code of Judicial Conduct.27 Rule 2.11 requires a judge to disqualify himself if his impartiality might reasonably be questioned as a result of contributions to his election campaign.

On April 3, 2009, England and Wales began to appoint the majority of their judges through a Judicial Appointments Commission (JAC). This independent JAC is responsible for selecting judicial candidates based solely on merit. There are approximately fifteen people serving on the English and Welsh JAC.

Most Commission members compete for each position during recruitment and ultimately appointment. However, the Judges' Council and/or the Tribunals' Council will choose three members to hold positions ex officio.

Independent JACs are spreading across the region. Scotland has established a similar body—the Judicial Appointments Board for Scotland—to select candidates for judicial appointments, as well as Northern Ireland—the Northern Ireland Judicial Appointments Commission—for the same purpose.

An independent judiciary is necessary so judges may act impartially for the benefit of the community, without prejudicial influence. Members of the legal community should be more conscious of ensuring that judges can work in environments which allow them to administer justice consistent with their country's laws without external influence.

Additionally, an independent, impartial, competent, and ethical judiciary is essential to the rule of law. It is necessary for the fair and impartial resolution of disputes; for the interpretation of a written constitution; the clear, just, and predictable application of the law; and for holding governments and private interests accountable. Ensuring that the judiciary is fit to perform these tasks—often in situations of considerable pressure—requires a sound institutional structure to support the courage and integrity of individual judges. For this to be possible, the legal framework for that structure, in any jurisdiction, must include: 1) the system by which judges are chosen and appointed; 2) the terms of their tenure; and 3) the mechanism for deciding whether a judge should be removed from office.

In light of these requirements, important questions arise, such as who should appoint judges and by what process, what should be the duration of judicial tenure and how should judges' remuneration be determined, and what grounds justify the removal of a judge and who should carry out the necessary investigation and inquiries.

II. The Southern African Chief Justice Forum: The Lilongwe Principles and Guidelines on the Selection and Appointment of Judicial Officers

The Southern African Chief Justices' Forum (SACJF) is committed to promoting the independence of the judiciary as well as the decisional autonomy of individual judges.

The SACJF credits judicial independence, in part, to the processes by which judicial officers are selected and appointed. To that end, the SACJF developed a Judicial Service Commission made up of individuals from the region. The SACJF considered varying international judicial appointment processes and research completed by the University of Cape Town's Democratic Governance and Rights Unit (DRGU).From these sources, it constructed a regional strategy that provides guidelines and principles for the appointment and selection of judges throughout Africa.45 These principles and guidelines contain jurisdictional directions for developing "legislation, policy, and practice[s][for] the selection and appointment of judicial officers." These guiding principles strive to secure a more independent judiciary with strong integrity.

The Commission noted that "judicial independence is ensured through the integrity of the selection and appointment process along with the security of tenure of judicial officers." Additionally, a process centred around integrity and transparency in judicial appointments bolsters trust and confidence of the public in judicial proceedings.

The implementation of the principles and guidelines are implemented subject to each country's national law.

Research by DRGU of the University of Cape Town, and other reputable International Research Centres, including International Legal Instruments, cite the following fifteen principles as extremely important in the selection and appointment of judges:

1. The principle of transparency should permeate every stage of the selection and appointment process;

2. The selection and appointment authority should be independent and impartial;

3. The process for the selection and appointment of judicial officers shall be fair;

4. Judicial appointees should exceed minimum standards of competency, diligence, and ethics;

5. Appointments of candidates should be made according to merit;

6. The appointment process should ensure stakeholder engagement at all relevant stages of the process;

7. Objective criteria for the selection of judicial officers should be pre-set by the selection and appointment authority, publicly advertised, and should not be altered during that process;

8. The judicial bench should reflect the diversity of society in all respects, and selection and appointment authorities may actively prioritise the recruitment of appointable candidates who enhance the diversity of the bench;

9. Candidates shall be sourced according to a consistent and transparent process;

10. The shortlisting of candidates shall be credible, fair and transparent;

11. Candidates shortlisted for interview shall be vetted and stakeholders invited to comment on the candidate's suitability for the appointment prior to the interview;

12. Interviews should be held for the selection of candidates for appointment to judicial office;

13. The final selection (decision) to recommend for appointment shall be fair, objective and based on weighing the suitability of the candidate for appointment against the criteria set for that appointment;

14. A formal appointment shall be made constitutionally and lawfully;

15. Provision shall be made for judicial officers to assume officetimeously once appointed.

It may be too early to assess the extent to which countries have adopted these principles. What is pleasing though is that they are being discussed and endorsed in an increasing number of countries, and one hopes that in the course of time they shall inform legislative reforms in the region and across the world.

Comparison of Country Appointment Practises

Botswana, Swaziland, South Africa, and Kenya

In recent years, the University of Cape Town and Bingham Research Centre, in connection with the Claude Leon Foundation, established an international research project to examine the selection processes and practices of Judicial Services Commission in the Commonwealth in greater depth. The project brought experts together from a number of the larger Commonwealth jurisdictions, where commissions have some role in the selection of judges.

The following comparative overviews are drawn from the joint research project by University of Cape Town (UCT) Law and Bingham Research Centre mentioned above. The project's primary aim is summarized by Justice Kate O'Regan, who served on South Africa's

Constitutional Court For Fifteen Years

Appointing independent, competent and trusted judges is central to ensuring the rule of law in a democracy. The last few decades have seen the establishment of judicial appointment committees in many Commonwealth countries that have diminished the power of the executive over the appointment of judges. The Cape Town Principles provide welcome guidance on the processes and principles that should inform the work of these committees, which should in turn contribute to the enhancement of the rule of law and independence of the judiciary across the Commonwealth.

The research findings enable a straightforward comparison of the commendable and concerning aspects of the JSC approaches in each of the countries under review. The research findings are summarized below, with respect to each country.

A. Botswana

After review of the previously mentioned reports, the areas of commendation according for the Botswana judicial appointment process are as follows:

Advertising vacancies – The JSC has begun to move away from head-hunting and is now publicly advertising vacancies for the High Court and the Magistrate Courts. This is a welcome move towards transparency and widening the pool of candidates for judicial office.

Role of the Law Society of Botswana – The Law Society of Botswana (LSB) has taken a keen interest in driving reform in judicial appointments in the country. The LSB has engaged in litigation to enforce constitutional compliance when it comes to appointments. The LSB sought to compel the President to appoint judges according to the recommendations of the JSC. This is because the President had been sitting on names for a year when the LSB decided to institute litigation. The LSB argued that Constitution requires the President to appoint judges on the advice of the JSC and to abide by the decision of the JSC. The LSB lost in the High Court but won in the Court of Appeal. The LSB has also developed a position paper of the appointments of judges in Botswana.

Public representation on the JSC – The Constitution makes provision for one ordinary citizen who is not a legal practitioner to be appointed to the JSC by the President. This allows for the public to be directly represented by an individual who is not formally part of the structures of government.

Adverse observations are as follows:

Lack of Transparency – The judicial appointment processes in Botswana are shrouded in mystery. Very few people know of the process and interviews are held in camera.

Court of Appeal vacancies not advertised – The JSC is still not advertising vacancies for the Court of Appeal. There is no rational basis for the differentiation between the High Court and the Court of Appeal appointment procedures. The JSC, therefore, could do better with the Court of Appeal appointment process.

Absence of JSC operating procedures or regulations – The JSC does not have guiding operating procedures and guidelines.

Shortlisting of candidates by the JSC – It is not publicly known who in the JSC does the shortlisting, and on what criteria. This makes the process less transparent.

Presidential influence – Judicial appointments in Botswana appear to be largely driven by political considerations, and the executive has much influence on who is appointed. As a result, there has been an outcry from both the public and the legal profession over the appointment of inexperienced judges.

Domination of JSC by Presidential appointees – The JSC is dominated by individuals appointed by the President. There is very little independent representation. It is recommended that, at the very least, the JSC must consist predominately of members of the legal profession. All members of the JSC are presidential appointees except the member of the Law Society.

Limited participation of members of the public and civil society – There is zero participation of civil society organisations and members of the public in judicial appointment processes.

Differences in the appointment of judges – The judges of the Industrial Court of Botswana are appointed in terms of the Trade Disputes Act as opposed to the Constitution. The JSC is not involved in their appointments, notwithstanding that the industrial court is of a court with concurrent jurisdiction with the High Court; so it is important that the appointments to that court mirror those of the High Court.

Questions of independence of JSC Commissioners – The LSB has been engaged in debate on whether a representative of the LSB on the JSC is not required to report to the LSB and to get directions from the LSB. There is a divergence of opinion on this aspect, and the Law Society, at one point, had to withdraw its representative from the JSC for failure or refusal to report to the LSB and to take instructions from it.

Judicial discipline – The constitution is silent on the process to be followed in disciplining judges. It was recommended that the law should be clear on the precise process to be followed when disciplinary proceedings are being instituted against a judge or judges.

B. Swaziland

The 2005 Constitution of Swaziland and the Judicial Service Commission Act, 1982 (JSC Act) establish the powers of judicial appointment, discipline, and removal. The JSC Act also requires that the Judicial Service Commission Regulations of 1968 continue to be enforced so long as its provisions are consistent with the Act.108 The JSC Act mentions such regulations; however, the regulations could not be found after a diligent search.

The curious relationship between the JSC Act and the 2005 constitution is complex, defying a simplistic explanation. The JSC Act defines the functions of the Judicial Service Commission.

However, it limits the scope of these functions by narrowly defining "judicial officers" to only include magistrates and the office of the Registrar or Assistant Registrar of the High Court or Court of Appeal. This language effectively removes judges from the definition, resulting in a vague definition that leaves room for manipulation.

For example, the Minister for Justice can unilaterally change the definition of "judicial office" by public notice in the Gazette.

Additionally, by terms of the saved portions of section 113 of the 1973 constitution, the JSC regulates matters of appointment, disciplinary control, and removal of magistrates. But, since the JSC Act deals with lower court appointments and mandates that the commission advise the King on judicial matters, there is a question of how effective such advice is without an independent judiciary under the present Act.

It is not clear whether any regulations have been passed that address these concerns about judicial appointments under the present JSC Act. If the 1968 Regulations do in fact exist, it should be as limited in scope as the primary Act, i.e., the JSC Act 1982. Assuming the regulations also purport to regulate how judges of superior courts are appointed, it is doubtful that those aspects of the regulations would be valid because the scope of the primary Act is confined to the judicial offices listed therein. This would leave no regulations to guide the JSC in matters involving superior court judges.

At any rate, and for reasons elaborated above, it is difficult to conceive the JSC as constituted under the Act carrying out functions allocated to it under the constitution.

A comprehensive review of the JSC Act may, therefore, be necessary in order to ensure that matters of judicial appointment, discipline and removal are comprehensively dealt with in legislation. The constitution is hardly the place to do this because by their nature, constitutions establish broadly framed general rules and principles regarding how things ought to be done.

For example, the JSC Act would need to be amended to include judicial appointments to superior courts and all matters relating to the administration of the judiciary in order to bring it into harmony with the constitution.

Additionally, the provisions of the JSC Act requiring that the JSC be constituted of five members would need to be amended to comply with the constitutional requirement of six members. Such small amendments to the JSC Act would help strengthen the judiciary.

C. South Africa

The post-independence judicial selection mechanism in South Africa radically differs from the apartheid era. The post-1994 shift to the democratic dispensation is rooted in the need to build strong and resilient institutions that support democracy and the rule of law. Despite these laudable aims, the judicial appointments process in South Africa faces many challenges.

These challenges include the transformation of the racial and gender composition of the judiciary; questions concerning the over-representation of the politicians and the subsequent impact on the independence of the judiciary; and questions of public confidence in an appointment process dominated by politicians.

To help answer these questions, a brief historical background is necessary to sharpen perspective. South Africa transitioned from a system of parliamentary supremacy under apartheid, where parliamentary participation was denied to the majority black population, to a post-apartheid constitutional democracy. The Constitution of the Republic of South Africa now vests the courts with extensive powers of review. The Appellate Division of the Supreme Court is now the Supreme Court of Appeal (SCA), an intermediate appeals court, and the Constitutional Court is now the highest court in the land.

Before the advent of democracy in South Africa, the judiciary was almost exclusively made up of white males. Black people, who constituted the vast majority of the populace, were excluded. The judicial appointment process was shrouded in secrecy and subject to pervasive political influence.

The process of judicial appointment has changed dramatically following South Africa's transition from apartheid to constitutional democracy.

The process of judicial appointment of judges in South Africa begins with a consideration of section 174(1) of the constitution, requiring a judge be "appropriately qualified" and "a fit and proper person." These are the two most essential requirements because a person who is not appropriately qualified or is not a fit and proper person cannot be appointed as a judicial officer. Although the constitution does not expressly detail the content of these criteria, it is the author's view that the JSC is obliged to take into account the provisions of section 165(2) of the constitution. This provision requires that the judiciary must be independent, protect the constitution and uphold rights, and "apply the law impartially and without fear, favour, or prejudice."

The JSC determines its own procedure. The JSC is comprised of representatives from "the judiciary, the legal profession including attorneys, members of academia, and advocates, political parties represented in parliament, members of the national and provincial executive, and presidential appointees."

While the JSC provides a collective definition, it is the responsibility of each of the above constituencies to define their role and approach. The procedures of the JSC are generally transparent, in that when vacancies arise, the general public is encouraged to nominate candidates. When the JSC plans to recommend a candidate to the President, interviews can be conducted publicly with media present to promote transparency. However, the media is not present for the JSC deliberations, resulting in media criticism about the deliberations taking place behind closed doors in order to prevent public scrutiny.

Under section 174(2) of the constitution, the JSC is required to consider "the need for the judiciary to reflect broadly the racial and gender composition of South Africa" during the recommendation process. This constitutional provision is meant as a remedy for the past racial imbalances within the judiciary. While section 174(1) only requires that a candidate for judicial appointment be "fit and proper," section 174(2) goes on to provide additional requirements to ensure that candidates from "previously disadvantaged communities" have the opportunity for consideration so long as they are also "fit and proper."

A questionnaire with a wide-ranging scope of questions is utilized as part of the recruitment process. Candidates who are already judges utilize specified forms that differ from the forms utilized by those who are not prior judges. The forms require candidates to provide information about: tertiary academic qualifications; employment particulars since leaving school or university; and membership of legal, political, community, and any secret organizations. Candidates are also compelled to list any publications in the field of law and to provide an explanation for the most significant publications. Candidates must indicate whether any writings have been cited in judicial decisions, indicating whether the citation was with approval or not, and must also identify who has reviewed the publications. All candidates are required to state what they regard as their most significant contribution to the law and the pursuit of justice in South Africa. The interviews are conducted in public and the process is transparent.

The report of the joint research project by University of Cape Town Law and Bingham Research Centre observed that, in relation to judicial appointments in South Africa, women are not sufficiently reflected.

There are allegations that the JSC considers race more heavily when appointing judges than it does merit. Additionally, there is a belief that the JSC is considerably influenced by partisanship when appointing judges. This belief is only furthered by the minister's authority to appoint judges outside the mechanisms of the JSC, and such exercise of this authority departs from the goal of judicial independence.

In South Africa, the JSC and/or the President's power of judicial selection has been subject to judicial scrutiny in the past. The following cases shed light on how the courts have insisted that the decisions of the JSC must be rational and reasonable and/or that the President should not do anything relating to judges that undermines judicial independence.

In JSC v. Cape Bar Council, the Supreme Court of Appeal of South Africa was confronted with two main issues. The first issue was whether the JSC properly interviewed candidates for vacancies in the Western Cape High Court, and if not, whether the decisions made were valid. The second issue was "whether... the decision of the JSC not to recommend any of the candidates to fill in the... [advertised] vacancies was irrational, and therefore, unconstitutional."

On the first issue, the court essentially held that the JSC was not properly constituted when it interviewed candidates for vacancies in the Western Cape because of the absence of the President of the Supreme Court of Appeal, among other reasons. Regarding the second issue, the court held:

(a) since the JSC is under a constitutional obligation to act rationally and transparently in deciding whether or not to recommend candidates for judicial appointment, it follows that, as a matter of general principle, it is obliged to give reasons for its decision not to do so; (b) the response that the particular candidate did not garner enough votes, does not meet that general obligation, because it amounts to no reason at all; (c) in a case such as this, where the undisputed facts gave rise to a prima facie inference that the decision not to recommend any of the suitable candidates was irrational, the failure by the JSC to adhere to its general duty to give reasons inevitably leads to confirmation of that prima facie inference. In the event, I agree with the finding by the court a quo that the failure by the JSC on 12 April 2011 not to fill any of the two vacancies on the bench of the Court was irrational and unlawful.

The court highlighted two important judgments related to the operations of the JSC.152 Primarily, before the JSC can make decisions, it must be properly established, and secondly, the JSC's decision must be lawful, equitable, and rational. In order to act equitably, the JSC must provide justification to unsuccessful candidates reflecting that the decision was made in accordance with the JSC's constitutional obligation to act fairly. When the JSC acts through delegation of constitutional authority, it allows the unsuccessful candidate a meaningful opportunity to challenge the decision.

The processes for judicial appointment are critical to the independence of the system. When appointment procedures are clearly stated in a constitutional manner, it ensures that appointments to the bench are done transparently and that judges are picked for the right reasons.

The security of tenure is another important, albeit controversial, aspect of judicial independence that has been the subject of litigation. "[A] judge of the Constitutional Court is appointed for a non-renewable term of 12 years or until the age of 70 years, whichever comes first."159 Judges who are not on the Constitutional Court "hold office until they are discharged from active service in terms of an Act of parliament." The Judges Remuneration and Conditions of Employment Act (Act) provides that Constitutional Court judges are to be discharged when they reach the "age of 70 years or after completing a 12-year term of office..., whichever occurs first."

The Act awards the President discretion to discharge a Constitutional Court judge, if reasonable, for incapacity resulting from ill health or at the judges own request. Additionally, should a judge fail to complete a fifteen-year term, his tenure is extended to meet the minimum twelve-year requirement.

Further, a judge who has completed his fifteen-year term and reached the age of sixty-five may notify the Minister of Justice should he wish to resign, and the President can then discharge him, accordingly.

The seminal case, Justice Alliance of South Africa v. President of South Africa, illustrates how South Africa subscribes to the independence of the judiciary. It highlights the importance of the non-renewability of a judge's term in office. The Constitutional Court compared the Act with the constitution and held that section 8(a) did grant the President the power to extend the term of office of the chief justice.

Further, the court held that section 176(a) of the constitution explicitly granted those same powers to Parliament. The court reasoned that the intention to delegate such power would have been clear if intended by the drafters of the constitution.

Because the President's extension was not an act of Parliament, it was-contrary to section 176(1), and thus, section 8(a) of the Act constitutes an unlawful delegation of authority. The court cautioned that the open-ended discretion in section 8(a) "may raise a reasonable apprehension or perception that the independence of the chief justice and by corollary the judiciary may be undermined by external interference of the executive." Additionally, the Constitutional Court held that "non-renewability is the bedrock of security of tenure and a protective mechanism against judicial favour in passing judgment," and non-renewable term limits "foster[] public confidence in the judiciary as a whole as judges can function without fear that their terms will not be renewed or inducement to seek to secure renewal." The court determined that the chief justice could not be singled out amongst the members of the Constitutional Court and such action is contrary to section 176(1) of the constitution.

The essential position taken by the court in this judgment is that the terms of office of Constitutional Court judges should be fixed. This principle establishes a means of providing stability and consistency to court functions.

Additionally, fixed terms aids in preventing any perceptions of bias thereby enforcing South African values regarding independence in the judiciary.

D. Kenya

Based on this author's review of Kenya's judicial appointment process, the areas of commendation are as follows:

Constitutional reforms on judicial appointments – The 2010 Constitution of Kenya brought about extensive reforms to judicial appointments. The JSC was expanded and given more powers, and the appointment process became more open and transparent. Today, the Kenyan judicial appointments process is one of the most advanced in Africa.

Development of detailed guidelines for the JSC on judicial appointments – Unlike most countries, Kenya has detailed operation procedures and guidelines for the JSC when dealing with judicial appointments. The First Schedule of the Judicial Service Act of 2011 provides step-by-step details of how the JSC should seek and recommend candidates for judicial appointment.

Relationship between the JSC and the Law Society – The JSC and the Law Society of Kenya ("LSK") have worked together on several occasions to ensure that judicial appointments are transparent and that competent and independent judges are appointed. When the LSK instituted litigation against the President for his failure to appoint candidates recommended by the JSC, the JSC applied to be joined in the proceedings and argued its case together with the LSK.

Active civil society and public participation – Civil society in Kenya is generally very active and engaged, and this is true of judicial appointments. Civil society organisations participate through making submissions on candidates to the JSC and attending and observing the public interviews.

Transparency and openness – Interviews are held in public and are streamed live on national television and radio. Members of the public are also permitted to attend and observe the interviews.

Wealth declaration – Kenya is one of the very few countries that require judicial candidates to submit wealth declarations. Candidates declare their wealth together with that of their spouses. This is done in terms of national legislation and applies to public officials at specified levels in the legislation.

Conversely, the following observations of Kenya's judicial processes that are of concern are as follows:

Presidential attempts to control the JSC – It is a matter of record that the President has on several occasions attempted to remove members of the JSC from the Commission or to strip the JSC of some of its powers, to refuse to appoint candidates recommended by the JSC. These attempts have successfully been resisted and thwarted by the JSC. There has been an attempt, twice, to change the law to give the President discretion during appointments. The Law Society of Kenya has been in the forefront in ensuring that the President does not succeed in interfering with the processes of the JSC.

Over-representation of the judiciary on the JSC – The judiciary is overly represented in the JSC in Kenya. This has led to problems in the functionality of the JSC, such as with judicial discipline, where junior members of the judiciary who sit on the JSC may find themselves having to discipline their seniors, or with promotions, where colleagues are considering the promotion of their colleagues on the bench.

Difficulties in instituting disciplinary processes against judges – It has been difficult for people to lodge complaints against judges with the JSC, and the JSC has been accused of being more interested in protecting judges than in investigating and acting on complaints of judicial misconduct.

Inadequacy of disciplinary procedures – The procedures in the laws of Kenya relates only to the removal of a judge from office for misconduct, and the issue of reprimand is not dealt with by the constitution. When a judge is thus found guilty of misconduct, but the seriousness of the misconduct falls short of warranting removal from office, it is unknown what process is to be followed. This is a gap in the legal framework and it seems to have been an oversight on the part of the lawmakers.

E. Comparative Observations on Judicial Appointments and Independence

It is fair to say that politicians all over the globe may sometimes feel tempted to seek to control the judiciary for varying reasons, including coming up with trumped up charges against judges. For example, in July 2015 the judiciary in South Africa held an unprecedented press conference with twenty-seven of the country's top judges, led by Chief Justice Mogoeng.

The judiciary sought to respond to what it called "repeated and unfounded criticism of the government." The chief justice believed it was necessary to reaffirm the judiciary's independence and protect the judges after the government failed to abide by a court order. Kenyan Chief Justice

Maraga, a strong proponent of an independent judiciary, has gone on record that he and other judges are prepared to pay "the ultimate price" to defend the constitution and thus the independence of the judiciary.

When the judiciary is under attack, history has shown that strong, independent judicial leaders are able to resist such attacks. One example is Chief Justice Maraga of Kenya who, as previously mentioned, is on record publicly defending the independence of the judiciary.

Additionally, professional judicial associations can tackle threats to judicial independence collectively. In Africa, it is fair to say that while some chief justices have exhibited signs of being captives of the executive, others have shown admirable courage to defend the independence of the judiciaries. The judiciary can withstand attack if it has a strong chief justice. Conversely, in other countries, it is the chief justices who join the executive to hound independent-minded judges out of office. In Swaziland, for example, Justice Thomas Masuku, who had been on the Swazi bench since 1999, was suspended in June 2011 after he was accused of insulting the Swazi king.

The suspicious end of Masuku's judicial career in Swaziland was largely attributed to the chief justice at the time who acted as both the judge and juror in the case. Masuku subsequently filed a complaint with the African Commission on Human and Peoples' Rights and has since been appointed a judge in Namibia.

In Swaziland, the leadership of the judiciary played a reprehensible role in undermining the institutional independence of the judiciary and that of individual judges by failing to protect and defend the same. A chief justice who goes so far as to issue a practice directive, abrogating fair process in allocating cases and allowing himself to intervene in allocating sensitive and political cases, fails the basic functions of the chief justice, namely, defending the independence of the judiciary. There have been recent developments in the Swaziland, Zambia, and Botswana in which the executive sought to purge independent-minded judges, requiring judges to close ranks and form judges' associations that can defend the independence of the judiciary.

The creation of regional networks among judges is important to strengthen independent judicial institutions. Judges are forming regional associations that serve to denounce acts of interference. During the sagas of Judges Masuku and Agyemang, judges from the region not only provided emotional support, but also lent their voices to the cause as advocates. The above-mentioned incidents were a precursor to the creation of the African

Judges and Jurists' Forum, which seeks to enhance the rule of law, good governance, and economic growth through standard setting, judicial and legal reform support, and rule-of-law-related capacity-development initiatives. Its creation shows that African judges are no longer satisfied with only being members of international bodies, such as the Commonwealth

Magistrates and Judges Association. They want a creation of their own, where they can have an authentic, indigenous voice on matters that are particularly contentious in the region, even if they may be happening elsewhere. The creation of such bodies sends a message that any undue interference with one judge interferes with the independence of all by harnessing the power of the judicial collective because judges are more vulnerable without allies. Once the bar, magistrates, academics, or civil- society organizations assert their influence, it is much harder for executives and chief justices to do as they please. Creating and maintaining relationships with stakeholders who are not part of the judiciary allows judges in the region to establish a sense of ownership in the judiciary and build a second line of defence for themselves.

Conclusion

A discussion of various methods of appointing judges should be assessed on the basis of whether they enhance the independence of the judiciary and whether they actually threaten judicial independence. After a review of various methods of appointing judges, the author is of the respectful view that one of the best methods of appointing judges is through the mechanism of an independent Judicial Services Commission. Particularly, one that operates in a fair and transparent manner, follows publicized guidelines, and is transparent regarding the criterion upon which judges are to be appointed. Where criteria are transparent and well known, candidates can assess their chances of success. It is also important that the JSC be granted all powers relating to transfer, suspension, and other disciplinary measures—short of removal—in order to guarantee the independent functioning of the judiciary.

Judges are the ultimate guardians of the law and must be appointed in a manner that engenders public confidence. Only judges that are a product of fair appointment processes can apply the law fairly, rationally, predictably, consistently, and impartially.

Chapter 20

Letter to The Editor – Human Rights, Tb, Legislation, and Jurisprudence

Source: Health and Human Rights Journal – June 2017 Volume 19 Number 1

People with tuberculosis (TB) experience infringements of their human rights on a daily basis. In far too many cases, they lack access to effective testing and treatment, face discrimination in employment and health care settings, and are unnecessarily detained and isolated against their will. Yet, even as TB has sur- passed HIV as the top infectious disease killer in the world and the global threat from multidrug-resistant TB continues to grow, the ethical and legal issues around TB remain largely neglected in national TB pro- grams and research agendas. New approaches are needed to address the social, economic, and structural factors the epidemic and drug resistance.

Commendably, this journal featured a special section on TB and the right to health in June 2016. As outlined in the editorial and a series of articles in the section, a human rights-based approach to TB establishes and protects the rights of people living with and vulnerable to TB, including the rights to life, health, non-discrimination, privacy, participation, information, liberty of movement, housing, food, water, and to enjoy the benefits of scientific progress. This includes access to the most recent treatments and diagnostic tools.

In addition, human rights law at the international and regional levels and national constitutions create corresponding legal obligations for governments and responsibilities for private actors, promoting accountability and access to remedies for rights violations.

In line with this rights-based framework, the Stop TB Partnership's Global Plan to End TB 2016–2020 calls for a human rights- and gender-based approach to TB grounded in international, regional, and domestic law. The Global Plan acknowledges that TB programming will not be successful unless global and national programs ground their work in human rights and gender equity.

As part of the Global Plan's implementation, the TB and Human Rights Consortium—whose members include the Stop TB Partnership, University of Chicago Law School International Human Rights Clinic, and KELIN (Kenya)—has launched an inclusive, consultative process to promote adoption of the Nairobi Strategy on TB and Human Rights. Led by people with TB, TB survivors, and other allies, the strategy aims to implement several streams of work to foster diverse, focused, and sustained advocacy efforts. The objectives of the Nairobi Strategy are as follows:

- Support networks of affected communities of people with TB, TB survivors, and civil society at the global, regional, national, and local levels.

- Enhance the judiciary's and legal communities' awareness of implementation of human rights- based approaches to TB.

- Expand legislators' and policy makers' capacity to incorporate human rights-based approaches into TB into laws and policies.

- Engage and advise international organizations and experts on the implementation of a human rights-based approach to TB in global policies and programs.

- Sensitize health care workers in the public and private sectors on the need to incorporate a human rights-based approach to TB in their work.

- Formulate and clarify the conceptual, legal, and normative content of a human rights-based approach to TB.

- Conduct qualitative and quantitative research to generate the evidence base for the effectiveness of a human rights-based approach to TB.

I was recently invited to give a keynote address at a consultation on the Nairobi Strategy organized by the TB and Human Rights Consortium with support from USAID on March 9–10, 2017, in Geneva, Switzerland. People affected by TB, communities, civil society, judges, lawyers, academics, clinicians, donors, and multilateral representatives engaged in a robust dialogue on the content and implementation of the strategy.

The meeting was a follow-up to the TB, Human Rights and the Law Judicial Workshop held in Nairobi, Kenya, in June 2016, where the strategy was first developed. My address is presented here below. It is my hope that the Nairobi Strategy is adopted widely in order to recognize, protect, and fulfil the human rights of people with TB. Without this, current efforts to combat the disease will continue to fall short.

Tuberculosis and human rights: A judge's reflections on human rights-based legislation and jurisprudence In a constitutional democracy, the primary lawgiver is Parliament—an assembly of elected representatives of the people. But Parliament is not the only lawmaker; judges too make laws, in the process of interpreting the law. It was once said that judges do not make laws; but that is a fairy tale. It is emphatically the province of the judiciary to interpret the law, and in countries where the constitution is the supreme law, the courts have the power to strike down legislation that is not in conformity with the constitution. This is one organ of the state which because of its independence, knowledge, and integrity of the justices can be the guardian of the constitution and ensure that the promise of the constitution is affected and that no one is excluded when it comes to the realization of human rights and freedoms.

In our last meeting in Nairobi, sometime last year, we heard heart-wrenching testimonies by many TB patients about widespread discrimination and stigma against TB patients and those affected by TB, as well as about other unacceptable violations of the right to liberty and freedom of movement that result in forced incarceration in circumstances where such incarceration is not strictly necessary to protect public health.

It is now widely accepted that many of the factors that increase a person's vulnerability to TB or reduce their access to services to prevent, diagnose, and treat TB are strongly linked to human rights. It goes without saying, therefore, that a human rights-based approach is the condition sine qua non to an effective TB response and that without placing human rights at the heart of the response, no meaningful progress can be achieved. It is also now widely understood that TB is rooted in poverty, as well as legal, structural, and social barriers that together collide and collude to deny patients access to TB services of the highest quality.

Yet despite the above understanding, the policy frameworks and national TB programs of most countries are not generally geared toward addressing human rights violations. In fact, most of the time, the focus tends to be biomedical and pays lip service to human rights, if at all. This is so despite the increasing realization that the promotion and enforcement of human rights is essential to overcome many barriers that stand in the way of

TB patients' access to critical services. A number of policies in our countries discriminate against marginalized people, such as prisoners, preventing them from accessing care and treatment. In addition, there is a lack of an integrated approach to TB and HIV.

Most policy frameworks appear oblivious to a number of documented challenges or barriers that hinder access to TB services, such as economic, geographical, socio-cultural, and health system barriers.

Economic and financial barriers relate to the direct or indirect costs of TB care, including costs related to travel, diagnosis, and treatment, as well as the opportunity costs of lost employment. Physical barriers relate to distance to the nearest health facilities and concomitant transportation challenges. And issues of stigma relate to community and individual prejudice that militates against access to services.

In my 14 years' experience as a judge, I have discovered that there is a plethora of policies governing issues of TB in many of our countries but that such policies are devoid of significant human rights content. This, accompanied with underdeveloped legal frameworks, makes the job of a judge extremely difficult.

To give but one example, I presided over an HIV-related case many years ago. At the time, I was serving as a judge of the Industrial Court, and there was no specific legislation governing the case at hand. At the end of the day, and having found no local legislative guidance—but only policy, which is not law—I had to invoke the aid of international law in a country where international law is not automatically part of the law, opening the court to charges of judicial activism and back-door legislating.

The question has often been debated as to whether we need TB-specific legislation. This is an issue in which there is no consensus—some experts support broader health legislation, while others think there is merit in enacting specific TB legislation. Whatever the case may be, the absence of legislation that comprehensively entrenches human rights with respect to TB is a matter of grave concern because it may lead to situations where the courts may simply say there is no law governing the situation at hand and therefore their hands are tied.

This has happened in my jurisdiction in the context of HIV/AIDS. There is an urgent need to sensitize countries on the importance of legislating on TB, whether specifically or as part of the broader health law. This legislation must be inspired by international human rights law and best practices on TB and human rights. Bringing human rights to the centre of the TB response is the imperative of our time.

In order to bring human rights to the centre of the TB response, we firstly need additional evidence to underscore the link between TB and human rights and to highlight how human rights violations or disregard for human rights-based approaches prevents people with TB (and often HIV and TB co-infection) from accessing services they need. For too long, TB has been a stigmatizing disease—this state of affairs is unsatisfactory and is clearly not helpful if we are to diagnose, treat, and cure those with TB.

Currently, in most countries, the country-level platform for TB control and management is through national TB control programs. These tend to be located within ministries of health and therefore tend to look at the national response to TB through a public health approach devoid of human rights. TB patients are bearers of rights. These rights are universal, interdependent, inalienable, and non-negotiable. Our governments must understand that as duty bearers they have a duty not an option— to protect, respect, and fulfil rights and must be willing to account for failing to do so. In order to give effect to this obligation, they must legislate comprehensively on TB so that there is little room for guesswork when it comes to human rights.

The right to health is one of the many rights implicated in the TB response. It comprises the right to access health facilities and protection against epidemic diseases. The right to health requires the realization of a number of underlying determinants, such as safe drinking water, food, adequate nutrition, housing, healthy occupational and environmental conditions, education, and so on.

The law, in its various forms, must underwrite and guarantee human rights. This is so because the ultimate objective of law is the welfare of society.

The legal enforcement of laws on TB is invariably a balancing act. On the one side are patients' rights. These include the rights to not to be discriminated against, to human dignity, to liberty, to freedom of movement, to privacy and autonomy, to access medical records, and to refuse medical treatment, to mention but a few. On the other hand, there are public health considerations, which include the obligation to prevent disease transmission and protect the public.

As a general rule, TB treatment should be provided on a voluntary basis, with the patient's informed consent and cooperation; and as part of respect for patients' autonomy, health professionals must explain the medication they are dispensing, including any side effects, to patients. This has a bearing on adherence. It is generally accepted that non-adherence is often the direct result of failure to engage the patient fully in the treatment process. Coercive measures such as detention should never be routinely utilized unless they are strictly necessary in the interest of public health. Involuntary isolation must be used only as a last resort—and since having TB is not a crime, any isolation must be linked to the legitimate purpose of preventing disease transmission and must take place in a health facility and not a penal institution.

Where it is considered necessary to effect involuntary isolation, the manner in which the isolation is done must comply with human rights as set out in international human rights instruments and guidelines, such as the Siracusa Principles, which require that measures must, among other things, be in accordance with the law, be based on a legitimate objective, be strictly necessary, and be the least restrictive possible.

We need to come up with laws that strike the correct balance between individual rights and the public interest. South Africa's National Health Act balances the confidentiality of a patient's health in formation against an allowance for the disclosure of such information to prevent a "serious threat to public health." In Zambia, the Public Health (Infectious Diseases) Regulation 8 restricts individual hardship to that which is necessary and unavoidable, which helps ensure that the government is limited in its authority to isolate and report people with communicable diseases.

This balancing of public interest and civil liberties is paramount in public health law, given the costs of excluding people from school, isolating them from social contacts, and disclosing their disease status.

In South Africa, a complex assortment of acts, regulations, and other policies governs TB infection control. The highest law governing health in South Africa, which may be cited as a good example, is

Section 27 of the Constitution, which states in part that "everyone has the right to have access to: (a) health care services."

In Botswana, the Public Health Act authorizes the isolation of persons certified to have communicable diseases on the order of a registered medical practitioner until such persons are determined to be free from infection or no longer pose a danger to public health.

The Public Health Act also addresses the reporting of TB, listing TB as a notifiable disease and requiring health officers to notify cases to the minister of health. Furthermore, Botswana's TB infection control guidelines call for the routine screening of all health care workers for TB and HIV infection. These guidelines use mandatory language (for example, "must"), raising the possibility of the guidelines being an instrument of coercion.

In conclusion, I reiterate the importance of strengthening the evidence on linkages between human rights, law, and effective national TB responses. While policies are good, legislation is far better. We need to involve people infected with and affected by TB in the planning, implementation, monitoring, and reviewing of TB programs—to ensure that the TB programs are based on human rights and sensitive to people's rights.

We also need to assemble a group of experts to work together with infected and affected people and other critical stakeholders to develop a guidance document on mainstreaming human rights into national TB programs. This can be carried out together with the development of tools, guidance documents, and policy briefs for key stakeholders, such as judges, parliamentarians, policy makers, and law enforcement officers.

It may also be a good idea to mobilize and support the idea of developing an international TB control framework similar to the Framework Convention on Tobacco Control. This may be a long-term vision, but it needs to be pursued with vigor and determination. This will ensure a strong political commitment to addressing TB. There are four distinct advantages to the development of an international framework. First, having a framework akin to the tobacco framework will institutionalize the strategy at the international level and make it obligatory for countries to sign it. Second, such a convention provides a point of reference for civil society organizations, the bar, and the bench for strategic litigation. Third, ratification of such a convention may make resources available for additional research and studies in the context of TB medication and so forth. Lastly, there is a link between smoking, chest infections, and TB prevalence so a convention linked to the tobacco framework may be a possible way to further advance global TB control.

It seems to me that the Nairobi Strategy is a timely and welcome intervention that seeks, among other things, to develop rights-based legislation and sensitize all critical stakeholders, including legislators, lawyers, and judges, on the development of a jurisprudence that is based on reasonableness and proportionality and is informed by empirical evidence and scientific advancement. It may therefore be a good idea for the Global Fund to encourage countries to include activities such as the above in their concept notes being developed this year.

I hope I have not exaggerated the value of law and given the impression that law is the panacea of all ills. On the contrary, what I sought to convey is that law in the hands of men and women of integrity and good will can be a force for good; but in the wrong hands, it can occasion serious harm.

In the right hands, law can help fight and dislodge stigma and wanton violations of human rights that ultimately endanger public health.

My very last parting word is this: for human rights to take root and endure, we need more than good constitutions, treaties, lawyers, and judges.

We also need a vigilant and active civil society. Constitutions and treaties are just promissory notes. Itis all of us—judges, lawyers, and civil society—who can ensure that the promise of constitutions and treaties is kept.

Chapter 21

Letter To The Editor - The Rule of Law as a Social Determinant of Health

Health and Human Rights Journal – December 2017 Volume 19 Number 2

(This letter to the editor is based on the author's address to the World Justice Forum in The Hague, July 10-13, 2017. The author spoke in his capacity as co-chair of the African Think Tank on HIV, Health, and Social Justice and president of the Africa Judges Forum on HIV, Human Rights, and the Law.)

The rule of law is increasingly understood as a foundational determinant of health; one which underlies other socioeconomic, political, and cultural factors associated with health outcomes. Strengthened rule of law and related human resource capacity are critical for achieving the health outcomes of the 2030 Agenda, Agenda 2063, the African Health Strategy, and other global and regional development frameworks in Africa.

The law and justice sector play a critical, though often unacknowledged, role in every health challenge. Universal health coverage (UHC) systems can only be established, financed, and monitored through processes and structures established by law. Good health systems governance also requires civil society participation, and government transparency and accountability.

Enabling legal environments are essential to reduce the burden of communicable and non-communicable diseases, as well as injuries, and to provide care, treatment, and support to people affected. States need legal powers and the human resource capacity to regulate production, marketing, and sales of tobacco and other unhealthy products, and to resist spurious legal challenges in national and international courts and tribunals.

A functioning criminal justice sector is essential to stem the flood of falsified and substandard medicines across Africa. It is also critical that the legal sector understands the international legal obligations to protect intellectual property, in order to ensure access to affordable medicines. Legal capacity to understand trade and investment treaties is vital for national regulation of the importation of unhealthy foods and beverages.

Public health law capacity broadly understood is critical to achieving 21st century health goals. The scope and depth of public health law capacity needed to achieve these goals is still poorly understood. Few law school graduates have the multidisciplinary perspective and capacity to support government action to achieve these goals.

Expanded legal education and partnerships between faculties of law, medicine, economics, and other sectors are urgently needed to support resilient systems for sustainable health. Civil society networks, including advocates for civil and political rights, must be engaged to ensure robust public debates on the allocation of resources for health.

Long-term capacity building plans are needed, as well as urgent short-term assistance. Enabling legal environments and public health law capacity must be acknowledged as building blocks of African health systems.

Access to justice, whether to courts, alternative dispute resolution mechanisms, or traditional justice systems can improve access to health services for girls and women and other vulnerable and marginalized populations.

Court action can challenge overly broad legislation on constitutional grounds, such as inappropriate public health measures to address infectious diseases. Court action may also advance group health rights, such as for HIV-positive pregnant women who need medication to prevent HIV transmission to their infants at birth. Conversely, competent and affordable legal advice and representation may help vulnerable groups fight discrimination. Key populations most at risk of HIV infection are one such group.

As court action often goes hand in hand with social mobilization, respect for civil rights is imperative. The global revolution in drug pricing and access to generic medication began in 2000 in South Africa, and was defended by civil society organizations of patients, communities, and legal activists. When global pharmaceutical corporations challenged the government policy, the court permitted civil society organizations to join the action in support of the government policy.

Mass social mobilization resulted in intense global media coverage, and the pharmaceutical corporations dropped the case. As a result, millions of people across Africa and around the world now have access to more affordable essential medicines for HIV and other diseases.

Effective laws and an enabling legal environment are as critical to a healthy society as clean water. Every public health challenge—from infectious and non-communicable diseases to injuries, from mental illness to universal health coverage—has a legal component. Despite this, in many countries, legislation, policies, and practices are antiquated, contrary to human rights obligations, and hostile to public health goals, threatening the achievements of SDG health targets in those countries and regions.

What are the social determinants of health? According to the World Health Organization (WHO), the social determinants of health are the conditions in which people are born, grow, live, work, and age. These circumstances are shaped by the distribution of money, power, and resources at global, national, and local levels.

Social determinants arguably play the largest role in determining the public's health. Our public health is determined by the policies and practices in place in our homes, schools, workplaces, and communities. Many of these determinants are difficult, if not altogether impossible, to control, such as economic standing, genetic predispositions or proclivities, and the customs, traditions, norms, and attitudes of the community in which we are raised. By developing policies that have a wide-reaching impact and improve both social and economic aspects of communities, social determinants of the public's health can have a positive impact, as well.

There is a great deal of research on the social determinants of health. Most of it points to three overarching factors:

Income inequality. Once a country has reached the point of development where most deaths come not from infectious diseases (tuberculosis, dysentery, cholera, malaria, flu, pneumonia, etc.), but from chronic diseases (heart disease, diabetes, cancer), the economic and social equality within the society is a greater determinant of death rates and average lifespan than the country's position with regard to others. The United States, for instance, lags behind Japan, Sweden, Canada, and many other less affluent countries in the life expectancy of its citizens.

The difference seems to be the size of the gap between the most and least affluent segments of the society Social connectedness. Many studies indicate that "belonging"—whether to a large extended family, a network of friends, a social or volunteer organization, or a faith community—is related to longer life and better health, as well as to community participation.

Sense of personal or collective efficacy. This refers to people's sense of control over their lives. People with a higher sense or stronger history of efficacy tend to live longer, maintain better health, and participate more vigorously in civic life.

Although few international laws have been adopted specifically to promote human health, many international laws have possible indirect effects on health as they may impact the social determinants of health (that is, the external conditions in which people live that may affect their health). Examples of social determinants of health include armed conflict, employment, empowerment, environment, finance, human rights, poverty, sanitation, social policies, trade, and water supply.

Social determinants of health can also be understood as the circumstances in which people are born, grow, live, learn, work, and age, which are shaped by a set of forces beyond the control of the individual. These are the intermediate determinants of health, downstream from the structural determinants. They include material circumstances, and psychosocial and behavioural characteristics.

They include the living and working conditions of people, such as their pay, access to housing, or medical care.

Structural Determinants

Structural determinants are the root causes of health inequities, because they shape the quality of the social determinants of health that people experience in their neighbourhoods and communities. Structural determinants include the governing process, economic and social policies that affect pay, working conditions, housing, and education.

The structural determinants affect whether the resources necessary for health are distributed equally in society, or whether they are unjustly distributed according to race, gender, social class, geography, sexual identity, or another socially defined group of people.

Good Governance and Health

While many public policies contribute to health and health equity, improving population health is not the sole purpose of societies and their governments. A lack of policy coherence across government can result in one part of government supporting the implementation of national strategies on malnutrition or non-communicable diseases, or international treaties such as the WHO Framework Convention on Tobacco Control, while other parts of the government promote trade, industrial development, and initiatives that can be harmful to health and well-being.

One reason that these inconsistencies arise is a lack of understanding across sectors about the linkages between health and quality of life, and the broader health determinants such as economic growth. They also arise because policies that appear to be unrelated may have unintended impacts that go unmeasured and unaddressed. These linkages are particularly important in understanding how these health inequities arise between population groups.

To contribute to policy coherence across government in order to address the social determinants of health equity, the health sector needs to understand the imperatives of other sectors and form common understanding of health, its determinants, and broader societal well-being or quality of life. This requires political will, as well as innovative solutions and structures that build channels for dialogue and decision making across traditional government policy siloes.

In practice, this means engaging in several actions, including:

- coordinating support to a network of trainers implementing the WHO training manual on health in all policies in countries, regions, and WHO programs;

- supporting and implementing workshops for improving the skills of government policy-makers, program leaders, and health provider groups to ensure coherence across sectors in policies, services, and programs responding to disadvantaged groups' needs; and

- supporting dissemination of information on intersectoral governance for determinants of health equity and exchange of evaluated case studies through the Intersectoral Action Case

Study Database for Health Equity (ISACS)

The rule of law as a social determinant of health Whether embodied in constitutions, statutes, regulations, executive orders, administrative agency decisions, or court decisions, the law plays a profound role in shaping life circumstances and, in turn, health. The ways in which this occurs can be broken down into four categories.

The law can be used to design and perpetuate social conditions that can have terrible physical, mental, and emotional effects on individuals and populations. One obvious example in this category is the "separate but equal" constitutional doctrine that allowed racial segregation in housing, health care, education, employment, transportation, and more.

The law can be a mechanism through which behaviours and prejudices are transformed into distributions of well-being among populations.

Health care discrimination and bias can take many forms: it can be based on race, ethnicity, disability, age, gender, or class (or socioeconomic status).

Class-related health care discrimination alone can take multiple forms. Laws can be determinative of health through their under-enforcement. For example, a perfectly good set of housing regulations aimed at keeping housing units safe, clean, and quiet are of little value to individual and group health if there is neither the will nor the resources to enforce them. Substandard housing conditions, including the presence of rodents, mold, peeling lead paint, exposed wires, and insufficient heat—all of which are common among low-income housing units—can cause or exacerbate asthma, skin rashes, lead poisoning, fires, and common illnesses, yet a clinical encounter cannot "cure" these housing problems. While their consequences can be treated medically, the causes require robust enforcement of existing laws.

Finally, the law can be used to structure direct responses to health-harming social needs that result from factors like impoverishment, illness, market failure, and individual behaviour that harms others.

Chapter 22

Judicial Selection and Judicial Independence

Source: Bolch Judicial Institute Duke Law School – Judicature International (2021 -22)

"The greatest threat to the independence of the judiciary in Africa and globally is the chronic temptation by political power to control judges." — Justice Dingake

Judicature: What role does the judicial selection process play in maintaining judicial independence? And what role does an independent judiciary play in a successful democracy and maintaining the rule of law?

DIingake: A fair, transparent, and merit-based system of selecting judges inspires public confidence. The life blood of any judiciary lies in the confidence the public has in it. A judicial selection process that is seen by the public to be unfair and not based on merit does not command the confidence of the people. Where the judicial selection process is not seen to be fair and not merit-based, the chances that such a process may not result in a judiciary that is independent are very high. This has been the case in many countries where the Executive authority, often in the form of the President, packs the court with its preferred candidates, at the expense of merit.

An independent judiciary is indispensable to a democratic society based on the rule of law. Only an independent judiciary can be an effective guardian of the rights of the people and ensure that constitutionalism and the rule of law prevails. Only an independent and impartial judiciary can protect society from arbitrary and unlawful state action — including, of course, unchecked private power. It is incontrovertible that the rule of law is not possible without an independent judiciary.

Judicature: Your article advocates the use of judicial selection commissions or committees (JSCs) in judicial appointments to assure judicial independence. Who should sit on a JSC? How do JSCs select judicial candidates? And what is the process by which candidates proposed by JSCs are confirmed?

Dingake: The JSC should be made of men and women of integrity and learning. Ideally, the JSC should include representatives of all the key stakeholders, namely: the legal profession, the judiciary, law faculties at universities, the legislature, and civil society. My preference is that the majority of members should be drawn from the legal fraternity (the profession, law faculties, and the judiciary) and chosen by the stakeholders mentioned above. Decisions of the JSC must be binding on the appointing authority, who may be the President. As far as practically possible, the selection process should be insulated from partisan politics.

Selection of judicial candidates differs from one country to the other. The modern trend is that a public advertisement for vacant posts is usually issued inviting interested and qualified persons to apply or members of the public to nominate candidates. This usually culminates in an interview of short-listed candidates. Thereafter the JSCs make recommendations to the appointing authority for confirmation. It is good practice that there should be criteria that guides the selection process. The criteria should not just be an imported criterion – but must be merit based and broad and suitable for domestic context. It is critical that selections should be based on competence and measured by objective standards.

The following considerations as part of the applicable criteria may be important:

Independence and impartiality

Commitment to the rule of law and the judiciary as a public institution

Demonstrated commitment to protection of human rights and democratic values

Integrity

Outstanding knowledge of the law

Analytical competence

Excellent oral and written communication skills

Ability to understand the social and legal consequences of one's decisions

Ability to strike a balance between delivering judgments timely and the quality of judicial decisions.

In my mind candidates should have the right to challenge the decisions of the JSCs, whose decisions should be subject to judicial review.

Judicature: You note that many Commonwealth countries — who by virtue of their membership in the Commonwealth presumably adhere to democratic principles — are shifting to the use of JSCs. Why are JSCs gaining in popularity?

Dingake: The shift to JSC is a result of increased recognition that an independent judiciary is better secured by a judicial selection process that is fair and transparent — and is not dominated by the executive. However, it is important to note that some JSCs are controlled by the Executive, which more often than not appoints judges based on political considerations rather than merit. There is nothing magical in the name JSC. What is important is that the body appointing judges, whatever name such body may be called, should follow a fair, transparent and merit-based process of selecting judges.

Judicature: Some democracies, including the United States, use very different methods of judicial selection. Do you believe JSCs are superior to judicial appointments by the executive branch or judicial elections by the populace? If so, why?

Dingake: JSCs cannot be superior by virtue of being called as such. Their superiority must be evaluated based on the process of selection (whether it is fair, transparent, and merit based), the extent to which the membership is representative of the society in general, and the quality of the membership. I believe JSCs may be superior only if they are not dominated by the Executive and are merit based. In my view, judicial selection processes that involve judges in campaigning for office risk politicizing the judiciary and compromising the independence, impartiality, and integrity of judges.

Judicature: In analyzing the judicial appointment processes of Botswana, Kenya, South Africa, and Swaziland, do you see common impediments to a fair and impartial judicial selection process?

Dingake: Yes. The common impediments have to do with executive dominance — the extent of which varies from one country to another. In Southern Africa, this dominance is more pronounced in Botswana, where almost two-thirds of the members of the JSC are directly appointed by and accountable to the President. The President therefore has the opportunity to influence or even dictate the composition of the judiciary. The Botswana situation seems even more glaring when compared to Kenya, where the JSC is made up of the Chief Justice, who is chosen through the mechanism of a representative JSC, and judges drawn from other courts who are elected by their own peers.

Judicature: What do you see as the biggest threats to judicial independence in Africa and globally? And what can judges do to protect against these threats?

Dingake: As I see, the greatest threat to the independence of the judiciary in Africa and globally is the chronic temptation by political power to control judges. In Africa and other parts of the world, judges who often don't toe the political line of the Executive are demonized, overlooked for promotion, arbitrarily transferred as a form of punishment, and forced to resign. And, often in desperation, criminal charges against them are manufactured to force them to jump ship. This usually happens when an independent judiciary attempts to curb the exercise of arbitrary governmental power by insisting that the executive must follow the constitution.

Chapter 23

Lgbti Equality – For a Fairer Future

Source: Commonwealth Heads of Government Meeting 2018 Report

In the African continent, there has been a very missed record of achievement on human rights and social justice for vulnerable and key populations, including LGBTI (lesbian, gay, bisexual, transgender and intersex) persons. It is correct to assert that the broad orientation of the legal frameworks in Africa regarding the rights of LGBTI persons can be described as hostile and anti-human rights.

It is a sad reality that in Africa, the lives of LGBTI persons, vulnerable groups and key populations remain both compromised and threatened in environments where they are criminalized and face ongoing stigma, discrimination, physical and sexual violence, victimization, abuse and denial of their rights, including their right to health. Moreover, social and economic inequality across the region places many other individuals and groups at risk of HIV, including women and girls, young people, people with disabilities migrants, and mobile populations.

In recent years, some African countries have moved to adopt punitive laws regarding homosexuality and same sex-relationships. Aside from the legal aspects of these developments, these counties have issued populist and incorrect messages that homosexuality is 'un-African' and that this is a 'western concept'. Yet homosexuality exists in every society across the world, and Africa is not an exception. In fact, Africans embrace that reality. The issue, I believe, is that Africans have challenges in dealing with the manifestation of homosexuality. All that this uninformed stance has achieved is the unwarranted violation of the right of LGBTI persons. This includes the outright denial of basic rights and dignity of LGBTI persons, including their access to HIV and health services. There is increasing evidence that lesbians, and transgender men and women are being targeted with sexual violence because of their sexual orientation and/or gender identity.

The serious nature of this reality was reflected in Resolution 275, passed by the African Commission on Human and Peoples' Rights in April 2014. The Resolution draws attention to the deplorable situation across the continent of ongoing violence and human rights abuses against individuals based on real or perceived sexual orientation. State-sanctioned persecution is specifically condemned.

Despite this ground-breaking resolution, the human rights of LGBTI persons across the African continent continue to be violated and undermined by repressive legal frameworks, hate speech and violence. Out of the 55 countries in Africa, 34 criminalise same-sex relationships. In many cases these laws were introduced under the British Empire, making this a uniquely Commonwealth problem.

In March 2015, under the leadership of the UNAIDS Regional office in Johannesburg, a diverse regional group of experts and advocates on HIV, human rights and social justice, including justices, lawyers, doctors, LGBTI persons and their networks, academic, faith-based organisations and policymakers, convened in South Africa, to form the African Think-Tank on Health and Social Justice. Our bold purpose is to function as a dynamic and engaged platform for strategic thinking, leadership and collaboration to support, expand and accelerate action on human rights and social justice for LGBTI persons, vulnerable groups and key populations across the African continent.

The African Think-Tank on Health and Social Justice is an innovative platform, the first of its kind, with a clear objective to address the institutionalized stigma and discrimination against LGBTI persons as well as the notion that homosexuality is 'un-African'. The fact that the think-tank is composed by Africans means it is in a unique position to lead the debate regarding sexual orientation and gender identity in the continent.

Our perspective comes not only from a human rights and social justice angle, but also through African contextual realities and lenses.

As such, there is an urgent need not only to debunk the myth that homosexuality is 'un-African', but also to engage in transformational dialogue with all stakeholders. Our aim is to assert the universality of human rights and the centrality of the dignity of all human beings without exception. African societies already subscribe to this notion through the philosophy of Ubuntu, at the heart of which is the idea that all persons are equally dignified.

The Commonwealth Heads of Government Meeting provides an important platform for African advocates to appeal to their governments for the right to equality for LGBTI people. Already important progress has been made on the African continent. Botswana and Malawi are slowly proceeding with removing their sodomy laws, while Mozambique and Seychelles have recently decriminalized homosexuality. The courts in other African Commonwealth member countries, particularly in Kenya, Malawi, and Botswana, have been at the forefront of implementing the promise of equality of all people entrenched in these countries' constitutions.

Part of my work at the African Think-Tank on Health and Social Justice is to use transformative roundtable dialogues, information sharing and best practices, and to work with key stakeholders and communities to bring down the walls of stigma, discrimination and prejudice. Through structured dialogues with key actors, it is possible to intercept and avert actions that could fuel further homophobia and violence against LGBTI persons.

There's a huge amount of work left to do, but slowly the walls of prejudice against the LGBTI community are crumbling. There is significant momentum and a critical mass emerging for resolving human rights and social justice challenges for LGBTI persons and other key populations across the African continent, led by trailblazing Africans themselves. What we now need is to leverage the positive changes alluded to above, and the opportunities provided by platforms such as the African Think-Tank and the Commonwealth Heads of Government Meeting. It's critical that we act on these opportunities to enhance collective impact regarding human rights and social justice for all in Africa.

I'm heartened by the progress made by some African governments on advancing equality for all in their countries. Leveraging on the positive presence of African LGBTI civil society leaders at the Commonwealth Head of Government Meeting, we can advance the vision of Africa that is free from discrimination and homophobia. I am confident we can keep this momentum going.